2009

D0176238

What people are saying about …

# READING YOUR MALE

"Mary Farrar combines meticulous research with heart-stopping facts that require her readers to face the truth about male sexuality. Any woman who seeks to better understand the thought patterns of her man will benefit greatly from *Reading Your Male,* but it should also be required reading for single adults and married couples who desire healthy relationships. This book is an essential reference tool for every Christian leader. I highly recommend it!"

**Carol Kent,** president of Speak Up Speaker Services
and author of *A New Kind of Normal*

"This is a powerfully inspirational and instructional book. We as women don't often recognize just how much male sexuality is under attack in this culture—or how central it is to how they feel about themselves. As you begin to understand and navigate this important and misunderstood subject, your eyes will be opened to the wonderful influence you have in the life of the man you love."

**Shaunti Feldhahn,** best-selling author of *For Women Only:
What You Need to Know about the Inner Lives of Men*

"Think you know it all when it comes to what men want and why? Then you're in for a shock if you'll take time to read this book. Mary Farrar shares insights that will inform you, change your relationship with your husband for the better, and help you train your sons to be the men God calls them to be. Do yourself a favor and gain a huge dose of understanding into how men view life, love, sex, and intimacy—and watch how that deeper understanding leads to the kind of positive changes you've been looking for in your marriage."

**John Trent,** PhD, president of StrongFamilies.com and
author of *The Blessing* and *The 2-degree Difference*

"Mary Farrar has written a profound book on understanding a man's sexuality. With strong authority and conviction, Mary addresses the chronic onslaught of temptation and destructive cycles, followed with a God-given, life-changing plan that works when undergirded by the strength of teamwork in a marriage. This is a powerful book. We have never read a book like it—ever. Get a book for yourself and one for every woman you know who has ever had questions about understanding what a man is thinking!"

**Gary and Barb Rosberg,** America's Family Coaches,
founders of The Great Marriage Experience, speakers,
authors, and national radio-program cohosts

"What a profound book for both women and men! *Reading Your Male* boldly uncovers the truth about our sexually skewed culture and examines a man's inner world. Most important, it uses God's rich truth to help every woman discover how to love her man the way he needs and longs to be loved."

**Jeff and Cheryl Scruggs,** authors of *I Do Again*, founders of Hope Matters Marriage Ministries, national speakers and biblical counselors

"Mary opens an insightful window into male sexuality and helps women understand how God can use them in His work to redeem the sexual hurt and misunderstandings that many couples know all too well."

**Steve Watters,** director of Family Formation, Focus on the Family

# Reading Your MALE

## AN INVITATION TO UNDERSTAND
### and influence
## YOUR MAN'S SEXUALITY

# MARY FARRAR

David C Cook

*transforming lives together*

READING YOUR MALE
Published by David C. Cook
4050 Lee Vance View
Colorado Springs, CO 80918 U.S.A.

David C. Cook Distribution Canada
55 Woodslee Avenue, Paris, Ontario, Canada N3L 3E5

David C. Cook U.K., Kingsway Communications
Eastbourne, East Sussex BN23 6NT, England

David C. Cook and the graphic circle C logo
are registered trademarks of Cook Communications Ministries.

All rights reserved. Except for brief excerpts for review purposes,
no part of this book may be reproduced or used in any form
without written permission from the publisher.

The Web site addresses recommended throughout this book are offered as a
resource to you. These Web sites are not intended in any way to be or imply an
endorsement on the part of David C. Cook, nor do we vouch for their content.

All Scripture quotations are taken from the *New American Standard Bible*, © Copyright
1960, 1995 by The Lockman Foundation. Used by permission. Scripture quotations
marked KJV are taken from the King James Version of the Bible. (Public Domain.)
Italics in Scripture quotations have been added by the author for emphasis.

LCCN 2008940794
ISBN 978-1-4347-6871-1

© 2009 Mary Farrar
Published in association with the literary agency of WordServe Literary Group, Ltd.,
10152 S. Knoll Circle, Highlands Ranch, CO 80130

The Team: Don Pape, Larry Libby, Amy Kiechlin, and Jack Campbell
Cover Design: Amy Kiechlin
Cover Photo: iStockphoto

Printed in the United States of America
First Edition 2009

2 3 4 5 6 7 8 9 10

110708

*To Steve,*

*my friend and partner,*

*and the reason I have come to treasure manhood*

## WHAT GAIN

What gain to womankind
When walks a man on earth
Who bears the image of his Maker
As you do.

What grace to children born,
When sheltered 'neath your god-like wings,
And tempered, yet ne'er abandoned,
Then, pinioned in their fledgling flights,
Are wooed and lifted upward
Towards Him, their heavenly Father.

What joy to this frail heart
When bound by your true love,
And knitted soul to soul,
Is strangely Godward kindled,
And gently drawn and welded
To Him, my soul's first Love.

What grace upon this world,
When guarded o'er its tower and bridge,
And by your princely walk
Is marked with every step,
And called to lift its eyes and gaze
On Him, their King of kings.

What gain to this rare man,
What joy to him ten-fold
Who bears the image of his Maker
As you do.

# CONTENTS

🔵 **Discover More Online**

FOR GROUP STUDY GUIDE QUESTIONS, VISIT
WWW.DAVIDCCOOK.COM/READINGYOURMALE

# SECTION I

## THE POWER OF A WOMAN
## WHO READS HER MALE

# *Chapter One*

# THE SECRET WORLD OF A MAN: AN UNFORGETTABLE INTERVIEW

*No signs from heaven come today—to add to what the heart doth say.*
*—Dostoyevsky*

I've seen plenty of interviews on *Oprah* and *Larry King Live*. But I was recently privy to an interview that will never make it to network television—even though it should.

In fact this interview happened entirely by accident.

It began as a conversation. And like many good conversations in our home, it evolved in my kitchen right after dinner. The guys were gathered around, watching me clean up as usual. But that's fine. Our best conversations have happened in just this way. I was cleaning—and listening and talking. The guys were just talking. (ADD people can't do two things at once.)

That particular night it was a hearty group of young men in their early twenties—friends of my sons, most of them slugging it out through the last years of college. As the night grew late, we got deeper into conversation, and they didn't seem to mind that I was the only woman still up with them. They had moved on from the light stuff about crazy friends and NBA basketball and the latest good music. They were talking about girls (which ones they liked and didn't like), careers (what in the world they were going to do after college), and the inevitable subject of marriage.

Then suddenly, we were into it. It happened really quite unexpectedly. But once we were there, we were riveted. We were talking about sex. Sex as it is only experienced in the masculine dimension of the universe. The problem of it. The temptation of it. The cloudiness of its boundaries. The destruction it can create.

Outside, the moon slipped silently across the shimmering sky as the world lay slumbering. Inside, the dishwasher swished and the clock ticked, eventually striking 2:00 a.m. There we were—huddled on our bar chairs, conversing quietly, importantly, and quite intensely. We were completely wide awake. Whatever exhaustion had tugged at us earlier had melted away.

We were Edmund and Lucy, who—having fumbled through an old coat closet in the professor's house—fell right into another land. We were in our own Narnia, that other world that always exists and is fully alive, filled with battles and wars and matters of great import, yet is rarely ever visited by strangers.

For some reason they allowed me in … even welcomed me. They seemed relieved, actually invigorated to be telling a woman about their world, to have her know and understand. They spoke in a kind of foreign language to me—a certain form of male dialect. But I was willing to learn. And I was permitted to ask the most probing of questions, questions that had been in my brain for years.

They answered me straight-out, no holds barred. For my part I was madly taking mental notes. Eventually, with their permission, I asked if I could write down what they were saying. "Sure!" they said. "Write away." They had never had a woman so interested in what goes on inside the masculine brain.

Now I'm going to give you a portion of this unplanned interview. You should know that they don't mind that I tell you, as long as their identities remain anonymous. But you should also know something else. These are all guys who love the Lord and are actively pursuing a relationship with Him. They want to have pure hearts and healthy marriages. They desire to be godly men.

I must also warn you that this is frank. But frank is what we need. Not a worldly, sick kind of frank, but an honest and helpful frank. And remember, I am letting you in on only a *sliver* of their inner world.

Q: How much do you think about sex?
A: Oh, quite a lot.

Q: Well, how much is a lot? Like a few times a week? Once or twice a day?
A: Oh no! Much more than that. More like *many* times a day.

Q: And you would say this is normal?
A: For guys our age in the world we live in, yes, it's normal.

Q: What makes you think about sex?
A: Oh, lots of things. It can be music, or a girl we see, or something on TV. Or just nothing at all. It can come right out of the blue, right in the middle of a worship chorus in church.

Q: How do you feel when that happens?
A: Well, it is the way it is. But it can really get bothersome. Sometimes we get really bummed out. I mean, what are you going to do with this intense desire to contemplate sex? We have to try to control it and not let it carry us away.

Q: Are you usually successful? I mean, successful in not giving in to those thoughts?
A: Ha! Good question. Sometimes we are, and sometimes we aren't. Lots of times we aren't, actually. It's tough when it's around you every day.

Q: Does the way that girls dress affect you a lot?
A: Totally. You try not to look, but most girls don't even seem to realize what we're dealing with. They really don't get it.

Q: Well, that's for sure. So what happens when you get pulled into those sexual thoughts and can't get them out of your brain?

A: It's pretty depressing. I mean, you don't want to think about it. And you're fighting it off. But then you blow it. It's hard not to feel guilty, you know? It's easy to get down on yourself and wonder if you can ever get it under control.

Q: So you feel defeated.
A: Absolutely.

Q: Can you describe what happens when thoughts of sex enter a guy's mind?
A: Well, you immediately want to dwell on it. Guys are just driven this way. Then it's not unusual to eventually want to masturbate. It's a real battle.

Q: How many Christian guys would you say have struggled or struggle now with masturbation? Maybe that's hard for you to say.
A: Oh no, that's easy: 99.9 percent of the guys we know would admit to having struggled with it. And everybody knows that the other .1 percent is lying. Trust us.

Q: That's a lot of guys struggling.
A: Yep. But that's how it is.

Q: Have any of you ever talked to your dad about masturbation?
A: Only two of us have. We don't know of anyone else close to us who has. That's pretty much not in the cards for most guys, including Christian guys. Our dads don't talk about it and we don't ask.

Q: The world says it's natural and okay for a guy to masturbate. Do you agree?
A: Well, the urge to go there at times may be natural, but otherwise—the world is wrong. It isn't good. It's addictive and destructive.

Q: You feel pretty strongly about that.

A: *Very* strong. We wish we could tell that to every young guy who is just beginning to think about sex.

Q: How is it destructive?
A: It causes a guy to think about sex as only sex—pure, unadulterated, self-fulfilling sex. It's the gateway to all sexual sin.

Q: So how does a guy get hooked into a lifestyle of sexual sin?
A: Well, it's a private thing that builds with a guy. It usually starts with an early natural and innocent experience of masturbation. Then somewhere he sees some pictures of naked women or he looks at some porn, and that stays in his brain. The next time those images come up in his brain, he thinks about them until he masturbates. That gives him a temporary physical high, a sort of release. But it doesn't last long. So he starts regularly looking at pornography while masturbating to get his high. This is when it becomes destructive. It doesn't happen overnight, but that's pretty much the routine.

Q: You said this is a gateway?
A: Well, at this point a guy is already compromising big-time, and it's already affecting his relationship to God. After awhile, just looking at porn and masturbating isn't enough. A lot of guys get sexually active with girls at this point. They need a real woman for a bigger high. They might get into a relationship, but they really want to have sex. In some cases, they'll even have sex with a prostitute. But for the majority of guys, there are enough girls around who will go all the way without a heavy commitment, so why look elsewhere?

Q: Have any of you guys had sex?
A: No, but we know a lot of guys who have. And we know a whole lot more who are very physically involved with their girlfriends and close to having sex. That's really common. When they're not with their girlfriends, they are masturbating.

Q: These are Christian guys?

A: Heck yeah, at least some of them. But, you know, they feel bad about it. They're really struggling, and they feel a lot of guilt.

Q: How do you think premarital masturbation hurts a future marriage?

A: Well, of course, none of us is married yet. But we know guys who are. And what we hear from them makes sense to us.

For one thing, a guy who habitually masturbates can get so good at satisfying himself that he can find that his wife isn't able to give him that same sensational high. That puts their sex on a performance basis, and that is just flat ungodly. It doesn't work very well for a wife, either. A man has to be willing to be patient and find out what pleases her.

The worst damage from the habit of masturbating with pornography is the mind-set it produces in a man—you know, a focus on sexual self-fulfillment without any relational effort at all. A woman becomes an object in this scenario. That's all. An object from which a man gets his own pleasures met.

So when a man gets married and has to work through things with his wife, it becomes much more of an effort than he's ever had to put out. He misses that instant pleasure.

But in a good marriage, intercourse is about fulfilling the other person's needs and having the surpassing experience of mutual satisfaction. The world can't even come close in that department. For this to happen, a guy has to be sacrificial and look for ways to please his wife's needs. You know, it's all about Ephesians 5. A guy has to love his wife as Christ loves the church. And this kind of love leads to sex that is so much better than the world's self-gratifying sex. That's why the Bible uses marriage as an illustration of the relationship He has with the church, His bride.

Q: Wow, guys, I am truly impressed. You've really thought this through. That's great stuff you're saying. So how does a guy get off the masturbation track?

A: It's all in the mind. It's inside a guy's head and heart. We have to get aggressive by starving it to death. You have to starve the bad stuff in your mind and feed on the good stuff. It's best if a guy never ever looks at pornography in the first place. Just don't put those images in your head. But if they are already there, and truthfully, it's hard to avoid them anymore, you have to consciously choose not to feed upon them.

Then you have to do something else. You have to feed on Scripture, and on the truth that's there. The Bible always brings perspective to the messed-up world we live in. We've noticed a real difference when we are feeding regularly like this and when we aren't. It's pretty amazing.

Q: So starvation and feeding.

A: Yes. But it has to be something even more than that. You have to get to a point where you just hate it. The thought of sexual sin has to make you feel disgusted, like throwing up. You're sickened by it, totally nauseated. You want to get away from it, have nothing more to do with it. That's the goal. That's what has to happen.

Q: Anything else you would say to a guy who's trying to conquer habitual sexual sin?

A: Well, you need a plan. You need to know what gets to you. What you can't watch and listen to. Where you can't be. Who you can't be around. That sort of thing. You need to know what you're going to do if the opportunity comes knocking, how you're going to "walk away" mentally and also literally. You have to know yourself pretty darn well and what brings you down.

It also helps to find other guys who are trying to defeat it. And it helps to be around girls who we respect and make us want to be godly guys.

The biggest thing is *hope*.

Q: Hope?

A: Yes, hope that there can be victory. If you've been defeated over and over, you lose hope. You need to know that somebody else has defeated it. To discover that "my dad doesn't do this," or "this guy I know hasn't done it for a solid year," or "this other guy hasn't done it for four years!"—that's incredibly encouraging.

Q: So what will you say to your sons?

A: We're going to be real straight-up, real early. We're going to talk about those women in pictures … that they are real people, somebody's mother, somebody's sister. We're going to tell our boys about the natural urges that we men have, and why they are good. But we're going to tell them not to give in to those urges. Those are meant to be fulfilled in marriage. They are for a very special woman. And when they find her, they will be so glad they didn't go down the other road.

Basically, we're going to try to coach them on how to develop a good defense. And we are going to advise them never to start down that path of masturbating. Just don't ever do it.

Q: Wow. That's very strict.

A: In this world, strict is necessary. We wouldn't have them smoking marijuana and playing around in the world of drugs. Why would we want them masturbating and messing around in the world of sexual indulgence? These days a guy's got to get a plan that works. And that works. We want our boys to talk with us about their struggles with girls and sex. It will make a big difference—just having a man they can talk to who's gone down that road and understands what it feels like.

Q: If I could tell women anything, what would you want me to say to them? What do you want them to know?

A: Tell them it's a lot tougher than they think for us. Tell them that they need to understand our struggle. Also, they need to think about what they are wearing and how they are acting around us. It doesn't solve the problem completely, but it would really help. It's hard to walk into a Bible study and be struggling because some girl is sitting there—excuse us, Mrs. Farrar, but—with her boobs hanging out in a revealing top and her pants down below her navel. They also need to be careful how they act. A girl that comes on to you doesn't realize what she is doing. We don't really respect her, but we can't help but be sexually aroused.

Q: What should I tell older married women?
A: Well, some of them are the same way. You can see a "loose" married woman a mile away. On the other hand, a woman should keep herself looking as good as she can, in a godly, feminine sort of way. It disturbs a young guy to be around married women who have just let themselves completely go. A guy can also tell if a married woman is cold and it's probably not happening with her husband. And that's a torturing thought. A younger guy worries that that could happen to him someday, and we have enough to be worried about as it is.

෫ර

I thought that after living with three very transparent men for most of my life, I understood men pretty well. But such honesty woke me up.

I didn't *really* know. I think most women don't really know.

This conversation was about sex. Men think about sex. But it revealed something important. Men who think about sex can also be very thoughtful, deep-thinking men. I sensed I had only scratched the surface of the male psyche. Several years later, I can confirm this to be true.

In the upcoming pages, we're going to go deep into the masculine mind. We will discover that men are profound, complex beings, and they possess profound, complex needs.

That's why, as you will discover, this really isn't a book about sex. It's a book about *male sexuality*—something much bigger and far more important than sex. It's true that sex is fundamental to a man's identity and self-expression.

It's also true that sexuality and sex are linked, for one leads very naturally to the other—like a river flowing into the ocean. But sexuality encompasses far more than its natural end result. It has to do with people and relationships, emotions and thoughts, inclinations and convictions. Sexuality goes to the very core of a man … and a woman. It is the headwaters from which the river of love and sex flows.

In truth, this book is about something even more encompassing than male sexuality. It is about *the difference a woman can make when she understands male sexuality.*

And that difference can be pivotal.

# Chapter Two

# FREE FALL

*When the people look like ants—Pull.*
*When the ants look like people—Pray.*
*—proverb of a skydiver*


*I have woven a parachute out of everything broken.*
*—William Stafford*


Sitting down to write a book about male sexuality was like jumping out of a plane without a chute. But personal passion overruled reason, and a compelling cause overcame shyness.

Let me assure you, I am not one to walk around casually discussing sex, especially male sexuality. I doubt if you are either. Sex is a delicate, personal, intimate subject.

So what was this passion, this compelling cause that enticed me to take leave of my senses, strap on my chute, and jump at ten thousand feet? It was an overwhelming sense of urgency brought on by an increasing awareness of three things:

1. a runaway *epidemic* that has targeted our boys and men;
2. the need for women to understand *why the male sex is uniquely vulnerable*; and
3. the *powerful role we play* in determining whether our men will survive and thrive.

A RUNAWAY EPIDEMIC

There is an epidemic of sexual sin that has swept across the evangelical world so quickly it takes the breath away. It is a virulent epidemic that leads to emptiness, confusion, hopelessness, addiction, and all its many adapting mutations. So powerful is this disease, it is destroying even the best of people who were once walking a path of serving Christ well. It is breaking up marriages right and left. It has Generations X and Y by the throat. And its toxins are spreading even to our children—the most vulnerable among us.

No one is exempt from its devastating infection. Not women. Not children. Not even our leaders, who seem to be dropping like flies around us.

If you work on the front lines of ministry and counseling, as my husband, Steve, and I do, you begin to grasp the true extent. I happen to be married to a man who speaks to thousands of men around the country every year. He meets with all kinds of men: pastors and laymen who are caught up in affairs or sexual addiction; men who are absolutely dying in their marriages; twentysomething guys who are searching for a template of manhood; midlife fathers who are in the throes of raising troubled sons; and men of all ages who are on their second or third marriages, still trying to figure out where things went wrong and why things aren't working this time around.

Then he comes home and tells me about these guys—anonymously, of course, without revealing confidences.

My world, on the other hand, is filled with women at the opposite end of the spectrum: wives of men who are addicted to pornography or are involved with affairs; women whose marriages are defined by conflict or distance and feel totally unable to intimately connect with their men; mothers who genuinely worry for sons whose fathers are distracted and seemingly unaware of their needs; and wives in loveless marriages who feel used in every way—including sexually. Then there are the hosts of single women who wonder if all the masculine God-loving guys have been shipped to another planet, or if such a man were to actually come along, could they trust him to stay?

The most recent mutation of this epidemic has been an astronomical increase in food disorders (yes, there is a connection) and an alarming rise in the number of women who are having affairs and simply walking away from their husbands and families.

You are a woman; you know how this epidemic of sexual sin and divorce is playing out around you. You know someone who has been devastated by it and whose children are the walking wounded. You may be among the walking wounded yourself. Even if you are blessed with a great marriage, even if you are both walking with Christ, you know that you are not invulnerable to attack. Anyone is fair game.

In a sense, it is beginning to feel like a free fall.

Despite all of our attempts to contain it through church ministries, twelve-step programs, books, counseling, conferences—this virulent illness rages on, seemingly out of control.

The stories aren't all bad. God can take a dead relationship and bring it back to life, and we have seen Him heal and restore some of the most hopeless of marriages. But the question before us is this: Why such an epidemic? And what—if anything—can we do about it?

Perhaps the story of another epidemic will shed a little light.

## THE MOTHER OF ALL EPIDEMICS

In 1918, the world experienced what has been called "The Mother of All Epidemics"—a pandemic viral outbreak of influenza that infected an estimated 40 percent of the world's population and killed what has now been estimated to be *100 million people.*

That is absolutely mind-boggling. Never before or since has there been such an epidemic. But what caused it to spread so quickly (it did this in *one* year) and so far (it reached the innermost regions and outermost corners of *every* continent), and what enabled it to kill the strongest among us (killing not only the old and very young but also men and women in their prime)?

It all had to do with five factors: *timing, misdiagnosis, cover-up, lack of containment*, and a particularly *powerful strain* of virus.

The story unfolds like this.

### Timing

In 1918, we were at war. Millions of soldiers were mobilizing and being shipped out to fight around the globe in World War I. One day in the spring of 1918, a group of soldiers at Fort Riley, Kansas, were burning tons of horse manure. A choking dust storm kicked up and swept over the prairie. The sky went black and all the soldiers ran for cover.

The storm raged for hours—and then suddenly it stopped. Fort Riley was covered with a dense shroud of dirt and ashes. The soldiers were then ordered to clean up the mess; so working through the night, they swept and raked and shoveled and coughed. Two days later, Private Albert Gitchell, a cook, became quite ill. By noon, the hospital was flooded with 107 cases. Within the month there were 1,000 sick men.

### Misdiagnosis

The cause of death was initially reported as pneumonia, but even an unschooled observer could see that its symptoms were far more gruesome and lethal than that. Victims suffered excessive fevers, depressed bodily functions, labored breathing, violent coughs, projectile nosebleeds, and eventual suffocation from bodily fluids filling the lungs. Most unusual of all was that this disease was not only infecting but also actually *killing* our hardy twenty- to forty-year-olds, something never seen before in such disease outbreaks.

Meanwhile, infected soldiers were being moved from base to base, where they lived in crowded conditions and then deployed across the sea into battle. They took the virus with them, by plane and boat and land, establishing beachheads from which it then spread to the interiors of all the major continents on earth. Doctors were alarmed and flummoxed. Not realizing they were dealing with a virus, they tried every possible bacterial vaccine, but of course, to no avail. So the disease just continued to spread.

## Cover-up

The most unfortunate factor was that the news of this alarming epidemic was quashed, completely kept under wraps, even though soldiers were dying by the thousands. In one single month during the fall of 1918, 25,000 American soldiers alone died from the virus. But belligerents didn't want the news to get out so that the enemy would learn of their weakness. The world was kept in the dark until Spain (which was neutral) finally began writing of its devastating outbreak among its people—giving the virus its nickname, the "Spanish flu."

## Lack of Containment

But by then it was too late. Utilizing the world's expanding transportation systems, the virus raced to the corners of the earth. Once it contaminated the water systems, there was no escape. Russia (which had initially avoided the outbreak) was decimated. India lost at least 20 million people. Even the most remote areas were affected, such as the Alaskan Eskimo settlement of Brevig Mission, which lost 80 percent of its adult population.

America was blessed, losing only half a million of its citizens to the disease (it is thought because we were better fed and healthier than most other people on earth). Yet memories of coffins of flu victims piled up on our city streets, along with the tragedies of a world war, marked the lives of our forefathers and mothers who managed to live through it. So many lives were lost that the reported average life span in the decade that followed dropped by ten years.

It is unthinkable that while the world lost 20 million people to this Great War (in which 25 countries fought), it lost five times that many people to a submicroscopic virus, which we never saw with our eyes until scientists recovered its genetic material from a frozen victim in Alaska in 1997. Many mysteries remain unsolved as to why the Spanish flu was so virile or what happened to it when it simply disappeared in 1919.[1]

## A Moral Epidemic

There are too many correlations between the epidemic of 1918 and the present-day sexual epidemic to cover here. But as this book progresses, you will begin to see them clearly.

The *timing* has been uncanny. Just as the convergence of the First World War with the Spanish flu made possible a worldwide epidemic, so the converging circumstances of the last fifty years have made this epidemic possible. The sexual revolution of the sixties set the stage for a complete underestimation of the seriousness of sexual immorality, with its *misguided belief* that there is actually such a thing as "free sex." In a span of a few decades, sex without boundaries had gone mainstream. Then came the World Wide Web. Cyberspace (with all its accompanying inventions) poured fuel on the fire by bringing sexual temptation to the everyday man (and child) with the click of a mouse. Wholly *uncontained*, it spread like lightning via a wireless network around the globe.

Most important, it has made for the perfect *cover-up*, for sexual sin thrives best in the dark corners of anonymity and secrecy. Its surprising *virility* lies in its addictiveness, the most tragic aspect of its nature. Like a poisonous toxin (which is what *virus* actually means in Latin), it has silently moved right into our homes and gained access to our most vulnerable and innocent minds.

But there is a difference in this epidemic.

We have one significant advantage: We know who the enemy is. *And we know how to defeat him.* We know his nature, his war plan, and his mode of operation. And, unlike the doctors of 1918, we have an exact diagnosis, we possess a strategy to fight the enemy, we have the means to immunize our own souls, and we have been given a pathway of recovery for those who are afflicted.

In this book, we will attempt to expose the enemy and the means to defeat him. But you should know what this book will *not* attempt to do. This is not primarily a book about sex addiction, though addiction is part of the epidemic. We will talk about how men get into addiction and some of the red flags, but the subject of sexual addiction is a book all unto itself, and there are many excellent books available on the subject. This is also not a how-to sex manual—of which we have plenty. Nor is it primarily a research or psychology book, though we will use these in our discussion.

In a nutshell, this is a book about the innate male sexual struggle and the role that women play in that struggle. We will not only plumb a man's inner world, but we will explore the gifts a woman brings to her man as the "other sex," his partner, and that complementary creature that God designed her to be. Engaging our men—sometimes in the most perplexing and difficult areas—is the end focus of this book.

But underlying our entire discussion will be the central question: What does God say? For He is the Conceiver and Creator of sex, the Lover of our souls, the One who gave sex to us as a tiny glimpse of His own unfathomable joy and pleasure! His wisdom on the subject exceeds any wisdom of man.

Oh, the depth of the riches both of the wisdom and knowledge of God! (Rom. 11:33)

For the LORD gives wisdom; from His mouth come knowledge and understanding. (Prov. 2:6)

Frankly, until I began to research this book, I had no idea that God had so much to say about the compelling questions that affect women today. Issues like …

- the upside and downside of our innate male and female wiring;
- what manliness means, and why it is so rare today;
- why men think and act the way they do in every part of life, including sexuality;
- how a woman can become strongly feminine at her core;
- what women bring into life that men really need;
- how we are to think about masturbation and pornography;
- what a healthy view of beauty looks like in a world obsessed with size 0;

- how to draw out our men and connect relationally; and
- how to walk through the fire of conflict and build healthy boundaries.

Not only are there biblical answers to these questions, but there is great hope for those who know God. Why is there hope? Because …

> How blessed is he … whose hope is in the LORD his God.…
> The LORD *sets the prisoners free.*
> The LORD *opens the eyes of the blind;*
> The LORD *raises up those who are bowed down …*
> He *supports the fatherless and the widow.…*
> Praise the LORD! (Ps. 146:5, 7–10)

With such a God, there is hope for you. And there is hope for your man.

## WHAT A MAN NEEDS MOST

Before we jump into this book and deploy our chutes, there is one great question that needs to be answered. It rose to the top as I interviewed men and women for this book. It came up with the publisher. It came up with people I met on planes and at social gatherings, beauty parlors, and doctors' offices.

The question is this: What does a man need most from a woman?

The answer from men was always first and foremost, *philandros.*

Before I tell you what this means, let me tell you that you are good at this. Women are exceedingly gifted at *philandros.* This is a Greek word that combines two words: *phileo* (meaning "love") and *andros* (meaning "husband"). It literally means "husband-lover." And it is found in one single place in all of Scripture, Titus 2:4, where Paul urges older women to teach younger women "to love their husbands," *philandros,* or literally "to be husband-lovers."

But there is more here than what first meets the eye.

Usually Paul uses the Greek word *agape* when he speaks of love in the New Testament. *Agape* means a God-like *sacrificial, unchanging, unmerited* love. When Jesus died on the cross, it was because of *agape*. We love God because He first loved us—*agape* (1 John 4:19). When Paul tells husbands to "love your wives" (Eph. 5:25), he uses *agape*. We are also to love our husbands with *agape:* 1 Corinthians 13 says that *everything* we do is to be done with *agape*. In fact, "If I give all my possessions to feed the poor, and if I surrender my body to be burned, but do not have [*agape,*] it profits me nothing" (v. 3).

That is a stunning statement.

But in the book of Titus, Paul chooses *phileo*. *Phileo* is an affectionate, personal, deep, even passionate love. It is a love that selects out the loved one and prefers him over others. It is often used to describe the love between very close friends—a David and Jonathan kind of love. It's where we get the name "Philadelphia" (the city of brotherly love).

*Phileo* was the love Jesus had for His dear friend Lazarus (John 11:36, "See how He loved him!"), and it was His love for "the disciple whom Jesus loved" (most likely John in 13:23 of his gospel). *Phileo* is also the deep, affectionate love of God the Father for His Son (John 5:20). Paul uses *phileo* in Romans 12:10 when he says, "Be devoted to one another in brotherly love; give preference to one another in honor," and John uses it in referring to God's fatherly love for His children (Rev. 3:19).

*Phileo* is a warm, tender, preferring, kindred-spirit kind of love.

What does this mean for us as wives? It means that we are to fix our hearts upon our husbands in a special one-man kind of love. Each of us is to prefer our man over all others, to express feelings of deep affection, to treat him as an intimate friend, understanding him and valuing him, caring for him and meeting his needs, treating him with respect and high regard—just as we would anyone we value as an intimate friend.

In short, when we love our husbands with *philandros*, we relationally connect with them and live with them in an understanding way. This we can do. Women are remarkable connectors. We were wired for this. You give us enough information and we are masterful at understanding.

Men have said to me over and over again: "When you write your book, please ask women to *understand* us. Tell them we need this most of all." Our men crave *philandros*. And we long to give it.

When you "read your male," you are using *philandros*. You are entering his world and learning his language. You are figuring out what makes him tick. You are discovering what goes on inside his head every blessed day of his life. You are appreciating his innate differences. You are beginning to grasp the inherent weaknesses that come with those differences. You are realizing that *understanding* does not mean *excusing*. On the contrary, in the case of destructive sin, a true friend is called by God to love with a tough love—oftentimes the hardest part of *philandros*. "Faithful are the wounds of a friend," says Proverbs 27:6, but such wounds can sometimes save a life, a marriage, a family.

Perhaps you are familiar with God's command to husbands to "live with your wives in an understanding way" (1 Peter 3:7). We women love that verse!

It could be said that Titus 2:4 is the corresponding command to women to "live with your husbands in an understanding way."

My guess is that you are reading this book because you deeply desire to understand your man.

There is power in that.

You can't even imagine how much power.

# Chapter Three

# THE POWER OF A WOMAN

*The mother forms the character of the future man;*
*the sister bends the fibers that are hereafter to be the forest tree;*
*the wife sways the heart, whose energies may turn for good*
*or for evil the destinies of a nation.*
—*Charlotte Beecher*

Women hold a certain power over men that is astonishing, even inexplicable. Sometimes we are totally oblivious to that power. Other times we are not.

We can breathe life into our men, or we can drain it right out of them.

We can nurture them or destroy them.

We can bend them or rend them.

We are a force to be reckoned with.

And we always leave our mark.

With all of his aggressive physical prowess, a man is surprisingly vulnerable to a woman. And his need for her is fundamental. If you are a mother or wife or girlfriend, you can be the making of your man. Or you can be the breaking of him.

That is a sobering thought.

By power, I do not mean authority. This is not about the feminist view of an individual right and power to rule over a man. Rather, I mean *influence*—an invisible, intense, magnetic, inspiring, iron-sharpens-iron, blazingly pleasurable (or utterly miserable) kind of force that inevitably occurs when a woman enters the world of a man.

*Mothers:* You possess an unequalled early influence over your boys, which, once embedded, can last a lifetime. It has been said that the formative period for building character for eternity is in the nursery. The mother is queen of that realm and sways a scepter more potent than that of kings or priests. We imprint our sons from the womb, shaping their character, their emotional intelligence, their perspective of women, and their healthy emergence into independent manhood.

Oliver Wendell Holmes once said, "Mothers carry the key of our souls in their bosoms." There is good reason why athletes look into the camera and say, "Hi, Mom!" instead of "Thanks, Dad!" The bond a mother builds with a son is deep and enduring. Mothers also have a remarkable unseen power over marriages-to-come (that is, who their sons will choose to marry and *not* marry, and how they will relate to their future wives). In fact, that influence goes on to affect the future children that will come out of those marriages. Mothers contribute uniquely to the process of preparing their sons to become great dads.

*Singles:* You have no idea how much influence you have on the men you date and work with. Single women have the potential collectively of influencing an entire generation of men. I am personally convinced that you have more influence over guys than do their own male peers. And that is saying a lot. Guys can get crazy when they are together, but something powerful happens when a woman is "in the house." We call men back from the brink of "untempered wildness" to a core center of healthy male responsibility. In dating relationships, single women set the tone (you truly do) and raise or lower the bar of character and manliness in your men.

You are able to woo or repel, pleasure or torture (often both), inspire healthy relational "oneness" or (out of your own lack of emotional health) impossibly entangle. When a single woman clings too much or lives and dies by a man (rather than by the Lord), she wields a strange, subversive, unhealthy power. No man can be God, but if he thinks *you* think he is, he's in trouble. If he flees, he is smart. If he stays, watch out. You don't want him to think he is the ultimate source of your well-being or happiness; that can lead to a downward spiral of control and disrespect (and many other variant dysfunctions) that will crush a woman and her ability to bloom.

When a single woman becomes comfortable in her own skin and finds her primary strength and purpose in the Lord, she possesses a very healthy, freeing kind of influence. Her man instinctively wants to be a better man and prove himself worthy of her. And that is good for everyone.

*Wives*: We possess a particularly powerful position. *We can literally enable or disable our men.* We do it in a hundred ways. But let us consider just a few:

- We do it by the *priorities* we choose; there isn't a man alive who can change his wife's core will or driving priorities.
- We do it by the *expectations* we have of our men—realistic or not—or by our sheer *lack of expectations* (which is just as powerful).
- We do it by *what we say* and how we say it, or *what we don't say* and how we don't say it. What incredible power resides in our words!
- And, finally, we do it through sex.

Sex may well be the place wherein our greatest power lies. It definitely comes out as number one in surveys among Christian husbands.

Let's take a moment to understand why.

## THE HIDDEN POWER OF SEX

We will talk at length on this subject later in this book. But let us begin the discussion here.

Sex is where a man finds his greatest pleasure. Hands down, no contest. We will repeat that enough in this book that by the end it will be ingrained in your mind. But sex is also where he is at his most vulnerable, which we will repeatedly say as well. This is because of several reasons.

(1) Sex is one of the primary ways a man expresses his emotions. For some men who have never developed emotionally, it may be the only way they are able to let out their emotions (though the right woman can help such a man to grow in those expressions). Showing emotion is, for a man, a vulnerable thing.

(2) Your husband is also called to exclusivity. He is to be a one-woman man (1 Thess. 4:3–8; 1 Cor. 6:15–20; Prov. 5:15–19). God has laid down a boundary that basically says your husband can have sex only with you.

So think on that for moment. If a guy chooses to follow God's all-wise plan, he will have sex only with one woman for his entire life—literally "until death do you part." Now in this culture that is outright laughable and unthinkable. But there it is. God has commanded our husbands to find their sexual release and satisfaction in the "wife of [their] youth," and in her alone (Prov. 5:18).

The wisdom of this God-ordained boundary is that it is only in exclusivity that a marriage can grow and thrive. Without it, a marriage collapses. Fidelity establishes trust and commitment through "sickness and in health," through "richer or poorer," through the heavenly and the hellish times every marriage goes through. (Did you get that? *Every* marriage goes through such ups and downs.)

(3) God has wired our men with a natural sex drive that is inherently stronger than a woman's, and He has placed within them an innate desire to initiate. (Don't worry; I know about the growing trend in certain guys having a lower sex drive than their wives, and I promise we'll get to that in this book. But you can see where this is going.)

A man's boundaries and sex drive place him in a very dependent, vulnerable position. In a very real sense, you hold the sexual strings. Let's say your husband follows his natural need and inclination to initiate sex (a vulnerable thing, in and of itself, since he risks rejection). You can say "yay" or "nay" or "ummm … wait" (which is really a "nay" in his book). And he is not permitted by law to force himself upon you. At least not in this country, where a woman's freedoms are protected. So he is at your mercy.

There is a common-sense truism that says that the person with the *greatest need* in a particular area of a relationship is the person with the *least power* in that area. This works out emotionally, relationally, and definitely sexually. If most men naturally have a stronger sexual desire than their wives (thus a greater need), let me ask you: Who then possesses the greater power in that area? We do.

That puts a guy in a fragile position. Our feminine position of power through sex affects our men deeply.

Should a woman therefore be all about sex, without any consideration of her own needs or the state of communication in the relationship? God forbid. Nothing could be further from God's desire. There are far too many marriages in which this is precisely the case. But sex without love or valuing or communication or patience or consideration of a wife's needs is devastating. It kills the soul of a woman and destroys relationships.

On the other hand, should a woman look down upon her husband's natural healthy sexual needs and turn her back in coldness or disinterest? Again we say, God forbid. It must not be. This, too, is becoming an alarming trend in marriages. God has said to both wives and husbands, in so many words, "Don't deprive your marriage partner of sex, except in a specified needed time of separation for prayer—lest Satan gets his foot in the door" (see 1 Cor. 7:5). In other words, while there are special times when sex is forgone for the sake of the spiritual/relational good, sex is always meant to contain a *sacrificial* element—on the side of both men and women.

My husband is constantly hearing from tender and caring men whose wives simply don't want to have sex. It is impossible to describe their angst and frustration. In fact, it is not uncommon to hear of marriages where there has been no sex for six months, a year, or even in some cases, years. Two people may live together in such an arrangement, but their relationship will be nonexistent at best, and a nightmare at worst. Please hear this: *Unwarranted continual denial* is a mortal wound to our men. The temptation for such a man to stray is excruciating.

But also hear this: In the end a woman must *never compromise dignity and healthy communication* on the altar of sex. Never. This is far easier said than done. It requires wisdom, maturity, depth in the Lord, and great balance (a balance we will seek to find later in this book).

### *The Influence of Every Woman*

You may think, *I have little influence on my man.* Think it not.

Your lack of influence *is* an influence in itself. Lack of influence—that sense that he cares little about what you think or feel, that he will basically do whatever he pleases in spite of you—does not remove you from the equation. You are still very much present, and your perspective and feelings are an integral part of your marriage, whether he cares or not. He may think he is arbitrarily free, and you may *feel* impotent, but in actuality, many women are unwittingly part of the reason their husbands are ignoring them. Without knowing it, they are *enabling* their men to dismiss them.

But our men *need* to care—for their own sakes as well as ours. They need to value our input and validate our feelings. If you go on passively (or reactively, by patterns of unwise emotional responses), letting him treat you like dirt (which happens in far too many Christian marriages), if you let him disregard your human dignity and God's commands for him to honor and love you, *you* are part of the problem. Men tend to dismiss women who are passive or overly emotional. Your passivity or unhealthy reactivity possesses a power all its own—a power of enabling, allowing, permitting sin. But if a man ignores his wife, Peter says God will not hear his prayers (1 Peter 3:7). And this is serious. A man with a brass ceiling between his prayers and his God is in deep trouble.

So in a very real sense, you are responsible before God to move out of such passivity or impotent reactivity. Does this make sense? Hard as this is for peacemaking or love-hungry women, you absolutely must.

Again I ask you to hear me well: *Every woman possesses a certain influence upon her man—even when she thinks she does not.*

Having said that, the question that arises is this: How in the world did we come to possess such influence?

God gave it to us.

## THE FEMININE SPARK

Man was created with a crucial part missing. You are that missing piece.

Adam was like a brand-new Lamborghini Murciélago LP640 Roadster, made of steel, carbon fiber, and leather, and packing a 640-horsepower midmounted V12 that can go from 0 to 60 mph in 3.4 seconds. Only this particular Lamborghini was missing the spark plug.

Now most of you have no idea what I just said. But my guys tell me that is a pretty big deal. Imagine plunking down $350,000 i, climbing into the cockpit of your new *Back to the Future* car, closing those gull-wing doors, turning the key, and nothing. No spark.

The spark plug supplies the spark that ignites the fuel so that combustion can occur. Women are a man's spark plug.

A man is a wonderfully designed machine. Testosterone courses through his veins, fueling everything from his brain to his muscles to … well, everything else. He is hardwired to move out into the world and conquer it. He likes power and drive and speed and a sense of mission. But he needs the spark plug to create combustion so that he can move out and accomplish his calling.

Adam knew instinctively that he was missing something. It wasn't that he couldn't live or think or function in the world. He could. But there was no spark, no combustion, no fire. When he looked around God's creation, his missing piece was nowhere to be found.

Adam was perplexed and lonely. He was perplexed because he had met and named every living creature and none of them fit him. He was lonely even though he had intimate communion with God. This was a unique kind of loneliness for a unique kind of companionship. And this loneliness was by God's design.

God said, "It isn't good for the man to be alone." It was really the first time God had declared that something *wasn't* good in His creation.

So God created an "XX" to fit Adam's "XY."

You are an XX. And the XX is the spark.

## DNA AND SEXUALITY

XY is part of man's basic chromosomal makeup. It shapes every cell, every system, every part of his physiology and brain. It programs him. XX is part of a woman's basic chromosomal makeup. It's what makes her different in all those areas, yet remarkably fitting and complementing to a man.

DNA was not discovered until the 1950s, right about the time when the feminist movement was gaining momentum. There was a brief period in which Western culture bought into the idea expressed by Simone de Beauvoir, who said, "One is not born a woman but rather becomes one."

But the discovery of DNA opened up a whole new universe of understanding. Remarkable scientific research in the last half century has shocked and awed our world and indisputably established that "male" and "female" are engraved in our chromosomes and genes, and that maleness and femaleness profoundly influence our natural identity, bents, and instincts. The evidence is so overwhelming that Beauvoir's thinking (an original core tenet upon which feminism was based) has now been essentially laid to rest.

As a recent *Psychology Today* article declared, "It's safe to talk about sex differences again. Of course, it's the oldest story in the world. And the newest. But for a while it was also the most treacherous. Now it may be the most urgent."[1]

### *The Male and Female Brain*

Science is now replete with evidence for the remarkable differences hardwired into men and women. Not least remarkable is recent research connecting sex genes to the male/female brain and behavior.

> Males and females, it turns out, are different from the moment of conception, and the difference shows itself in every system of body and brain.... Sex differences ... unfold in the most private recesses of our lives, surreptitiously molding our responses to everything from stress to space to speech.[2]

The differences are astonishing and unmistakable. And they have powerful implications—physiologically, psychologically, relationally, and emotionally.

Scientists are learning, for example, that a person's sex influences *physical and emotional health*. The male Y chromosome spurs the brain to grow extra dopamine neurons (which in turn affect the motor skills that go awry in Parkinson's disease, an illness that afflicts twice as many males as females). These neurons are also involved in reward and motivation (which underlie addiction and novelty seeking). The Autism Research Centre at Cambridge has also found that the male XY chromosome is more vulnerable to autism (which overwhelmingly strikes males) and Asperger (which strikes males over females ten to one).[3]

Meanwhile at the Virginia Institute for Psychiatric and Behavioral Genetics, scientists have discovered that women's bodies respond to stress differently than do men's; they pour out higher levels of stress hormones at lower adversity levels, and their sex hormone progesterone blocks the system from turning off readily. This helps to explain why females outnumber men in cases of unipolar depression three to one.[4]

Research is also revealing a connection between the sex genes and our *mental and relational skills*. Neuroscientists have learned that sex genes influence aggression (in men) and maternal behavior (in women).[5] And while almost everyone has a mix of skills, there is a marked propensity in men to compartmentalize and excel in spatial cognition, and a marked propensity in women toward language development and verbal expression of emotions—all traceable back to the effects of our genetic ordering in the brain. The "social brain" and language centers are more developed in females, while fibers in white brain matter inhibit "information spread" and allow harder spatial tasks in the male brain.

Male and female minds are innately drawn to different aspects of the world around them....

Women's perceptual skills are oriented to quick—call it intuitive—*people reading*. Females are gifted at *detecting the feelings and thoughts of others, inferring intentions, absorbing contextual clues* and responding in emotionally appropriate ways…. Tuned to others, they more readily see alternate sides of an argument. Such empathy *fosters communication and primes females for attachment….*

Men focus first on minute detail, and *operate most easily with a certain detachment*. They construct rules-based analyses of the natural world, inanimate objects and events [italics mine].[6]

Scientists are also realizing that the "boy brain"—that kinetic, sometimes disorganized, maddeningly rough-and-tumble behavior in young boys that drives mothers and educators crazy—is actually not a defect; it is hardwired and advantageous. "Boys are biologically, developmentally, and psychologically different from girls," we are told in a cover story of *Newsweek*, and our lack of recognition of this has put our boys at a severe developmental disadvantage.[7]

It should not surprise us, therefore, that children tend to choose certain toys (humanlike dolls versus mechanical trucks), or that interrelationships between boys are markedly different from those of girls. Nor should it surprise us that grown men and women think and react differently throughout the whole of life.

We have been aware of our differences for centuries. Now science is verifying and explaining why this is true.

But there is one thing science does not explicitly say: God is at the heart of our differences. With His great inimitable forethought, God purposefully created Adam with his loneliness. And He wove the XX genetic code of Eve with something grand and majestic in mind.

### The XX Factor

A woman's extra X chromosome is pretty amazing. Like a brilliant diamond necklace, it is studded with an additional 1,000–1,500 genes.

Together, her complex double-X creates a magnetic attraction for the male of our species.

That is why when a woman enters a room, men *look* (italicized, underlined, bold print) at her. Men are drawn to our physical bodies. They remember our smell. They visualize us when we are gone.

We are soft. We have curves. We arouse something "other." We tap into a deep, enduring need. We move a man. We bring something new to the world that they need: a nonmale touch and perspective, a feminine softness and strength, an intuitive relational bent, a drive for intimacy.

This generates an alternate drive within men to want to be with us, to enjoy us—in every sense of the term—to be adored and respected by us, to be connected on a level that they can never find with a man.

But God created woman to be more than a magnet to a man. She was also designed to be a "helper suitable for him" (Gen. 2:18).

This is no weak or insignificant role. The Hebrew word for *helper* is a strong term. Scholars agree that it does not imply inferiority in a woman so much as it refers to the inadequacy of the man in his lonely state.[8] This very same word is used in describing God, the Helper of His people (Ps. 10:14; 30:10; 54:4).

The expression "suitable for him" means there is a complementary relationship. Eve "fit" Adam, supplying what he needed just as he supplied what she needed. Man and woman were designed to be *inter*dependent beings, each needing what the other innately possesses, and supplying what the other innately lacks.

To summarize, this means that even though she was the "second sex" (Beauvoir's title to her famous book), being second did not mean the woman was less. Rather, it meant that she was the counterpart.

So it was that when Eve was brought to Adam, he exclaimed,

This is *now* bone of my bones, and flesh of my flesh; she shall be called Woman. (Gen. 2:23)

You get the impression that if the ancient Hebrew language had used punctuation (which it didn't), there would be several exclamation points at the end of that sentence. She fit him like a glove. She was exactly what he needed.

Let me put this in concrete terms for us.

As a wife, you were meant to fit, complement, strongly help, and meet your husband at his point of need. God intended for you and your husband to be complementary partners in the task of filling the earth and subduing it (Gen. 1:28). As a mother, you were meant to be that warm, strong "other" by which your son could measure healthy femininity and embrace his own manhood. As a woman out in the world, your very presence was designed to be a gift to the men around you—a healthy XX in their otherwise XY world.

Dr. James Dobson once wrote that a woman "gives [a man] a reason to harness his masculine energy—to build a home, obtain and keep a job, remain sober, live within the law, spend money wisely, etc. Without positive feminine influence, he may redirect the power of testosterone in a way that is destructive to himself and to society at large."[9]

Women are a stabilizing force in a man's life. Without a woman's positive balancing and counterbalancing influence, a man can fall off the high wire.

But we can also just as easily push him off ourselves.

## For Ill or for Good

The greatest problem for all of us as women—even more than realizing the natural power we have been given—is in having the wisdom to use it well.

A woman needs the wisdom of a surgeon in wielding her feminine scalpel. Wisdom is the difference between …

- demanding/manipulating change—*or* becoming an astute catalyst for change;
- using passive-aggressive "signals"—*or* communicating your heart openly without malice;
- prematurely judging a man's intentions—*or* stepping back, asking good questions, and listening well;

- putting our men in their place (like, say, blasting them sky-high or nailing them to the wall)—*or* learning the fine-tuned art of arguing well;
- allowing sin to destroy your husband through passivity/emotional neediness—*or* courageously entering the fire of healthy biblical confrontation.

Do you see the stark contrast? One way of utilizing our feminine power is destructive; the other is redemptive.

What woman is able to be so balanced, healthy, or adept? You can be sure I have failed on every single count. A woman must mature to such a place of balance. We have to be humble enough to see and admit to our "stuff" and be brave enough to work at it. It takes great wisdom to develop the art of using our power well. Becoming a wise woman is like learning to build a fine piece of furniture. Or raise beautiful roses. Or sail a boat. You need excellent instruction and a great deal of practice. I don't know about you, but I don't want just any doctor cutting me open with his scalpel.

At a crucial moment, Eve influenced Adam. All she did was hand him the apple (or pear or passion fruit) after biting into it herself. But sometimes it is the small, simple choices that can make a pivotal difference. Her decision changed human history. Were they both responsible? Absolutely. In fact, according to Scripture, Adam was ultimately held more responsible than Eve (a subject that must be left for another book).

But talk about influence … now *there* was a moment.

It's important how we use our God-granted position of influence. We forget sometimes that Eve was a normal woman who lived, worked, made love, gave birth, and endured the grief of a murdered son, as well as countless other events not recorded in Scripture—without any mother of her own or any other mentor to advise and comfort her. We have to believe that she grew and increased in wisdom in her long lifetime. The experience of failure often gives birth to wisdom.

Since her day, women have continued to powerfully influence through their choices. Whether highly visible or quietly obscure, we have put our indelible—oftentimes decisive—mark upon history.

Two particularly fascinating stories in more modern times can be found in the biographies of Abraham Lincoln and Winston Churchill. The contrast between these two men and the women who touched their lives is worth the telling.

It is safe to say that few men in recent history have carried greater weight on their shoulders. Civil War tore Lincoln's country asunder from within, and Churchill's Great Britain was the last domino in Hitler's quest to rule Europe. It was questionable as to whether either of their nations would actually survive the conflict.

But what about their women?

### Nancy and Mary

Lincoln's mother was a saint. His wife was not.

Of his mother, Nancy Hanks Lincoln, the president once said, "All that I am or hope to be, I owe to my angel mother." On another occasion he said, "I remember my mother's prayers and they have always followed me." Nancy Lincoln was a wise, self-educated woman, but was ever poor and obscure. She died at the age of thirty-five when Abe was only ten. Not until her son became famous some thirty years later did anyone attempt to learn much about her, and by that time most of those who had known her were dead.

One neighbor and close acquaintance of Mrs. Lincoln who did remember her well was William Wood. Wood was an industrious, reliable man who had sat up with her all night during her final illness before she died. When asked of her, he said,

Abe got his mind and fixed morals from his good mother. Mrs. Lincoln was a very smart, intelligent, and intellectual woman; she was naturally strong-minded, was a gentle, kind, and tender woman, a Christian of the Baptist persuasion, she was a remarkable woman truly and indeed.[10]

Then there was Mary. Regarding his marriage to her, Lincoln wrote, "Marriage is neither heaven or hell; it is simply purgatory." Unlike his mother, Mary Todd Lincoln was born wealthy, well educated, and fiercely ambitious. She once told a friend she wanted to marry a man who would be president someday. She loved the fact that Abe had brought her status, importance, and the identity of first lady.

When Lincoln became president, Mary Todd intended to be her husband's chief advisor, but history reveals that instead she became his chief thorn in the flesh. She yelled, screamed, threw things, accused him of abandoning her when he traveled, and embarrassed him with her extravagant spending. Sadly, while presiding over a nation deeply divided, Lincoln's own house was also deeply divided. During the war, Mary became more erratic and demanding, while Lincoln grew more distant and withdrawn.[11]

I have yet to read a historian who looks upon her kindly.

Question: How does a man endure such a woman?

Answer: With great difficulty.

One wonders if he could have held up under the strain had his mother not so faithfully ingrained in him as a child the importance of strength of character and a deep trust in God.

## Jenny and Clementine

Winston Churchill also had two very different women in his life.

His mother, Jenny Churchill, was a notorious flirt and adulteress. In fact, there was widespread speculation that Lord Randolph Churchill was not actually Winston's father. Whatever the case, Lord Churchill treated his son with distance and disdain. And his mother, always the glamorous social gadabout, was entirely absent from his early childhood. Were it not for his loving nanny, Mrs. Everest, Winston would have grown up quite destitute of any adult nurturing or care.

One newspaper wrote candidly at Jenny's death that she was "one of the liveliest and most controversial women of her time."[12] When Churchill looked back and wrote of his lonely years growing up, he remembered his mother in those days as some distant being for which he had little feeling or attachment. Her lack of love or attention left a hole in his young, boyish heart.[13]

Clementine Hozier became the saving grace in Churchill's life. From the moment they fell in love and married, their friendship was cemented—and it only grew stronger over the long, hard years. Even with all the great men around her husband in his years as prime minister, Churchill considered her to be his greatest confidante, wise counselor, and most ardent supporter.

Clementine didn't know everything about the war, but she knew everything about her husband. It is really impossible to summarize their relationship here or its importance to Churchill. From the beginning, she was constantly tuned in to her husband's needs. If he was sick, depressed, exhausted, or troubled, she was keenly aware and did whatever she possibly could to care for him. When all were against him, he always had Clemmie to come home to. They were constantly jotting affectionate, thoughtful notes to be passed along to one another, sometimes within their very own home during the thick of the war. They used little nicknames—"Kitty" and "Pug"—and addressed one another as "my darling" or "my tender love." In one letter during a long separation, she wrote to Winston:

My Darling, Every time the post came yesterday I ran down to the hall for the letter … I crept downstairs thro' the sleeping house & there on the hall table was the much wished-for blue envelope …

Winston, who was weighing a most important, irrevocable decision, jotted to her soon after:

My dearest soul, You have seen me very weak & foolish & mentally infirm this week. Dual obligations, both honourable both weighty have rent me … I cannot tell you how much I love and honour you and how sweet and steadfast you have been through all my hesitations & perplexity.[14]

It is difficult to imagine such an exchange between Abe and Mary Lincoln. Winston and Clementine certainly had their struggles: He was terrible with money and led a furiously busy life; she anguished over and even sometimes strongly disagreed with some of his biggest political decisions. But she was a class act and never demeaned him publicly. Together, they were truly a team. They pondered political and personal decisions together, worked side by side in the war effort, and continually expressed their unwavering love for each other.

Clemmie could read Winston like the morning paper. And Winston often said he could not have led the nation in such a dark time without her.[15]

I would submit to you that in the midst of the horrors of war for these men, Lincoln's mother proved to be his saving grace, while Churchill's wife became his single greatest ally.

## THE WAR AT HAND

Our men are very much in a war of their own. We know this because their language is filled with fighting words like "battle" and "weapons" and "defense systems." It's as if our men practically live in full combat gear. They talk of an "enemy" who implements brilliantly deceptive "strategies." They are constantly reading books with titles like *Every Man's Battle*, *A Winnable War*, *The Warrior Man*, and *Tender Warrior*. My husband's first book to men in the nineties was titled *Point Man*, which refers to the most dangerous position on a patrol of men heading into enemy territory.

There are no volunteers in this war. Every man is called to duty. And every man has his own vulnerabilities.

The good news is that the majority of godly Christian men have not relinquished the battle. They care deeply about their wives and marriages and families. They don't want to become one more name on the long casualty list.

Is there hope for our boys and men? Absolutely.

*There is great hope for our men.*

There is hope because God fights for them. "You come to me with a sword, a spear, and a javelin," cried David as a ruddy youth to Goliath. "But I come to you in the name of the LORD of hosts.... For the battle is the LORD's and He will give you into our hands" (1 Sam. 17:45, 47).

God understands what our men face, day in and day out. He knows where each one is vulnerable. He is looking for men who will wholly trust Him and—like young David of old—dare to take up their sling and five stones, and with a warrior's skill, engage the enemy.

But we women are not to be passive bystanders in this arena. We are right in the thick of it with them. As their closest companions, we are their most powerful allies, their buddies in the foxhole. What's more, we are their *secret weapon.* You or I could be that one smooth stone our man will use to bring the enemy down.

We cannot be their God and Savior. Many of us are fixers and need to remind ourselves of this truth from the Lord: "There is no savior besides Me" (Hos. 13:4). Only God can change the human heart and remove blinders from eyes.

But we can be a catalyst for change, a partner in arms, a saving grace.

The first line of defense is *philandros.* This we know.

But how are we to understand a creature whose drives and inherent makeup are so different from ours? Let me put it to you in the form of a question: Next to being understood, what do you think a man needs, desires, and craves most from a woman?

You will be surprised at the answer.

Let me give you one hint: It isn't sex.

## Chapter Four

# DIFFERENT LANGUAGES, EQUAL NEEDS

*Men are from Earth, and women are from Earth.*
—Daniel Akin

The question that often arises among men today is, "What *does* a woman want?"

The question that often arises among women is, "Why do men want *that*?"

We mystify our men. They frustrate us. And vice versa.

One day as I was sitting in the chair at the beauty salon, a middle-aged *GQ*-type sat down in the opposite chair. He began to talk about his business, and we realized we had some common friends. He was very chatty for a man. So it wasn't long before he had told me that he was in his second marriage to a much younger woman who (contrary to his first wife) believed a husband and wife should "live and let live."

My female hairdresser and I exchanged knowing looks as she clipped.

Then he asked, "What do you do?"

"Well, I'm a writer," I said vaguely.

"Really? What do you write about?" he asked.

I hedged around about writing books for women from a Christian perspective. "Wow!" he said, beaming.

I was now an intriguing point of interest. "What are you writing about right now?" He had me in a corner.

"Well, I'm writing a book to women explaining male sexuality."

"Really?" He was completely engrossed. "Why on earth would you want to do that? Men are easy to understand. Women are the ones who are a complete mystery!"

"Ah," I said, "then it will be an easy book to write."

But he pursued the conversation, grilling me on every point of the book. He was checking my facts. To his surprise, he had to admit they were right on target. "How did you figure all of that out?" he asked.

"Oh, I didn't," I said. "My husband taught me everything I know."

"Well, then," he said, "could you please ask him to write one on women?"

Men tell me regularly that they can't seem to crack the feminine code. It's as if we speak a complex language that requires highly specialized cryptography. "I've worked with female patients every day for over twenty years," one doctor told me recently, "and I still find them to be indecipherable."

Even Sigmund Freud despaired: "Despite my thirty years of research into the feminine soul, I have not yet been able to answer the great question that has never been answered: What does a woman want?"

We women on the other hand sometimes wonder if Woody Allen represented all men when he said, "My second favorite organ is the brain." Surely men are not that simple and shallow. One woman aptly said, "When it comes to sex, a man's 'on' button is never off."[1]

There is a humorous story about a man who became ill and was growing steadily worse. So his wife took him to the doctor for tests. When he finally appeared in the waiting room, she asked about the doctor's diagnosis. "He didn't say," said her husband.

"Well, how serious does he think your condition is?" she asked, growing anxious.

"He didn't say," he replied.

"Well, that is unacceptable," she said, and with that she stormed past the front desk right into the doctor's office. Standing before him, she said, "Doctor, I just need to know! Is my husband going to live or die?"

"Take it easy," said the doctor. "All he needs is three good meals every day and sex twice a day, and he'll be just fine."

When she reentered the waiting room, she sat down in silence.

"Well, what did he say?" her husband asked.

"He said you're going to die," she replied.

Women are quite certain that sex does not solve everything. Sometimes it doesn't solve anything.

How different could we possibly be?

John Gray, author of *Men Are from Mars, Women Are from Venus*, has made a zillion dollars off the idea that we come from different planets.

And sometimes one does have to wonder.

## MEN ARE FROM PLANET SEX, WOMEN ARE FROM PLANET LOVE

Men do love sex. They like it better than sports or cars or gladiator movies, which is saying a whole lot. So of course they tend to think about it a lot. If you are married, your husband thinks about having sex with you when he wakes up (he's rested then), when he's in the middle of a business deal, when he's driving home at night, and even when he's arguing in the kitchen with you after dinner.

We women really don't fathom that. We are mystified by such a fixation on an "act," such an intense urge to merge.

We women tend to think a lot about love. We love the thought of being loved—and loving in return. We like a good girly movie, a Jane Austen novel, a strong man who looks deeply into our eyes. We like the idea of being pursued and wooed. We like candles and music and holding hands and cuddling. And intimate conversation is huge for us. Oh, and we also enjoy hugging and kissing. Our men are happy about this last part, but they really don't fathom our fixation on relational intimacy and our urge for presex connection.

I recently read about a new concept that is revolutionizing people's love lives. It's called PSD, and even though it first appeared in *Wired* magazine, it has nothing to do with computers. PSD was first put forward by Roger Libby, sex therapist at the Institute for Advanced Study of Human Sexuality in San Francisco. Now this is nothing against you people from San Francisco; but PSD stands for "presex discussion." This revolutionary idea (I am totally serious) is that "if you get to know the person you're about to have sex with, even a little bit, the sex is improved."[2]

Amazing. Do these brilliant minds not realize that women have been practicing PSD for aeons? But let us move forward.

I am often asked, how much *should* a man think about having sex? While there is a trend of lowered libido among a certain population of men,[3] the majority of men have a healthy sex drive, even when they are unhealthy! It boggles the mind, actually. We should probably ask the alternate question, which is, how much *should* a woman think about romantic, relational love? Lots of men honestly wonder.

Here is the important thing. God wired men to think about sex, and He wired women to desire loving relationship. But these two drives don't completely define us. Not by a long shot.

## MEN ARE LOVERS, WOMEN ARE SEXUAL BEINGS

Despite their drive toward sex, men do desire love. They write about it in eloquent poetry and beautiful songs. The classics, mostly written by men, are filled with great and tragic love stories. Men often dream of finding a woman to love and protect and cherish, and they think about being great lovers themselves. God intended that the sex drive within men should draw them into loving relationship.

It is true that many men have abandoned this inclination in pursuit of raw sexual pleasure. But such pursuit is a misdirection of the male sex drive—and inevitably ends up on the ash heap. Even Woody Allen's wanderlust character, Alvy, admits to Annie Hall that indeed, "Sex without love is an empty experience."[4]

In his book *False Intimacy*, Dr. Harry Schaumburg describes men who get addicted to the pursuit of sex without intimate love:

> They create a self-perpetuating hell of unremitting anguish that demands *moments of illusory relief* through more sexual behavior and the *fantasy of being loved* [italics mine].[5]

In the end we can say that men, too, are seeking to find love in the sex act. They desire and need—indeed, they *require*—loving relationship.

Likewise, despite our drive toward emotional and romantic love, women truly enjoy sex. Granted, our sex drive is different from our men, for we do not possess the physiological makeup that creates the same drive. But this doesn't mean that we have no desire. The male testosterone-type hormones create an "assertive" sexual desire, while higher levels of estrogen in women lead to a "receptive" type of sexual desire.[6] In her most natural feminine state, a woman really does prefer to be the pursued, rather than to be the pursuer.[7]

What a freeing concept. Today's relentless media image of the aggressive, body-obsessed, sexually charged woman (primarily churned out by men, by the way) is *abnormal*. And in the end, as with her male counterpart, her life is an equally empty one.

So we can say this: *While women are sexual beings, we are not carbon copies of our men*. We are responders. This difference goes very deep (for instance, we tend to naturally have a lower libido, are more profoundly affected by nonsexual aspects of life, and need a bridge from the kitchen into the bedroom). But this does not negate our desire for sex. Rather, it defines the *nature* of our desire. Even among women whose libido happens to be higher than their husbands', the majority of them would prefer for their husbands to be the primary initiator in marriage.

This is only a taste of the sexual differences between us. Later we will explore our differences in depth. But let us answer a few natural questions that immediately come to mind.

Do men wish their wives would initiate lovemaking sometimes? Absolutely. They love it when that happens. But joyful as it may make a man, his primary desire is that his wife would be the warm responder God created her to be.

Can normal women lose interest in sex at certain times in life? Certainly. Many factors affect us, such as childbirth, sickness, hormonal imbalance, or pressures of life. But even in these times, most women still *want* to be interested. The majority of women truly desire to have a great sexual relationship with their husbands.[8]

Can a woman lose her ability to respond sexually? You bet. An unhealthy marriage relationship can do that to a woman. *A responder has to have something to respond to.* If a man is unloving, a woman's screen goes black. She moves emotionally into "shutdown." Our need for love and connection is hardwired into us by God. It is a gift we possess! The truth is that even though a woman can fake it and set aside her wounded feelings to please her husband, he will intuitively know. And the lack of real connection will affect them both at a very deep level.

Even so, unless she is riddled by bitterness and self-absorption, a wounded woman still *desires* to experience healthy sexuality in the way God intended it to be. Women were designed by God to enjoy sex. And when we are loved well by our men, we truly do.

This is exceedingly good news!

Men desire love (which is the greatest news on earth for women!), and women enjoy sex (which is unbelievably exciting news for men!), even though our natural inclinations and drives are fundamentally different.

Yet—and here is the amazing thing—as different as we may be in our innate wiring, *we share far more similarities than we do differences.* This is a striking, oft-unrecognized truth. We are not from other planets. Men and women are both from planet Earth, as Daniel Akin wisely points out in his book *God on Sex.*[9]

## MEN ARE FROM EARTH, WOMEN ARE FROM EARTH

Man and woman are *homo sapiens*, made in the image of God. We are cut out of the same cloth, so to speak. And that makes us far more alike than different.

> God created man in His own image, ... male and female He created them. God blessed them. (Gen. 1:27–28)

In our humanness, we are equal in our *ability* to feel, think, reason, contemplate God, and make moral decisions. We are equal in our *assignment* to rule over creation (Gen. 1:28) and in our *innate dignity and value* bestowed upon us by our Creator (Ps. 8:4–6). And among those who are believers, we are equally blessed as *joint heirs* and *gifted members* of the body of Christ.

But our equality goes deeper still—to our core underlying needs.

When it comes right down to it, we may speak different sexual languages, but we share the same fundamental needs:

- a mutual longing for connection;
- a need to be valued, respected, and understood; and
- an inescapable desire for a loving, lifelong partnership with the opposite sex.

While we are hardwired differently, we are headed in the same direction. And the implications are vastly important:

- Women need to be *loved*. So do men.
- Men need to be *respected*. So do women.
- Women need *connection*. So do men.
- Men need to be *admired*. So do women.

It's an amazing thing to discover that when all is said and done, your husband has the same fundamental needs as you do. Even more stunning is the fact that we share the single most fundamental need of all. What is that need? In a word, it is *intimacy*.

## INTIMACY: THE UNDERLYING NEED

Sexual (or *eros*) love and romantic love were never meant to be an end in themselves. They were meant to be elements of—and a drive toward—something much deeper and enduring. That something is *intimacy*. Intimacy is the underlying drive in both sexes. In fact, it is the fundamental connecting drive we both share. Women crave it, and so do our men.

Intimacy is another word for *oneness*—emotional, spiritual, relational, and physical. It is what we were created for:

> For this reason a man shall leave his father and his mother, and be joined to his wife; and they shall become *one flesh*. (Gen. 2:24)

Hebrew scholars open our minds to this idea: "'One flesh' speaks of a spiritual *oneness*, a vital *communion of heart as well as body*, in which it finds its consummation [italics mine]."[10] Theologian H. C. Leupold writes, "Becoming 'one flesh' involves the *complete identification of one personality with the other in a community of interests and pursuits, a union consummated in intercourse* [italics mine]."[11]

In other words, though consummated in sex, *oneness* is an intimate connection of mind, body, and soul. Adam "knew" Eve when he had sex with her (Gen. 4:1 KJV; from the Hebrew *yada*, meaning "to know and become known, to investigate and clearly understand"). Marital *oneness* is a kind of "knowing" unlike that of any other human-to-human knowing.

### Men and Intimacy

Everybody knows that women are wired for intimacy. But men? Perhaps the biggest surprise for women is to hear men express it themselves. In his book *What Men Want*, Dr. H. Norman Wright reports from his nationwide survey of Christian men and counselors that …

Men do want more from sex than sex! They want complete relationships. Complete—meaning *intimate*—sexually, emotionally, spiritually, and relationally. Men do *hunger for intimacy*, despite the fact that many substitute sex for sharing and emotion [italics mine].[12]

A landmark study conducted by Dr. Archibald Hart was equally revealing:

Believe it or not, men want to be joined in *close, intimate companionship* with their partners.... We seek a partner from the opposite sex as if to restore our completeness. Sexual attraction is the force that drives this attraction aimed at restoring our wholeness [italics mine].[13]

Men were made for intimacy. They not only need it, but they also are ever on the search for it.

### The Winepress of Intimacy

When you and your mate enter into such intimacy, it is much like being put through a winepress. Husband and wife are each like a cluster of grapes, pressed and crushed until each one is turned into a delectable cup of wine that can then be poured and drunk together. If you stay in the winepress day after day and year after year, your love (and your lovemaking) grow better with age, just like a fine wine.

In his brilliant little masterpiece *The Mystery of Marriage*, Mike Mason uses this poignant image of the "winepress of intimacy":

There is nothing like the experience of being humbled by another person and by the same person day in and day out. It can be exhausting, unnerving, infuriating, disintegrating. There is no suffering like the suffering involved in being close to another person. But neither is there any joy nor any real comfort at all outside of intimacy, outside the joy and the comfort that are wrung out like wine from the crush and ferment of two lives being pressed together.[14]

This is what we were made for! We hunger for it as a baby hungers for her mother's milk. But like anything precious and lasting, it does not come without hard work and some degree of pain. Is it humbling? Oh yes. Nothing is more terrifying or humbling than for another person to become privy to the previously clothed and hidden, but now naked and exposed, person of your heart. And nothing is more difficult than to have this very same person pressing ever so gently against you in an iron-sharpening-iron call for change.

Intimacy is costly. By its very nature it confronts our pride and moves us toward a disquieting but wonderful kind of metamorphosis. It is like the emerging of a caterpillar from its earthly cage into the sky. Or like the moving of a baby through the birth canal into a new world of oxygen and light. Or the bursting forth of irises in spring at the end of a bitter winter. Or the shaping of a beautiful diamond—which occurs only in the deep places of the earth, under great pressure, over long periods of time.

Mason also writes,

Naturally it is painful to be sharpened, painful to have one's dullness filed to a point.... [But] who ever heard of being sharpened against a warm, familiar body of loved flesh? Only the Lord could have devised such an awesomely tender and heartwarming means for men and women to be made into swords.[15]

But when two people enter the winepress of intimacy, we become far better people, and we experience a love more indescribably wonderful than anything else known to man this side of heaven.

So what holds us back? Why do we find it to be so incredibly difficult to achieve in marriage? There is a very simple but conclusive answer.

It is because of the Fall.

## OUR SEXUAL TOWER OF BABEL

The Fall occurred when Adam and Eve sinned. And it was our undoing.

Before sin, intimacy was natural. Adam and Eve were "naked and unashamed"—physically, spiritually, emotionally, relationally. Adam felt understood by Eve. Eve trusted Adam. Both partners appreciated their differences. There was no pressure in sex, only pleasure and oneness. Love in Eden was a pure, unadulterated thing.

But when Adam and Eve sinned, death entered the world. And our nature became tainted by a proclivity to sin. And that changed everything.

- We became separated from God and from one another.
- Our minds became darkened.
- We felt shame and hid ourselves ("The man and his wife hid," Gen. 3:8).
- We began rationalizing and excusing our sin ("I was afraid," 3:10).
- We blamed one another ("The woman whom You gave to be with me, she ..."; "The serpent deceived me ...," 3:12–13).
- Jealousy entered the picture; then lies; then anger at man and God; then murder (4:1–9).
- Soon there was open infidelity (Lamech was the first to take more than one wife, 4:19).

By Genesis 6 there was so much sexual immorality (vv. 1–2) and so much wickedness ("Every intent of the thoughts of [man's] heart was only evil continually," 6:5) that God became sorry He had ever made man on the earth (6:6).

In other words, it all went very bad.

The effect of the Fall on male/female relationships was catastrophic. In a very real sense, the Fall became our *sexual Tower of Babel.* Our sexual languages literally became confused and inevitably separated us.

- Pride replaced humility.
- Fear of exposure replaced openness and transparency.
- Self-gratification replaced patience and sacrifice.
- Hurt and anger replaced conflict resolution.
- Denial or escape became our method of coping.

We suddenly found that we couldn't "read" one another; we had lost the ability to speak one another's language. "Why can't a woman be more like a man?" cried men. "Why can't men be more sensitive and transparent?" cried women. While our sexual attraction continued to thrive, our sexual understanding became illusive and frustrating. Sin had done its divisive work.

As Schaumburg writes, "The fall didn't diminish our capacity for intimacy; it created a distortion and an agonizing disruption of it."[16] The barrier between men and women became a language gap akin to, say, French and Russian, or Chinese and English.

In other words, not only did sin touch our personalities and backgrounds, it created a chasm of innate *mis*understanding between the sexes.

## A CANYON AND A BRIDGE

Picture yourself standing at the Grand Canyon. You are on one ledge. Less than a quarter mile away stands your mate on an opposite ledge. It appears that you are really quite close. You're only a little over a thousand feet apart—as the crow flies. If you are a young couple newly in love, you feel much closer—more like one centimeter apart.

By the way, enjoy that! It is a wonderful time of life. I love Mason's description of the ecstasy of new love:

> In a person about to be married there is a quality of footloose derailment, as if an old rusty locomotive had suddenly sprouted wings and soared away from its tracks. Being engaged is like entering a new stage of childhood, right down to the feeling of strange new chemicals being released into the body. It is, in fact, like having a *new body,*

like being a brand-new creature just emerged from a cocoon, with shining skin not quite dry. It is like a baptism. The world is so *bright*, and this crazy new body is so incredibly *sensitive* to everything.[17]

But of course, love cannot remain in this state forever. It must grow roots and rise tall; it must withstand the wind and rain; it must endure through the heat of summer and the cold of winter. As Mason says, "Sooner or later, love throws its pail of cold water in our faces." Every couple discovers that if their love is to survive and thrive, there is hard work to be done. There are risks to be taken. The canyon must be bridged.

For some of you, that canyon is very deep—with cliffs and precipices, rugged rocks and ridges and perhaps even a river, with treacherous turns and white-water rapids. The canyon valley beneath you has separated you by miles and miles. There is so much pain from your past and so much hurt in your present, it appears to be unbridgeable. For years you may have lived in a state of being physically close yet emotionally disjointed and relationally disconnected.

For others of you, the canyon may not be so deep, nor the distance quite so far. Yet even in the best of marriages between the most blessed of people, the bridge must still be continually built. Intimacy can't survive on thin air. It has to be fed and nourished.

There are times in marriage when you find yourself in such a lonely place, when the chasm of misunderstanding is so great, when trust is so eroded and love is so wounded that it honestly feels like you could fall and perish. There is no greater loneliness than the loneliness of a broken "two."

We need help. We need a steel-corded rope to carry us across. We need a Herculean scaffold upon which to build our bridge. Man cannot give us this. Which one among us—no matter how scholarly or credentialed—has the wisdom and power for such a task? If we have only ourselves, we are lost.

Unless the LORD builds the house, they labor in vain who build it. (Ps. 127:1)

Only God can be that rope, that scaffolding. He alone can build the bridge. He is the Missing Piece without which we will never find true purpose and meaning or capacity for "oneness."

### The Centerpiece of Intimacy

God created every man and woman with a *unique need for intimacy with Him*. Because of the Fall we are born with a void, a central piece, a missing inner gear of the soul that enables the female "spark" and the male "engine" to connect and move in sync.

God Himself is the great "Other," the Missing Piece of the human heart. And no man or woman or thing on this earth can fill that great divine void. The seventeenth-century Christian thinker and philosopher Blaise Pascal wrote of this "infinite abyss" within us all:

> What else does this craving, and this helplessness, proclaim but that there was once in man a true happiness, of which all that now remains is the empty print and trace? This he tries in vain to fill with everything around him, seeking … the help he cannot find in those [things] that are, though none can help, since this *infinite abyss* can be filled only with an infinite and immutable object; in other words, by God himself.
>
> God alone is man's true good [italics mine].[18]

God created us to know Him and walk with Him. J. I. Packer writes in his classic book *Knowing God*,

> What were we made for? *To know God.*
> What aim should we set ourselves in life? *To know God.*
> What is the "eternal life" that Jesus gives? *Knowledge of God.*
> "This is life eternal, *that they might know thee*, the only true God, and Jesus Christ, whom thou hast sent" (John 17:3).

What is the best thing in life, bringing more joy, delight, and contentment, than anything else? *Knowledge of God* [italics mine].[19]

The Lord Himself says,

Let not a wise man boast of his wisdom ... the mighty man boast of his might ... a rich man boast of his riches; but *let him who boasts boast of this, that he understands and knows Me.* (Jer. 9:23–24)

When God is missing in our lives, we are disoriented, out of sync, ever reaching, and, in the end, quite wretched. Even if you have found a great love and friendship with another human being, apart from God you're still like two people adrift, two castaways on a raft that eventually washes up on some empty island. You may be together, but you are lost together. It is only in knowing God that we can become grounded and oriented. It is only in knowing Him that we can begin to understand life, including how to function as men and women.

He must be our centerpiece, our means of survival, the rock of our security, the hope upon which we ultimately rely.

Do you know God? Is He your greatest love? Is He your primary source of sustenance and significance? If so, then you have a foundation upon which to build the bridge of intimacy with your man. If not, you *can* know Him. He is there, He knows your heart, and He is ready to meet you where you are. He came into this world to save you and to give you a new life. The prayer of the woman who says, "God, I want to know You. Help me!" will be heard. Have you been living a life far from Him? "Seek the LORD while He may be found; call upon Him.... Let the wicked [*which is every last one of us*] ... return to the LORD, and He will have compassion on him, ... for He will abundantly pardon" (Isa. 55:6–7). When you call upon Him, He will hear your cry:

Let us draw near with confidence to the throne of grace, so that we may receive mercy and find grace to help in time of need. (Heb. 4:16)

*A Male Lexicon*

The "bridge" we speak of is another word for communication.

Now, we women are great communicators. No one is better at bridge-building. We could build the Golden Gate if you just give us the right tools.

But we have to have the tools. And the first tool we need is a lexicon. A "male lexicon."

A lexicon explains the words of an unknown language; it translates that language into our own. So just as the Hebrew and Greek lexicons translate those languages into English, a male lexicon translates a man's inner sexual language to a woman. Interestingly enough, the male lexicon is embedded in the Greek and Hebrew lexicons (for they are the languages of the Bible). It is in the pages of Scripture that God gives us a foundational understanding of our men.

Consider the next two sections of this book as a kind of male lexicon. Section II will open our eyes to the two modern battlefronts in the ongoing male sexual war. Section III will take us deep into the male mind and explain four inherent struggles unique to our men. Section IV will highlight the gifts women bring to the table and seek to equip us to be wise partners in this great struggle.

So let's put on our fatigues and field glasses and, armed with God's Word—our compass, map, and light—let us begin our journey into their world.

# SECTION II
## READING THE ENEMY'S TACTICS

# Chapter Five

# IN SEARCH OF MANLINESS (I):
# THE LOST MALE TEMPLATE

*Our manhood has been emasculated,*
*and that has sterilized our ability to reproduce.*
—*Edwin Louis Cole*

*Be on the alert, stand firm in the faith, act like men, be strong.*
—*1 Corinthians 16:13*

You have undoubtedly heard of MI6, the Britain's version of our CIA. But you may have never heard of Genevieve Touzalin, a secret member of its early version (MI5) in the 1940s. Genevieve was actually her French undercover name during World War II. Her real name was Pearl Cornioley, whose undercover operations behind enemy lines in France were only finally released upon her death in February 2008.

Pearl was a nervy young British woman who spoke fluent French and proved to be one of Britain's most effective spies throughout the war. She parachuted into France and, posing as a cosmetics saleswoman, passed on secret messages to Resistance members by hiding communiqués in the hem of her skirt.

After the capture of her French cell leader (who ran the Resistance in the Loire River Valley—about 240 miles from the Normandy beaches), she assumed control out of necessity and went on to coordinate a total of 3,000 French Resistance fighters in a host of guerilla warfare missions.

They interrupted the Paris-Bordeaux railway line more than 800 times and attacked convoys in June 1944, the month of the D-Day invasion.

Her pivotal underground role proved so vexing that the Nazis issued a reward of 1 million francs for her capture. But remarkably she escaped France via Spain to England. Her bravery, for which both England and France eventually awarded her highest honors, was astonishing.

"She goes through Gestapo lines, helps airmen escape to safety, and battles the Nazis in the field," wrote World War II historian Mark Dunton. Yet despite her seamless transformation into the streetwise Genevieve, she never forgot her family back home, sending handwritten notes to them via London officials throughout her time as a spy.[1]

In this section, Reading the Enemy's Tactics, you and I are parachuting behind enemy lines. We are doing it because we love our families and deeply care about our men. Satan does not want us to know what he is up to, and he certainly doesn't want us to use our feminine skills to thwart his efforts. But just as Pearl bravely entered enemy territory, so can we. So *must* we. That is our mission in these next four chapters.

## TWO FRONTS

There are two fronts in the male sexual war.

The first is in the area of *masculine identity.*

The second is in the area of *sex.*

On the one hand, our men have lost their template for masculinity. On the other, sex itself has become a problem of epidemic proportions. Exacerbating the situation is the fact that we women are in an identity crisis of our own (which we will explore in upcoming chapters).

We begin with the first front in the male sexual war: the search for manliness. Why is this so important? Because the loss of a male template in our culture has set the stage for a sexual crisis among our men unlike anything seen in Western civilization.

## *Wanted: A Manly Template*

Young single women today often say to me, "Where are all the 'manly' men?" The relational reluctance among single guys drives them crazy. Many married women express the same kind of frustration over a husband who is ill inclined toward leadership at home or moving intentionally toward them. And mothers are watching their boys grow up in a world woefully lacking in healthy male role models.

Writer Regis Nicoll observes,

> Whether it is Alpha male, Metro male, or the Uber male, each is a dwarfed ideal whose shelf-life is determined by popular whim. Together they form a kaleidoscopic vision that has left a generation of men clueless about their masculine identity.[2]

It is important to understand what has happened to our men. Quietly but surely over the last century they have undergone an acute identity crisis. Like a pilot flying in fog without instruments, our men have found themselves in a mixed-message, upside-down world without a clear template. And the resulting masculine disorientation has affected us all.

When we speak of "manliness," we are referring to the natural, God-given proclivity toward *courage*, healthy *aggressiveness*, and *readiness to lead* in personal relationships when it is proper to do so.[3] Such manliness was commanded by God: Be *men* (1 Kings 2:2; 1 Cor. 16:13); be *leaders* (Eph. 5:23; 1 Cor. 11:3; 1 Tim. 3:1, 4–5); be *warriors for good* (1 Tim. 1:18; 6:12); be *strong* and *courageous* (Josh. 1:6–9; 2 Tim. 1:7).

Manliness was held up as a model for men throughout the pages of Scripture. Daniel—a captive in a dangerous heathen land—exemplified remarkable courage. Moses—an impulsive late bloomer—learned aggressiveness tempered by patience. Nehemiah—wise but never reticent—led his people strongly amid outer conflict and inner turmoil. The prophets fought the good fight, declaring truth even when it sometimes meant losing their lives. Jesus—ever tender yet brazenly bold—was the ultimate Man.

Boldness and leadership are the hallmarks of good men throughout the Bible. Even our word *manliness* is derived from one of these traits. Dr. Harvey Mansfield explains that the Greek word for manliness, *andreia*, is also the word the Greeks used for courage, the virtue concerned with controlling fear. The idea is that while a manly man still carries fear, he wrestles with it and rises above it.[4]

### From the New World to the Modern World

In the early history of our country, manliness was taken for granted. Our early explorers and frontiersmen did not struggle with their masculine identity. Being manly was as natural for them as breathing. They climbed mountains, rode river rapids, and killed grizzlies. They pursued a woman, built a home for her, and went out to provide for her. They saw themselves as a buffer of protection between their families and the harsh world.

It is true that they were men building a new world in a rough and violent land where everything tended to extremes. And it is also true that in these situations manliness shows itself most vividly. But manliness doesn't require marauding Indians or mountain lions in order to be needed; life under the curse of sin has always carried elements of danger, violence, and the herd mentality. There has always been a great call for courageous leaders and tender warriors.

For their descendants (until full-blown industrialization), manliness was easily passed on. Were all of them manly? No. Nor did every man handle his manliness with temperance. But temperance was expected by culture, and the natural male traits of taking initiative, welcoming responsibility, leading at home and in the world, confronting and fighting evil, protecting and providing for those in his care—these were assumed and embraced as desirable by the majority of men and women in our culture. It was simply what a man did.

So what happened?

### Three Giant Waves

Manliness came under heavy assault in three consecutive waves, each crashing one upon the other in a monumental tsunami of change. The first great wave was the *industrial revolution*, which removed fathers from a young son's world and distanced him from his needed male template. The second was the *feminist revolution* (or second-wave feminism, a movement taking root in the 1950s and '60s), which degraded manliness and insisted on androgyny—or sameness—between men and women. And the third was the *sexual revolution*, which destroyed moral boundaries in sex and led to the culture of divorce.

With that culture came the postmodern mind-set, which imposed passivity and denounced the drawing of moral judgments and boundaries. It took a healthy environment in which right and wrong, sin and morality, and good and evil were readily recognized and addressed, and replaced it with an environment in which godly manhood became seen as uncool, imposing, harsh, and insensitive. Men were no longer emboldened to rise up and counter the evil around them. In reality, postmodernism neutered manliness and turned it to putty.

It is impossible to describe the devastating implications of this last wave upon our men. Not only did the boys of divorced homes grow up wounded and confused, but *their template became a predominantly feminine one*. The preponderance of their generation of boys found themselves not only surrounded by postmodern thinking, but they were now being reared in a female-dominated world.

The result has been the rise of the feminized male.

## THE FEMINIZED MALE

Hang in here with me while I briefly explain. If you get this, it will shed light on the guys you date, the men you are married to, and the sons you are raising.

Dr. Stephen Clark, in his masterful classic *Man and Woman in Christ*, was one of the first to observe this recent loss of manliness, referring to it as "feminization."[5] Feminization, he explains, is *not* to be confused with "femininity" or "effeminacy."

(Pause. As we enter into this discussion, we must allow for certain generalizations. We are not speaking here of temperament. There is much variety arising from temperaments. But normal and healthy masculinity [or femininity] can be characterized by certain overriding tendencies, recognized for centuries and now underscored by modern research. And while these tendencies may show up in different degrees among individuals, they are nonetheless generally true. Back to Clark.)

Clark defines *femininity*:

> *Femininity* is a natural womanly quality. A woman is "feminine" when she has an appropriate womanly personality, when her strength, assertiveness, and interests are expressed in a womanly way.[6]

By "womanly personality," Clark is referring to a woman's natural, God-given proclivity toward nurture, sensitivity to people, and gentleness. It is womanly to be more of a responder by nature, to tend toward being more verbally expressive, more driven toward intimacy and connection. And all of these innate traits contribute to our ability to fulfill our natural calling as wives and mothers. It is also womanly to possess a healthy strength and assertiveness, and when these are expressed in the context of genuine femininity, they are wonderful things.

*Effeminacy* is a condition in which a man not only emulates a woman but actually prefers to be one; he is usually fearful that he cannot successfully be part of a group of men. This is a developmental condition (which we will not take the time to tackle in this book). For now, we only need to know that feminization is *not* effeminacy. Feminized men don't reject being men. In fact, they *desire to be manly and respect those who are.*[7]

So if feminization is not femininity or effeminacy, what is it? In short, it is an inner worldview propagated by growing up in a woman's world. Clark explains that *feminization* is an inward prism, or worldview, in which a man sees things more from a womanly perspective. And it tends to come out most clearly in relationships. *It occurs when a boy's father is absent during the formative years* of his life and he is *surrounded, influenced, reared, trained, and educated by women* who either intentionally or unintentionally shape him into their mold. In such an environment of female domination, a boy's natural masculine instincts (the drive to be physical and aggressive, to overcome fears, play rough, take risks, and step into confrontation) are either squelched or left to languish. More feminine traits like kindness, sensitivity, gentleness, and concern with what others are thinking and feeling (all good traits, in and of themselves) are elevated and become his primary template. As a result, *a boy learns to value womanly traits over manly ones* and learns to see and react to the world as a woman tends to see and react to it.[8]

Marion J. Levy Jr., a sociologist who has studied extensively the effects of this phenomenon on our modern world, writes,

> Our young are the first people of whom the following can be said: if they are males, they and their fathers and their brothers and sons and all the males they know are *overwhelmingly likely to have been reared under the direct domination and supervision of females from birth to maturity.* No less important is the fact that their mothers and their sisters and their girl friends and their wives and all of the ladies with whom they have to do, have had to do only with males so reared. Most of us have not even noticed this change, nor do we have any realization of its radicality.... To put the matter as dramatically as possible, we do not even know whether viable human beings can over any long period of time be reared in such a fashion [italics mine].[9]

This is a stunning observation. Never has there been a generation of men with so little direct influence from their childhood by a strong and healthy male template. And once a generation of men is raised in this female-controlled environment, the sequential male template is marred. The next generation of fathers passes down this feminized template to their sons and the problem is compounded.[10]

Now, a healthy man always possesses soft traits (Jesus certainly did), just as a healthy woman always possesses a certain assertiveness and strength. But soft traits in a man are desirable only when you find them in the context of manliness (just as assertiveness in a woman is only desirable in the context of true femininity). Jesus was the ultimate man's man, though He possessed the softest of traits. Joseph, who wept with his brothers, had all the traits of godly manhood. Jonathan, the tenderhearted friend of David, was every bit the man his father was not.

Softness in a strong man is a wonderful thing. But when a man takes on these softer traits as his *primary* modus operandi, things get turned upside down.

### Earmarks of Feminization

What are some of the earmarks of feminization (which can be seen in varying degrees in different men)? According to Clark …

- Compared to men who have not been feminized, a feminized man will place an unbalanced emphasis on *how he feels* (and how other people feel), in turn becoming highly visceral in his personal thinking and reactions.
- He will be much more gentle and *handle situations in a "soft" way.*
- He will be much more subject to *the approval of the group*, and thus significantly affected by how others feel and react toward him.
- Sometimes he will relate by preference to women or other feminized men, and will have a more *difficult time with an all-male group.*
- He will tend to fear women's emotions; in his family and at work he will be more *easily controlled by a woman's emotional reaction.*
- He will tend to idealize women, and if he is religious, he will see women as ideal Christians and *identify Christian virtue with feminine characteristics.*[11]

Feminization is not about persona or personality. A macho personality may hide a feminized inner worldview, while the most sensitive and poetic personality can carry a very manly inner worldview. Jacob, for example, was the sensitive, family-connected twin brother of the rugged outdoorsman Esau. Yet it was Esau who turned to jelly at the aroma of a bowl of soup. While of Jacob we learn that "in the womb he took his brother by the heel, and in his maturity he contended with God. Yes, he wrestled with the angel and prevailed; he wept and sought His favor" (Hos. 12:3–4).

Another example is Saul, the good-looking, masculine first king of Israel. Yet beneath lay a hidden feminization. Saul was overly concerned with the feelings and approval of people. "I feared the people and listened to their voice," said Saul when he disobeyed God (1 Sam. 15:24), and he lost God's anointing because of it. Yet hidden away in Saul's courts was an unimpressive poet-musician who possessed a surprisingly strong inner core of manliness. It was of this man, David, that God spoke when He said, "Man looks at the outward appearance, but the LORD looks at the heart" (1 Sam. 16:7).

External appearance and personality are not the determining factors. It's how a man interacts with his world—and his God—that counts.

### Feminized Men in Relationships

Feminized men can be highly aggressive in their careers—for they have learned this well from their male templates. It is in a man's personal relationships that feminization tends to be most evident, in spheres such as the home, the church, and his network of friends in society at large. These are the places where the father/male template has gone missing and women have been left to do the shaping. *If a man has never seen healthy manliness in these environments, he is operating in a vacuum.*

How does feminization show up in a man's relationships? It shows up in …

- a passiveness when it is appropriate to initiate and lead;
- a reluctance to confront or fight when a situation calls for it;

- a reticence to take on the responsibilities of a wife and family;
- an overconcern with the approval of peers;
- a lack of drive to protect and provide;
- a reluctance to risk or take action out of fear of failure.

Though a feminized man may not possess all of these traits, he will possess enough of them to give him a more feminized approach to his world.

## Feminization in the Church

The modern church—and this is important—has contributed to feminization by idealizing more womanly traits as the pinnacle of Christian virtue (like gentleness, sensitivity, tenderness, and greater concern with emotions and feelings), and shrinking back from the more masculine traits of courage, aggressiveness, boldness, and confrontation. Men are made to feel that their first and best response should be the more feminine one.

Yet healthy manliness by its very nature tends to be *insistent* and *intolerant*—insistent in the manner that Jesus was insistent regarding righteousness, honor, and holiness, and intolerant as He was intolerant toward evil and injustice. Biblical masculinity takes charge and leads, is unafraid to call a spade a spade, and takes the fight to the enemy, all the while *tempering such strength with patience, kindness, sacrifice, and sensitivity.*

I once read a book titled *Passive Men, Wild Women,* which is exactly how a woman who lives with a feminized man begins to feel. Feminization drives women nuts. Even though women can easily control a feminized man, in the end we lose respect for him. And even though we may chafe against healthy manliness and sometimes make our men miserable for it, deep down we still want them to be manly. When they aren't, we become exasperated. We can also tend to step into their role and fill their shoes.

## Countering Feminization

The good news is that feminization is easily remedied. *It is not some kind of complex psychosis that needs years of counseling.* It only requires (1) the permission/encouragement to be manly and (2) a template, or masculine mentor—a man who visibly models healthy biblical masculinity.[12]

Men want to be manly. It resonates with their innate design. And they can learn manliness quickly if they are given the model and live in an environment that encourages the expression of it. While men can learn manliness from reading a good book on the subject, it is far better for them to see it fleshed out.

What is a woman to do when a man has feminized tendencies? Right off the top, let me say there is one thing she must *never* do, and that is to accuse him of being feminized. If it were possible, I would underscore and put this in red. This chapter was written to give insight into what our men are up against, not to be used as a tool of chastisement. The last thing any man needs is to be told that he is not manly. It could very well bury him. So don't do it. Period.

There are, however, two extremely positive things you can do.

*Chapter Six*

# IN SEARCH OF MANLINESS (II): THE FEMININE SUMMONS

*The girl he loved was in that house … depending on him.*
*Then within him he felt it….*
*Suddenly doubt and fear and waiting were shed from him,*
*and in that moment he was what he had been created for:*
*a fighting man—*
*a fighting man alone, facing great odds,*
*and fighting for the things he valued.*
—Louis L'Amour, Utah Blaine

Michelangelo was born with a gift. He used to laughingly say that he took his hammer and chisel from the milk of the stonecutter's wife who wet-nursed him as a baby. But it was quickly apparent even as a young boy that no one had to teach him how to sculpt or paint.

One day as a child, he was visiting a chapel where the artist Domenico had been working. The artist was gone, so he picked up a sketchbook and began to sketch the scaffolding along with some stools and tools of the craft, and even some of the men at work. When the artist returned, he said in amazement, "This boy knows more about it than I do." This was the kind of work one would expect from someone who had been studying and practicing for many years.[1]

One of the most amazing skills Michelangelo possessed was his ability to bring a single giant piece of stone to life in such brilliant and exquisitely detailed form that it needed only to breathe. When he shaped a man, you saw every muscle, nerve, tendon, and emotion. Anyone who has viewed his nineteen-foot *David*, poised in his sinewy youth with one stone in his right hand and a sling in the other, can see why Michelangelo had a special affinity for this work (sculpted when he was only twenty-six years of age). Later in his own diaries, he described his *David* as having "eyes watchful ... the neck of a bull ... hands of a killer ... the body, a reservoir of energy."[2]

Yet while Michelangelo could sculpt a man out of marble, a woman has the capacity to shape a man in his very own flesh. This is the gift with which we have been born. God makes the man, but He gives the woman to be his mother, his friend, and his wife. And by our very gift of femininity, we possess the ability to call our men to rise up to full manhood.

Women bring two gifts in summoning forth their men's potential. The first is a strong *counterimage* of healthy femininity. The second is a *reason to attain* to full manliness, for manliness is what every woman really needs and wants in her man.

## THE COUNTERIMAGE OF HEALTHY FEMININITY

Our men need to be around *healthy* femininity—women who are simultaneously strong and unashamedly feminine.

In order to explain healthy femininity, however, we have to look at its unhealthy version. Unhealthy femininity shows up in a least two forms, which I will describe in the extreme:

(1) On one end is the unresponsive, self-focused, critical, Amazon-type woman who discourages—even shuts down—healthy manliness. A man is reduced to rubble by such a woman.

(2) On the flip side is the easily manipulated, overly sensitive, pleaser-type woman who cannot set boundaries or enter into healthy biblical confrontation. A man loses respect for such a woman and is unchallenged to grow into healthy manhood.

The first type appears to have few needs, while the second is far too needy, always seeing herself as the problem. The first type has no sense of healthy interdependence. The second has no sense of her own separate individuality. We could go on, but you can see the idea.

What a man needs is an emotionally grounded, God-dependent, soft woman who understands her husband, loves him deeply, knows how to draw healthy boundaries, and—most important—encourages every step he takes toward true manliness. This means that we women have to grow just as much as our men do. In later chapters we will study healthy femininity and how to achieve it. But for now, let us simply say that the more healthy we are in our femininity, the more we can encourage our men in healthy manliness.

True femininity stirs the embers of manliness. It awakens a man's calling and breathes life into his manly quest.

Our men and boys need such women.

## ENCOURAGING MANLINESS

The second most important thing you can do is to provide an environment of *encouragement*. In this feminized world, where else will your men be encouraged toward healthy manliness? Your encouragement will be like rain in the desert.

The Hebrew word for "encourage" means "to strengthen." And the Greek word carries the idea of "putting courage into." That's what every man and boy needs from us.

*There is nothing more encouraging to a son or a husband than a woman who believes in him.* One man put it this way: "It's all about whether my wife thinks I can do it. A husband can slay dragons, climb mountains, and win great victories if *he* believes his *wife* believes that he can."[3]

Oftentimes men don't step up because they feel it will involve a battle. Or they may simply find it is much easier to be enabled by a wife who will do their job for them.

May I tell you what many men from around the country have expressed to my husband? An astonishing number who awaken to their call to godly manliness and decide to make a serious change in their lives face surprising resistance at home. Not long ago Steve received an e-mail from one bitter wife:

> My husband has left me in charge of the house for so long that I will not give it up.… I REFUSE TO GIVE THAT UP. THIS IS MY HOUSE AND CHILDREN. I'm the one who has been reading the Bible to the kids. I defaced the book my husband bought from you, and hid it in a place he won't find it. If he really wants to be a leader of the house, then he has to KILL ME FIRST, OR YOU CAN.

Okay. Is it any wonder that this man didn't feel overly inclined to attempt his manly role sooner? As over-the-edge as this e-mail was, it represents a certain kind of control that kills a man's spirit. A man needs to know that if he is attempting to step into godly manhood, he is not going to have to face a continual counterattack. Or be killed. If your husband expresses a desire to become the man he has not been in his home, love him for it and give him all the space he needs to grow into that role.

Most of us, however, are guilty of enablement. We have allowed our men to depend on us to discipline the children, oversee their education, make family decisions, and basically determine our social, financial, even spiritual lives. The single best thing an enabling woman can do is to *step back*. Way back. And we must do it graciously, without great drama.

*If you never step back, he will never step forward.*

This doesn't mean that you drop everything or cease being his helpmate. Think of it rather as gently laying the mantle of leadership at his feet. Where once you would have led the charge, you are now turning to him. Let your husband hear, see, and feel by your actions that you are serious about stepping back. Dead serious.

"What if I do this and he does nothing?" you may ask. Give it time. Hold off. Let the void be felt. Let the chips fall where they may. Pray for him. Let God have an opportunity to work in the void. *Your children will not die, and your marriage will survive.* Men need time and space and all kinds of encouragement.

Is this easy? No. It may be the hardest thing you have ever done.

But it is the first—and possibly most important—of many steps you must take in being a catalyst in helping your man to grow into his manly role.

Does this raise hard questions? You bet. It raises a boatload of questions. And we will try to tackle at least some of them later in this book. But for now, think on this: There is a distinct difference between *demanding* manliness (which attempts to manipulate and change a man) and *encouraging* it (which expresses need and verbally appreciates manly behavior when it shows up). It is entirely possible to express a desire for manliness in a way that emboldens a man rather than making him feel like he is a complete failure.

## PERMISSION GRANTED

One evening I was in a situation where this was vividly illustrated. My oldest son had invited a group of friends over to watch the Ultimate Fighting Championship. If you are not twentysomething, let me explain. The UFC is a combination of kickboxing, Greco-Roman wrestling, and hand-to-hand combat. It is highly tactical, requires extreme conditioning, and can get a little gory at times. It's sort of a modernized gladiator last-man-standing kind of sport … though no one has been killed in it yet.

That's probably all you need to know.

I have watched several competitions at the behest of my guys largely because one of them was training in the sport for a while. (This son, by the way, was my most fearful child in his formative years.) He loved the ultimate intellectual-physical challenge; he also loved the fact that contenders didn't talk trash (which has since changed) and the loser always ended up congratulating the winner and hugging or shaking hands. If a guy got banged up and a little bloody, oh well.

I will admit to you, my first reaction to the sport was horror. I could not fathom any sensible person actually being interested, much less invigorated, by such a sport. Such brutes, these men. It was only over time with the tutoring of my men that I began to recognize the attraction. *Sports are one of the few places outside of the workplace where a man can express his innate manly aggression, fighting spirit, and courage—without being penalized for it.* But men also like the fact that in sports there are certain rules and boundaries as to how far a man can go. Even in the UFC.

On the night aforementioned, we all gathered in the family room to watch a series of competitions. Among us were men of every stripe and age, along with wives, girlfriends, and girls who were friends—some of them athletes in their own right. We even had a newborn baby girl in our midst.

As the first fight began, the guys were riveted. They were pointing out this move and that, "oohing" and "ahhing" over certain kicks and punches (much like a woman "oohs" and "ahhs" over a baby). The women in the room were more muted. Female grimaces were simultaneous to male outbursts. Some women were completely repulsed and disgusted; one hardy feminine soul was actually pale, verging on nausea. A few minutes into the final fight, the older, smaller, but more skilled fighter broke the nose of his young and powerful opponent. Blood gushed (I mean, literally *gushed*) while both contenders continued on for a full two more rounds until a winner was declared.

The entire room erupted in cheers when the old guy won. It was a fight to remember. Or forget, depending on who you were.

It was the heated conversation that followed which was most enlightening. Every man in the room (including one guy whom I happen to know is terrified of spiders) defended the value and integrity of the sport, while the women pointed out the obvious defects of such brutality. But here's what I noticed. While the men were focused on the character of the fighters (such as discipline and courage and skill and endurance), the women were focused on the nature of the fight itself.

I also noted something else very telling. By the end of our conversation, the guys expressed appreciation for why relational and nurturing women would innately shrink back, while at the same time the women expressed appreciation for their manly invigoration in seeing a skillful, well-fought battle. There was a mutual appreciation, even valuing, of our innate differences. And that is important.

Women can be repulsed by the natural joys of men. We don't see the point. (Who cares about a car that can go five hundred miles an hour when you can never legally drive it that fast?) We don't comprehend the rush. Of course the reason we don't get it is because we are women. But if men are to be men, we must let them be men and appreciate the underlying drives of their manliness. A man needs a place where his manliness is understood and encouraged.

## TOO WILD AT HEART

There is a darker side to lost manliness, which can be seen in the rise of the socially irresponsible, disruptive male. Not only has popular culture glorified such men, too many impressionable boys have seen it modeled by the men in their lives. When a young man grows up with a dad who is irresponsible, unfaithful, selfish, or dishonorable, why should the world expect him to be different? This is his template for manliness.

Left to itself in a sinful world, masculinity has a natural tendency to run amok—just as femininity does. And because *a woman was never meant to control a budding young man*, it makes sense that when there is no man to discipline him and instill a sense of honor and responsibility, his masculinity can run wild. Add to that (1) the father-wounds inflicted by harsh, detached, or abandoning fathers and (2) the mother-wounds inflicted by overcontrolling, overnurturing mothers who have often depended upon their sons to emotionally replace their dads, and you have a growing population of hurt, confused, and angry young men. The results can be lethal.

A boy requires an older man's focused involvement and firm discipline. Deuteronomy 6:7–8 commands a father to be focused and engaged. Ephesians 6:4 commands wise fatherly discipline, warning dads against being harsh and excessive. Biblical fathering is so important that even if an otherwise good man fails to do it, he can bring judgment on himself and his sons.

Eli, the priestly mentor of the prophet Samuel, incurred God's divine discipline for failing to rebuke his sons for their grievous sins against the Lord (1 Sam. 3:13; 4:17–18). Both sons died. Interestingly, Samuel became guilty of the very same thing (1 Sam. 8:1–5), and as a result the people turned away from prophetic leadership in favor of having a king. First Kings tells us that Adonijah, David's oldest son, wreaked havoc in the household as well as the nation because "his father had never crossed him at any time" (1 Kings 1:6).

The illustrations are numerous. According to Scripture, the curbing of a son's sin nature by a father's wise discipline and training is an absolute necessity.

Do women play a role in that discipline? Yes, they do. Proverbs is clear on that point. Never underestimate the importance of your role in your young son's training and discipline. But it's no coincidence that the rise in absent, uninvolved fathers has coincided with an increase in irresponsible, out-of-control young men.

Being manly, therefore, involves learning how to restrain the sinful expression of aggression and act honorably in this world. The very term *gentleman* refers to a man of honor who is gentle out of policy rather than weakness.[4] A gentleman is chivalrous and can be trusted to protect rather than attack a woman. He recognizes his penchant for masculine intemperance and is endeavoring to master the art of self-control.

## RETICENT GENTLE MEN

One trait of manliness is an eagerness to embrace the responsibilities of being a husband and dad. But many of our best young single men today have a reticence in forming intimate, committed relationships. It isn't because they don't desire them. They have an overwhelming desire to put a new link in the chain and become the men their fathers were not. But having grown up in a culture of failed marriages and lost templates, they feel profoundly inadequate at pulling that off.

I cannot emphasize how normal, natural, and prevalent this is. These men want a good woman, yet they are reticent to move close to her out of a sense of inadequacy. They wonder if they can ever be the man she needs. *What if I turn out to be like my dad? What if she discovers how little I really know about being a leader? What if my weaknesses become exposed?* The sense of inadequacy and fear of failure can paralyze them. That's one reason why we have an increasing pattern of young men in the church who can't seem to initiate or commit.

Do you want to know the truth? Most men have a deep fear of failure.

They don't show it, but it is always there lurking beneath the surface. And understandably so. For most men—including those who have a healthy manly identity and know what it means to be courageous—life is a "Peter and the waves" experience. Every day they jump out of their boat into the winds and waves of life that threaten to take them under. Any normal man will have times when he has to fight off a terrible sense of inadequacy. Every man has to learn how to look toward Jesus instead of the waves.

If you are a single woman living in a world of God-loving, reticent men, what do you do? Should you chase them and throw yourself at them (as many women do, and you have probably felt tempted to do yourself)? Please hear me well. Manliness—which you desire and he wants to possess—will not happen when you take on the role of the "man." Yes, you may get a man this way—but what kind of man will he be? Don't compromise your woman-hood. He needs for you to be a feminine woman—neither passively inert, nor anxiously overt.

*Be strong in your femininity, for that is what he needs most in you.*

If you have a teachable guy who genuinely loves Christ, there are some concrete things you can do. And these come straight from what single guys have told me themselves:

- *Become his friend.* A friend is not a man-chaser who calls a guy every day. A friend is someone who very obviously cares about a man's well-being and enjoys his company for the sake of true friendship. A real friend is relaxed because she doesn't care if anything more comes of the relationship. (And a guy can pick up on this from a mile away.)

- *Notice his good qualities, his gifts, his tender heart toward God.* And make a point to *compliment him verbally.* Men today have an astonishing need for verbal encouragement.

- *Be vulnerable with him.* Not a gushy, emotional, weepy kind of vulnerable. But an open, genuine vulnerability about your doubts and fears, about the hard things you struggle with in your own life. You are weak. You have needs. You fail. You don't have it all together. Men have a hard time believing that about a strong Christian woman. Let him see the chinks in your armor. Let him see how completely human and weak you are—just like him. This is hard for a lot of us who were brought up to "have it all together" and to "need no one or nothing." But if you want a man to be vulnerable with you, you've got to be vulnerable with him.

- This one might surprise you. But *don't quote Scripture verses and tell him of your vision to reach the world for Christ.* At least not right off the bat. That can wait. Am I saying not to talk about spiritual things? No, absolutely not. I am saying that the majority of guys feel very weak in this area. You can be honest about your love for Christ without one-upping him spiritually. Encourage his manliness by asking him what *he* thinks and getting at the heart of *his* strengths. Every good man has the ability to be manly, and leadership flows naturally out of manliness. The very idea of "spiritual leadership" has become an elusive, mystical, unattainable thing to men today. *But what is "spiritual leadership" really? It is godly manliness in the context of caring friendship*; that's all. You may be the woman to help him discover that.

- *Don't expect immediate vulnerability from him.* But do *gently encourage it.* We women can be open books. Men tend to need more time, and they need to be drawn out skillfully, as we will see in the last part of this book.

- Most important, *when he is transparent, let him know how much you value and respect that.* Men think that exposure of their inner struggles lowers them in a woman's eyes and makes them appear weak. But it takes a strong man to be transparent. Unbeknownst to our men, vulnerability actually *elevates* a man in a woman's eyes. This is unfathomable to a man. So tell him what this does for you. Tell him you have never respected him more. It will shock him.

When all is said and done, know this. The wise encouragement of a good woman can make all the difference for a young man who loves the Lord.

Can you change him? Don't even try. But what a difference when a young man senses that a woman believes that he can put a new link in his family chain. She is no longer a threat; she is an asset.

Should you marry a man who doesn't have your respect and can't lead you? No. Don't lower a wise standard. But let your men be human, recognize what they are up against, and encourage them in their aspirations for godly manhood.

$$\infty$$

The less successful a man is in his quest for healthy manhood, *the more vulnerable he is in the next great battlefront of the male sexual war:* the war against sexual temptation.

- His wounds will drive him to search for an anesthetic for pain.
- His inability to draw close in relational intimacy will drive him to seek a false intimacy.
- His search for a manly identity will tend to drive him to look for it in the all the wrong places.

But even among our most manly of men, this second battlefront is by far the most intense. It is every man's Normandy.

So for their sakes, let us take up our Night Vision binoculars and zoom in on this dark and dangerous front.

# Chapter Seven

# HOOKED (I):
# THE RISE OF PORNOGRAPHY

*The bird hunting a locust is unaware of the hawk hunting him.*
*—old proverb*

*I think that the major message of my life and what I hope*
*to be remembered for is someone who managed to change*
*the social sexual values of his time absolutely.*
*—Hugh Hefner*

The skies were jet blue and eerily quiet. There had been no sign of the Super Cub for two days, or *any* plane at all. Not even the commercial flights that daily arched over Alaska with destinations of continents westward.

The hunting crew huddled together in the freezing snow. Things were not looking good. They were stranded out in the Alaskan wild—surrounded by huge bloody packs of freshly killed moose, with no satellite phone, and a very hungry grizzly nearby. A pack of wolves had cheated that grizzly out of the moose carcass the day before, and he was bound to catch up to the scent of their fresh cache of meat.

Rocky McElveen had promised to pick them up two days ago. What could have gone wrong? He was the best wilderness guide in Alaska, and they knew he would move mountains to get back to his guys. Could the Cub have crashed? But even then, surely *someone* would have come looking by now.

Something of serious magnitude had gone wrong. There is an old saying in the Alaskan wild, "If nobody is flying, somebody is dying."

Then against the glare of the morning sun a tiny speck appeared, and soon the puttering of the Cub's little engines reached their ears. Within moments it was banking and gliding in for a soft landing at their site.

Rocky's pilot, Joel, jumped out to embrace the ragged but elated crew, and then he quickly explained. The morning of the Cub's expected return, America had been attacked. Four planes had been hijacked. Two of them had hit the World Trade Center in New York City, the third had hit the Pentagon, and the fourth—headed for Washington, D.C.—had crash-landed in a field just outside of Shanksville, Pennsylvania. Immediately the FAA had grounded all planes of every kind indefinitely throughout the United States—a first ever in U.S. aviation history.

As many as eight hundred people had been stranded in rural Alaska without any knowledge of why they had been abandoned. McElveen had pleaded with the FAA for permission to rescue his crew, but only dire emergency medical flights were being allowed. Not until this Thursday morning of September 13 was Joel released to fly. Rocky was back at the lodge busily handling the needs of stranded pilots and others who had been unexpectedly grounded.

At that moment, the threat of a hungry grizzly paled in comparison to this new, more insidious and dangerous enemy—human beings just like us, who would hide among us with the sole intent of silently emerging and killing thousands of innocent people.[1]

Men love to hunt. There is something innately male about that ancient pastime.

But our men are also the hunted.

Just as 9/11 forever changed the rules and tactics of modern American warfare, so the year of 1973 would forever change the rules and tactics in the war against sexual temptation. That was the year the Internet was born. And within a few short years, temptation—unparalleled in its nature and extent—would come hunting our men and boys through an inconceivably accessible wireless network via a new world called "cyberspace." Most important, it would be aimed at their greatest Achilles' heel.

## AGE-OLD TEMPTATION, NEW-AGE APPROACH

The Achilles is the thickest and strongest tendon in the body. Its name comes from the handsomest and greatest warrior among the legendary Greek gods. According to legend, Achilles was completely invulnerable to injury or death, with one exception. When his mother dipped him as an infant in the river Styx, every part of his body touched by its waters was rendered invulnerable—except for the heel by which she held him. And it was an arrow to his heel that eventually killed him.

That is why from the days of the Greeks we have referred to our place of greatest vulnerability as our personal Achilles' heel. What is the Achilles' heel of the male sex? It is sexual temptation. Without question, this is the single greatest place of vulnerability in the male armor.

In the next section of this book, we will begin to understand why. But this struggle is as normal as the rising of the sun and as common as rainfall in a rain forest. Our men want us to know that their struggle is normal and inevitable. Every budding male comes face-to-face with it. And every man lives with it his entire life.

The men in your life are no exception, no matter how long they have walked with the Lord or how committed they may be to purity.

### Fear Not

My greatest fear as we broach this subject is that you will become overwhelmed by the power of the enemy and the magnitude of the struggle. I don't want that to happen. Women have said to me, "You know, I would really rather not know what is going on in that world. I'm afraid I will worry even more and feel less secure as a wife."

I understand. The dark world of sexual sin is a violation to the senses and an assault on the soul. To be frank, there were times while researching this chapter that I wanted to walk away and not even write about it.

But how can we love our husbands and sons well if we make no attempt to understand what they're up against? Just this week one wife of a troubled husband said to me, "The world of sexual temptation was so troubling, so sick, that I just wanted to pretend it wasn't there. But I wish I hadn't. I could have helped him when he needed me."

Our men need for us to know.

And God wants us to know. His words to us through the apostle Peter are about as graphic a warning as you could construct: "Be on the alert. Your adversary, the devil, prowls around like a roaring lion, seeking someone to devour" (1 Peter 5:8).

More than that, God wants us to *expose* the enemy:

Walk as children of Light.… Do not participate in the unfruitful deeds of darkness, but instead even *expose them*.… But all things become visible when they *are exposed by the light.* (Eph. 5:8, 11, 13)

May I encourage you? There is something remarkably freeing about truth. The more you know, the better you will be able to love your husband or son or single man in your life—and the smaller will be the gulf between the two of you. And in the end *the less mystery will exist* to fuel unfounded fears.

So don't fear the truth.

We would be fools to underestimate the enemy. But we shouldn't overestimate him either. Our enemy is not omnipresent (present everywhere), nor is he omniscient (all knowing) or omnipotent (all powerful). These attributes belong to the Almighty alone. Don't allow this enemy to paralyze, intimidate, or cause you to despair. Our enemy's greatest power lies in our dismay at his roar. But our God is able to seal the mouth of the lion and completely subdue him. The enemy can be beaten. He *is* being beaten every single day by those who walk wisely.

Knowing this, let us fearlessly expose this insipid enemy and the modern-day methods he is employing to entrap our boys and men.

## WEB OF TEMPTATION

"Come into my house," said the spider to the fly.

"Come into my Web site," said the porn producer to the child.

Strangely enough, the Internet was first developed by the U.S. Department of Defense. It was created in the aftermath of World War II to help in the event of a nuclear disaster, as well as to put us on the cutting edge of modern warfare.[2] In short, the Internet began as a weapon of defense.

By 1983, the World Wide Web had been created and cyberspace was opened up to the everyday man on the streets.[3] For the rest of the '80s, it was used mostly by "nerds" who had access to computers with modems. But in the early '90s, the Internet went mainstream and began to reshape our world. As with every great advancement of history, the possibilities it created for good were beyond our wildest dreams. The Web has been an undeniable gift. But the possibilities it has created for evil have taken us places we could have never foreseen.

From the very beginning, the industry of pornography saw its opportunity for ...

- uncontrolled, easily moved, and elusive sites (thus evading the law);
- immediate, private access to a fast-growing segment of the population; and
- untold fortunes to be made.

For the pornographer, the potential in the cyberspace market was practically infinite. With lightning speed the porn industry moved in and set up shop. And overnight the Internet went from being a weapon of *self-defense* to becoming a tool of *self-destruction*.

The first article warning of the problem of child porn on the Internet was released in 1985,[4] and by the '90s, there was an onslaught of studies and books related to the negative social impact of Internet porn. Since then, the speed with which it has morphed and exploded has been nothing short of breathtaking.

"The Internet is changing everything," said Patrick Carnes, pioneer in the field of sex addiction. "We have people who were already [sex] addicts who got on the Internet and just immolated.... The impact it is having on people is extraordinary."[5]

David Hiltbrand writes,

The Internet's ready availability is also making sex addicts of people who previously would have resisted temptation. Procuring pornography used to entail visiting an adult video store or lingering by the seedier side of the magazine rack. The threat of exposure was enough to discourage many people. But now anyone with a modem has access to a vast storehouse of cyberporn without leaving the house. The inhibition of social censure has been obliterated because the behavior takes place in private.[6]

So it is that with all of its great and unimaginable good, the Internet has also proven to be the perfectly conceived web. Al Cooper, leading researcher in the field of cybersex addiction, explains why:

It's a Triple-A engine: *access*, *affordability*, and *anonymity*. Those three factors turbo-charge the Internet, giving it a power that is hard to match in other venues. The number of people being arrested for child porn has increased phenomenally. I'm convinced many of those people wouldn't have gotten involved if it wasn't for the Internet.[7]

## PORN'S METEORIC RISE

Let me make a suggestion as we look at the meteoric rise of Internet porn.

As you read the next few pages, *speed-read* over the statistics. Don't get bogged down in the details. The point is for you to be aware of the almost incomprehensible availability of porn and how the industry so quickly adapts in its tactics to capture victims. The statistics cited in this book will be old news the day after they go into print; by the time you read these pages, new tactics will already be in play. But the more aware you are of how the porn industry thinks and works, the more tuned in you will be to your men and boys. This is what they need for you to know.

Let us begin with pornography's strides in becoming *accessible* on the Web. The number of pornographic Web pages jumped from 14 million in 1998 to 260 million in 2003 (representing a nearly 2,000 percent increase of pornography available online in just five years).[8] In the year of 2007 alone ...

- there were 420 million *Web pages* of pornography and 4.2 million known *Web sites* worldwide;
- there were 68 million *daily requests* for porn, making up a quarter of all daily search-engine requests;
- 2.5 billion *pornographic e-mails* had been sent out;
- pornographic Web sites were *visited three times more often* than Google, Yahoo!, and MSN combined; and
- studies showed that 42.7 percent of *Internet users overall* had viewed porn.[9]

Many of those visits were inadvertent. The tricks pornographers play particularly on our children are viciously evil and deceptive. But many of those visits were quite intentional. In early 2007, there were over 100,000 official *adult-oriented subscription* sites in the United States alone (maintained by 1,000 major firms, with another 9,000 operating as affiliates), while there were some 400,000 subscription sites globally.[10] Worldwide commerce in the porn industry is booming, made easier because sexual images need no verbal translation.

And, yes, subscription sites are exactly what they imply!

In his book *Microtrends: The Small Forces Behind Tomorrow's Big Changes*, Mark Penn (who is quite happy about the rise of Internet pornography) documents that 40 million adults in the United States *regularly* visited Internet porn sites in 2007. Penn says,

This marketplace is so large that porn [has become] the norm. There is hardly a hotel room in America without easy access to porn. It is just a click away for everyone.

A startling number of people view their porn at work. According to Web-sense, a vendor of Web security and filtering software, *70 percent of porn is downloaded between 9 a.m. and 5 p.m.* And 20 percent of American men admit accessing porn while at work. Are there five men who work where you do? Try sneaking a glimpse of their computer screens when they're hunched over them, looking like they're working. Chances are, at least one isn't gazing at spreadsheets.

What's remarkable is that these are people who otherwise cleave to really high moral standards [italics mine].[11]

As I write, the fastest-growing market for hard-core porn is through peer-to-peer (P2P) downloads. *One-third of P2P downloads* in 2007 were pornography. And take note, parents. With P2P file sharing, kids can now download a triple-X-rated movie from a friend free of charge, and more often than not, the installed Internet filter will let it right through. (Due to the nature of the technology, filters are basically bypassed.) Once a purchase has been made and downloaded by a single person (a minor needs only to lie about his age), then the hard-core movie becomes available to anyone with a PC and can spread very quickly, which of course it has. As with any new technology, parents have been behind the curve on this one, while kids have, as usual, been very savvy to it. P2P is widely used today among minors, and among those downloads is a growing number of hard-core porn productions.[12]

But how did the porn industry make such strides in so little time?

## HOLLYWOOD, THE WHITE HOUSE, AND WALL STREET
Money talks.

And the early financial windfall to the porn industry via the Internet was astronomical. There was so much money being made (and so much more to be made) that the industry soon led the field in cutting-edge cyberspace technology. It takes money to fund development. In fact, the porn industry proved so quick and adept that Hollywood decided to sit back and let these companies create, test, and refine new technologies before picking them up and taking them mainstream. "Why not let them deal with the headaches and foot the bill?" they reasoned.[13] *Hollywood's eagerness to make money* from this quickly morphing technology provided a porn media boost. And cable networks (along with the movie industry) quickly began to air their products for the same reason. They attract. They sell.

But a shrewd political move also contributed to the rise of porn. Before 1992, Wall Street wouldn't touch porn companies with a ten-foot pole. Public companies were too concerned about lawsuits and obscenity prosecutions— understandably, since there were tough laws against pornography. But then in the '90s, prosecutions plummeted. Why?

According to a 2001 Hoover Institution report, shortly after taking office, President Bill Clinton fired all (not some, but *all*) sitting U.S. attorneys, an audacious power move never made by any president in history. In doing so, he wiped out an experienced cadre of prosecutors who had made obscenity a priority. There ensued *an eight-year period in which the sex industry went virtually without prosecution.* At the end of that period, Dennis Hof, associate of *Hustler*'s Larry Flynt, said this:

> We've had eight years of lack of prosecution.... So the [adult] film industry has gone from 1,000 films eight years ago to 10,000 last year. Ten thousand pornographic movies. You've got Larry and [*Penthouse* publisher Bob] Guccione doing things that 10 years ago you'd go to prison for. Then you've got the Internet stuff—dogs, horses, 12 year old girls.[14]

It didn't take long before *reputable brokerages* on Wall Street began help-ing porn-related companies win public listings on U.S. stock exchanges.

And close behind, *mainstream companies* that previously wouldn't have been caught dead being associated with the porn industry decided to climb aboard this cash cow. The report reveals,

> Visa and Mastercard play a large role in the industry by processing its payments. ([In 2007,] American Express ... stopped processing charges for "adult" sites, but the reason was the inordinate volume of "chargebacks" by customers who denied patronizing the sites when the bills came due.)
>
> Though they don't advertise the connection, respectable companies like AT&T, Time-Warner, and the Hilton hotel chain have quietly become major players in porn distribution. A few years ago the cable TV folks wouldn't go near the stuff ... [but] the cable industry's resistance has now completely crumbled.... Since its launch in 1999, Hot Network has taken the cable world by storm....
>
> Whole genres of pop music are now in the process of coalescing with the "respectable" porn industry, most notably represented by Vivid, whose stable of Vivid Girls is much in demand for autograph signings at Tower Records and local video outlets.[15]

Since this report, the economic and technological prowess of the porn industry has only increased.[16]

One example was the accessibility of pornography to iPods within twenty-four hours of the iPod launch. CEOs of the two top porn firms readily admitted to targeting the iPod retail market, and they made no bones about their intentions of financing other cutting-edge innovation in the delivery of content.[17] (Profits from the transmission of porn to mobile phones in that year topped $100 million.)[18]

Another example is porn's power to make or break companies in the world of new media technology. In the '80s, VHS nudged out Betamax (becoming the videocassette standard) largely *because it had the X-rated movie business* on its side. Today, HD DVDs *alliance with the "adult industry"* is at present giving it the new generation edge against Blu-ray Disc.[19] Porn money is giving these companies the edge they need to be on top.

In short, pornography has gone mainstream.

I recently picked up the April 7, 2008, issue of *Forbes Magazine* only to find Marc Bell, Penthouse Media Group chief executive, featured in a front-cover article. He was being called one of today's hottest new entrepreneurs because of his brilliant moves in taking a sagging magazine company and turning it into a raging entrepreneurial success. Giving this explicit men's magazine a new "tame front," he also bought a racy collection of 27 social-networking Web sites for $500 million in cash and stock. The biggest of these sites is the X-rated AdultFriendFinder (with 22 million members), which is a Match.com-type site for people who want to find sex-mates. In addition, he also acquired Passion.com and Bigchurch.com (a site for Christians who want prayer-mates). That's what you call "diversification." Then Bell signed a deal with New Frontier Media to make *Penthouse Video On-Demand* available on TV in 59 million homes.

Surrounded by seminude front covers of his newly improved magazine, Bell says with a smile, "Sex is recession-proof."[20]

For the last decade, income from pornography has exceeded that of professional baseball, basketball, and football combined—making it the most popular sport by far among men.[21] (This may not mean much to women, but it speaks volumes to men.) And out of all its services, adult video sales and rentals have proven by far the most profitable (with much of their distribution being done via the Internet).

To sum up the damage:

- In 2005, there were some 800 million porn videos and DVDs available for public consumption;[22] and *Adult Video News* (porn's trade magazine) boasted $12.6 billion in revenues.[23]
- In 2006, revenue from I-porn exceeded the combined revenues of ABC, CBS, and NBC.[24]

- And in 2007, porn revenues exceeded the combined revenues of the top eight technology companies: Microsoft, Google, Amazon, eBay, Yahoo!, Apple, Netflix, and EarthLink.[25]

Short of an electrical shutdown of the planet, one can only imagine where things will go from here.

෧෨

I will pause to let you catch your breath.

It is worth pausing to consider this question: Is pornography really that bad?

# Chapter Eight

# HOOKED (II):
# WHAT PORNOGRAPHY DOES

*The mass of men lead lives of quiet desperation.*
—*Henry David Thoreau*


*Do not bite at the bait of pleasure till you know*
*there is no hook beneath it.*
—*Thomas Jefferson*


If you were born post-1950s, you may not fathom the extent of earth-shattering change that has occurred in the area of sexuality in the last fifty years. Perhaps this little poem will be enlightening. It is more than nostalgic; it is true. Ask your mother or grandmother.

In 1949
Young girls blushed.

Virginity was a treasure—
A vial of perfume,
Which once opened was poured over its opener
And then forever lost.
Yet it was not a sad loosing,
For its fragrance lingered over the marriage bed.

In those days
The gentle grasp of a hand meant something,
And a kiss wrought commitment.
Eyes spoke without guile,
Seeking not vacuous attention
But the knowing of another's soul.
Inner thoughts lingered upon feelings aroused,
The memory of a look,
A caressing touch,
An intimate conversation of self-revelation.

In those days
Common language was restrained—
As if spoken in a hushed temple
Where intimacy was sacred
And consummation was a holy mystery.

Outside a storm brewed.
The rumblings of revolution quaked beneath our feet.

As in our thriving childhood
We thought not upon our terminality,
So in our unspoiled wooing
We heard not the distant death-knells of love's requiem.
But modesty was fated to die,
And virtue to be lost and forgotten,
Casualties in the coming tectonic shift.

Looking back,
I long for those days
When innocence was preserved,

The air was clean,

And love was a cherishing thing.[1]

Those years were not without their problems; the sexual revolution of the '60s was a reaction to the mounting problems of our postindustrial, soon-to-be postmodern world. But it was never the answer. In its elusive search for happiness, it led us down a dark, unthinkable path.

Which brings us to the present.

Pornography has become so commonplace in our day, many Christians have begun to wonder what the big deal is. Some wives have said to me, "I am confused. My husband looks at porn. He says it helps him in our sexual relationship. Is that okay?" And some husbands even ask their wives to watch it with them "to make our sex lives better."

How are we to think of porn? We need clarity.

## ORIGINS OF DEATH

The word *pornography* comes from *pornia*, the Greek word for immorality, explicitly sexual immorality. Rabbis of the first century often used shorthand phrases, such as "the law and the prophets," when referring to Old Testament law. *Pornia* was one of those shorthand words, and it encompassed all the sexually immoral acts listed in Leviticus 18, from incest to bestiality to adultery to homosexuality. In Matthew 15:18–19, Jesus teaches that all of these acts in Leviticus 18 are still to be considered immoral. (Likewise, Paul refers to the very same *pornia* in numerous passages, such as 1 Corinthians 6:18, where he says, "Flee immorality," or *pornia*.)

Internet pornography spans the scope of *pornia*, introducing every conceivable, perverse, even violent form of sexual immorality.

But even in its mildest form, pornography is deadly. It fuels lust. It alters a man's mind. And it calls him into a dark, addicting world.

In Matthew 5, Jesus cut right to the chase. He said that when a man lusts after a woman in his heart, *he has committed adultery already.*

You have heard that it was said, "You shall not commit adultery"; but I say to you that everyone who looks at a woman with lust for her has already committed adultery with her in his heart.

If your right eye makes you stumble, tear it out and throw it from you; for it is better for you to lose one of the parts of your body, than for your whole body to be thrown into hell. (Matt. 5:27–29)

Lust is serious, says our Lord. So serious that it can doom a man to perish. A moth approaching the glittering web of the glowworm does not imagine the death that awaits him. "Then when lust has conceived, it gives birth to sin; and when sin is accomplished, it brings forth death. Do not be deceived, my beloved brethren," says the writer of James (1:15–16). Five times in the early chapters of Proverbs we read that the "strange woman" or the "harlot" or the "adulteress" takes a man to his death (2:16–19; 5:3–5; 6:26–33; 7:6–23; 9:17–18). Therefore "drink water from your own cistern" and "rejoice in the wife of your youth" (Prov. 5:15–23).

What then shall we say? Pornography is sin. Pornography is treacherous. Pornography leads to death—emotional, relational, and spiritual. Pornography comes straight from the pit. It is deceitful. It promises what it cannot deliver. It carries a man to places he never intended to go. It feeds off personal immolation. It is the brainchild of Satan, the father of lies, who has been a "murderer from the beginning" (John 8:44).

These are strong words.

But let us think wisely, clearly, and biblically. Pornography leads into a blind, cavernous pit of death.

How does pornography lead to death?

## WHAT PORNOGRAPHY DOES TO THE MIND
*Pornography poisons the mind.*

When our oldest son was seven, one of his friends wanted to show him a magazine with some pictures of naked women. John was so disturbed that he came to his dad. Steve realized the time had come to prepare this little guy for something he would deal with for the rest of his life. First, he told John about God's unbelievable plan for sex, which is exactly what John thought of it: unbelievable. ("Can you believe God thought of *that*?" he said to me later, eyes like silver dollars.)

"Sex is great, John," Steve told him, "and someday you will find that out when you get married." Then he went on to explain how God's great plan for sex can be ruined and turned into something dark and ugly.

"Think of it this way," he said. "Would you go in that bathroom and drink out of the toilet?" The thought made John sick. "Well, when you look at that stuff it's just like putting sewage in your mind. And, John, those women in those pictures are someone's daughter or sister or wife. Somebody is using them to make money. And he doesn't care about those women or what happens to the guys who look at those pictures. I know you don't want to put poison in your mind. And you would be upset if someone were to ever use your mom or your sister like that."

John has never forgotten that conversation.

What does porn do to the mind? It starts by *changing perception of reality*. It *lowers human beings to objects*, and *turns sex into a self-centered, vacuous, addictive rush*. Like cocaine, it leaves a man empty, yet strangely craving more. The propagators of porn know this. They understand how our men are wired and what turns them on. They know exactly how to hook a man (or a boy, as the case may be); and they know he will want to come back for more.

### Women and Pornography

Do women get into porn? Yes. But the numbers of men so far outnumber women that pornographers purposefully target men. A man's mind is profoundly affected by visual image, as we will see later. Pornographers assume (and rightly so) that the women who do seek pornography will arrive by adopting a male mind-set and mirroring male behavior.

Obviously without women the porn industry would crumble; we *enable* pornography. But research shows that the typical woman who gets pulled into online sexual activity does so in search of *relationship*. Men online are far more likely to seek out pornography, while women online gravitate toward adult chat rooms.[2] And even though there has been a large influx of women seeking counseling for cybersex addiction in recent years, they tend to be seeking help in the area of relationship/love hunger.[3]

It is true that with the rise of the "hook-up" generation, we are seeing an increasing number of young women actually obsessed with sex. Yet even these young women privately admit that when it comes down to it, they really desire relationship and commitment; they just fear that if they expect and ask for it, they will be shunned by their male peers and shut out altogether.[4] This is tragically what the porn generation has brought us to. But inevitably, we women find that we are creatures of relationship. We always have been and always will be.

## WHAT PORNOGRAPHY DOES TO RELATIONSHIPS
*Pornography kills relationships.*

It *distances a man from God* and darkens his ability to think wisely. A Christian who looks at porn habitually begins to split in his personality. In one life he is seemingly pure and unadulterated, publicly faithful to his wife; in the other he carries great guilt and simultaneous craving. The deeper he moves into sexual lust, the less capable he is of keeping his personality intact. All the while his soul is becoming numbed, callous, hardened to the Spirit of God. Eventually he may reach a breaking point in which he can no longer keep his private world private. Some men go on to act out their fantasies in real life, risking everything—personal reputation, family, job. But long before the public split, their hearts have experienced a spiritual and moral split. And God has become a distant Being with little relevance at their inner core.

Pornography also *distances a man and a woman*. It creates a false world of airbrushed images, virtual women who are always there, cyberaffairs that consist of highs without hurts, ecstasy without expectations, fulfillment without exposure of faults. One counselor says,

> What happens is people are being tutored by pornography, taught to objectify others.… So some men say, "Even when I try to focus [sexually] on my wife, I can't get these pictures out of my head." It can be very destructive to relationships.[5]

A single guy who looks at pornography and masturbates reaps a wealth of problems. His expectations for sex in marriage are distorted (even though he may not realize it). And his desire for premarital sex is intensified. He hopes that when he marries, his wife will deliver him and solve his craving. But marriage alone does not solve the problem. Let me try to explain.

In my interviews of Christian men, they have described what I will refer to as "consumer high" syndrome. When a guy habitually views porn on the Net, he becomes used to moving from one woman to another. He will spend time fantasizing with one woman for a while (some of these women have become quite famous in the world of pornography); then when things become less interesting, he will move on to someone new.

It's a little like the consumer high that comes with buying a new car. The rush and initial exhilaration of the new car gradually wear off until he finds himself wanting a new one.

In the same way, the early period of a marriage can also be a "high." But just as the new car loses its "newness," a wife also loses her newness. Pornography feeds the unhealthy desire in a man to seek that rush of something—or someone—*new*. Never mind the fact that enduring and satisfying pleasure in sex comes through the deepening of communication and the genuine growth of love in a long-term committed relationship.

Porn disconnects sex from relationship and communication. And that is what is most disastrous for marriage. When there are struggles (and *every* marriage has them), the temptation to seek fulfillment elsewhere rather than working through the struggle is an enormously powerful one. A wife is also asked to compete with images; she is expected to become like the "prostitute"; her role turns into a purely physical one. This is humiliating to women and devastating to a marriage relationship. And it is a complete defilement of God's rich, pleasurable, meaningful gift of sex.

## PORNOGRAPHY AND ADDICTION

Finally, Internet pornography is *highly conducive to addiction.*

We could add to Al Cooper's triple-A engine a fourth "A": *addiction.* Studies have shown that I-porn taps into the pleasure centers of the brain and creates a chemical reaction much like that of a drug.[6] The draw with this particular addiction is that there is little financial cost, no hangover, and no difficulty in getting more. Sex-addiction researcher Patrick Carnes has called the Internet "the crack cocaine of sexual addiction." It accelerates the spiral of self-destruction and even captures some who might otherwise resist.[7]

One counselor explains, "A taste of pornography can grow to an out-of-control obsession with alarming rapidity. The sexual buzz they experience is as strong as any derived from alcohol or drugs—and just as destructive."[8] Dr. David Greenfield, author of *Virtual Addiction*, says that men who surf the Net regularly for sexual fulfillment find that they not only crave more, but they soon crave novelty, even the bizarre.[9] It is a vicious cycle in which the computer becomes to the addicted what the bottle is to an alcoholic.

In his 2001 report to congress on the scientific research indicating brain alteration in sex addicts, Dr. Mark Laaser said that out of the more than one thousand sex addicts he had treated, "almost all of them began with pornography."[10] Laaser is cofounder of the Christian Alliance for Sexual Recovery and he counsels many sexually addicted pastors. He writes, "Just like alcoholics, sex addicts tell themselves that they can quit tomorrow if they want to. They like to think they are in control, but they are not."[11]

There are strong psychological and emotional factors in sex addiction.

It is a rare man who says of pornography, "That really doesn't do anything for me." Most men are significantly affected. The power of those images on the mind—especially the young, male mind—is difficult to translate. But it is *comparable to the experience of being in a war and seeing your buddies blown up*. It's that powerful. And that enduring.

But porn is different in that as potent as its images are within the male psyche, it is also strangely comforting. That is why, of the guys who do look at porn, a large percentage of them end up looking at it habitually. Pornography *temporarily fills a need*. When there is an unmet need—a lack of nurturing and fulfillment, a feeling of inadequacy or great loneliness, for example—a man may turn to porn to meet that need. And when that happens, the next time he feels that need, the desire to return to porn is triggered. (One guy told me that a lack of female attention and admiration was his trigger. Wives and moms, we should take note.) Thereafter this need-trigger cycle creates a pattern of returning again and again. It is this ingrained trigger and resulting compulsion that a man must overcome if he wants to be freed from this deathly web.

A man can do lots of things to find companionship, comfort, and pleasure—many of them healthy and good. And many Christian men consciously choose to turn to those things. But here's what we have to understand: Out of all the ways a man can have those needs met, porn has become the *easiest* and possibly the most *instantly gratifying*.

To sum up, we can say this: Although everyone who looks at pornography does not get hooked on it, everyone is altered and affected by it.

## CHRISTIAN MEN AND THEIR SEXUAL STRUGGLE

Research among Christian men is largely dependent on the transparency of those men being surveyed, and since porn thrives on the element of secrecy, it is impossible to know the complete story. But we can get an inkling of what is happening.

The earliest major study of men in ministry came out in a 1998 *Leadership* journal. It was a wake-up call to the church. Of the 300 pastors who responded, 23 percent indicated that they had done something sexual with someone other than their spouse. Twelve percent reported having intercourse with someone other than their spouse, and 61 percent admitted to fantasizing occasionally about having sex with someone other than their spouse. Twenty-five percent said they sexually fantasized weekly or even daily.[12]

Men in ministry are still men; their Achilles' heel has not been removed or turned into titanium. During the succeeding porno boom, the trend among Christian men continued downward:

- In several nationwide surveys among Christian men in the 1990s, sexual temptation consistently topped the list as their single greatest struggle.[13]

- In 2000, one in seven calls to Focus on the Family's Pastoral Care Line were about struggles with Internet pornography.[14]

- Sixty-three percent of men attending "Men, Romance and Integrity" seminars admitted to struggling with porn in that previous year. Two-thirds of these were in church leadership, and 10 percent were pastors.[15]

- In 2003, *Today's Christian Woman* reported that 53 percent of men at that year's Promise Keepers Convention admitted visiting a porn site the week before.[16]

- That same year, 47 percent of Christians said that pornography was a major problem in the home.[17]

That was several years ago. Since then the situation has only intensified.

How do I know this? I have learned it from men who work on the front lines with Christian men, from the increase of public failures among addicted men in ministry (and those at the top are always a tiny reflection of what is happening in the pew), from the continuing reports by young single guys in the Christian world, and from counselors who are working with troubled couples. As sexual temptation has exploded, the ensuing struggle among Christian men has become all the more fierce.

But it is the news about our children that is the most compelling of all. This we know: The earlier the exposure, the more lasting the effects.[18]

## Boys and Internet Pornography

"What we have here is really kind of the new Wild West. Nobody is really in charge," said researcher Anne Collier in the January 2008 documentary *Growing Up Online*. She's right. Our children are living in a virtual Wild West, conducted through cell phones, MySpace, Facebook, YouTube, and a host of other new technologies. But if Christian parents in the Wild West found a way to raise up their children, so can we. The principles of biblical parenting are timeless.

The last thing our children need for us to do is overreact or obsessively overcontrol their lives. This is the world our children live in and we cannot go back. The Internet is at school, in the homes of their friends, at the nearest library and bookstore and Starbucks. Their social world increasingly revolves around it. Their studies draw heavily upon it. Their future includes it and may even depend upon it.

Therefore, we must *get to know it, appreciate it, be savvy to it, refuse to be bullied by it* (who says you cannot be privy to your underaged child's password?), and *use it as positively as we can.*

And we must work extra hard at being close—genuinely close—to our kids.

It would be crazy to try to keep them out of that world. They will find their way there anyway, one way or the other. Wisdom tells us to step into the arena with our children and walk the tightwire of mentoring them well.

One of the best things you can do is to be aware of what is going on. Get on Facebook (or whatever network your kids are using), use YouTube, interface with your kids and their friends on the computer, let them teach you the ropes. And stay tuned in to the backdoor routes that pornographers use to get to your kids. Being involved, ever learning, and on the offensive will give you a learning curve that can make a difference.

Obviously child pornography and sexual solicitations are a well-publicized danger: In 2007, there were 100,000 known Web sites offering illegal child pornography; and the number of youths being solicited in chat rooms had grown to 89 percent.[19] But in truth the greater danger lies in *the secret nature* of the Internet world, the *separation* that it creates between a parent and child, and the indiscriminate and *deceptive* manner with which the porn industry pursues our kids.

Kids are open season for pornographers and they are the most vulnerable prey. As it is with men, it is also with boys. *Boys are the most easily snagged.* And research is unanimous: The younger the boy, the more profound the effect, and the more highly addictive pornography is.[20]

How effective has the industry been in reaching our kids? In 1999, 50 percent of teens had visited porn Web sites. By 2003, the number of 8- to 16-year-olds viewing I-porn had increased to 90 percent. That is an astonishing statistic.

Another astonishing statistic is the *average age of exposure*, which is in the single digits. Dr. Laaser reported to a U.S. congressional committee in May of 2000:

> We are seeing research that is telling us that, whereas in my generation of men, the average age a person first saw pornography was age 11, *now it's age five*. [Children] are seeing things that in my extensive history with pornography I never saw. Pornography that is being seen is violent. It is degrading. It humiliates people, and it's teaching our children very immature, immoral, and damaging roles about themselves.
>
> All psychological theory would certainly confirm that this kind of material, even if it's in its softest form, has the ability to affect a child's attitude, sexual orientation, and sexual preferences for the rest of their life. Internet pornography also can become very addictive. Addiction is progressive, and leads to more destructive forms of sexual acting out later in life [italics mine].[21]

Age *five*? Had this report come from a person less credible, I would not have believed it. For kids at age five, moms are still the primary parent;

perhaps it is time fathers played a much bigger role in the lives of their very young sons! But we mothers need to be equally aware. Early soft-porn exposure is a precursor to early hard-core-porn exposure. This is evidenced in a 2007 report that found that *80 percent of 15- to 17-year-olds today are having multiple hard-core Internet pornography exposures.*[22] You read that correctly. This is an unthinkable state of affairs.

How are these minors exposed? A decade ago kids were most often inadvertently exposed while doing homework.[23] However, today there is a full-scale blitz to deluge a child with temptation. Teen boys have become a particularly desirable target, but anyone with a computer will do.

Besides spam e-mails, there is a large, ever-changing bag of tricks pornographers use to hook children today. The brief addendum in the back of this book will tell you about five of them: *porn-napping, cybersquatting, misspelled words, doorway scams,* and *entrapment.* If you are a mom, let me encourage you and your husband to read this so that you can better mentor your children.

Four of these tricks are aimed at getting your child to end up involuntarily on a porn Web site. But once there, entrapment is the goal. There are many forms of entrapment, but the most vicious form I have learned about is called *"mousetrapping."* Some sites actually alter the "back" or "close" button, preventing a person from exiting the pornographic Web site. This is called mousetrapping because it renders the mouse useless.

When I interviewed a Focus on the Family counselor, he told me that there were numerous times as he was doing important research when he would inadvertently find himself on a porn site and then not be allowed to exit. The only way to exit was to shut down his computer. Children can get caught in the same mousetrap: 26 percent of those who were inadvertently exposed to pornography while surfing the Net reported that when they tried to exit, they were *brought to another sex site.* A 2001 survey revealed that two-thirds of those porn sites *did not indicate the adult nature of that site* up front, and most disturbingly, 25 percent of them *hindered the user from leaving.*[24]

It's all the more reason to establish wise boundaries and become proactive. Know your children's friends—and the parents of those friends. And team up with those parents in a united effort to inform and protect the innocent among us.

## WHATEVER IS TRUE, WHATEVER IS GOOD

Are you angry? Good. What you are feeling is righteous indignation—the same indignation Jesus felt in Luke 17:

> It is inevitable that stumbling blocks come, but woe to him through whom they come! It would be better for him if a millstone were hung around his neck and he were thrown into the sea, than that he would *cause one of these little ones to stumble.* (vv. 1–2)

Pornographers face a severe judgment. But until then, we must tell our children the truth about the enemy and his traps. They need to be warned just as if there were a bomb in the backyard. Don't let the enemy keep you from exposing him early, fully, openly, and honestly *before* the trap is sprung. An enemy exposed is an enemy more readily disarmed.

We must also focus on what is true and good about God (Phil. 4:8).

*Our God sees and knows all.* All is laid bare before Him (Heb. 4:13). He knows our boys and men even better than the enemy. He sees all of a man's ways and counts all his steps (Job 31:4; Prov. 5:21). He also knows the strategy of the enemy. God knows every dart, every stratagem, every vulnerable moment. And while the enemy works in the remote corners of the dark, our God sees in the dark (Ps. 139:12). Ask God to lead you through the darkness (Ps. 119:105), shed light on Satan's activities (Ps. 112:4), and blow his cover.

*Our God never sleeps* (Ps. 121:3). He watches over you even as you sleep. He is actively at work for you 24-7, and He does not grow weary. When you are not there to see, He is ever-present. Pray that He will impress your heart when something is wrong and that He will supernaturally intervene and protect your children at the times they are most vulnerable.

*Our God knows the future.* He knows what Satan and his cronies plan to do the next 31,449,600 seconds of the coming year. He knows in advance what their next trick will be. What surprises us is no surprise to Him.

*Our God limits the power of Satan.* God has him on a leash (Job 12:16), and the demons tremble at His name (James 2:19). Therefore cling to the Lord, for He is on your side (Rom. 8:31). The battle is His (1 Sam. 17:47), and He fights for you and those in your care.

> But you are to cling to the LORD your God ... for the LORD your God
> is He who fights for you, just as He promised you. (Josh. 23:8, 10)

Feed upon all of these things, for they are good and true.

## A Final Insight

There is one thing more to ponder.

God has given *you* to your men. "Two are better than one; a cord of three strands is not be quickly torn apart" (Eccl. 4:9, 12). And knowing the enemy well equips you to fight arm in arm alongside your men. Your multilayered relational skills, your intuitive sense and discernment, your ability to get inside a man's heart—all of these womanly gifts make you the best comrade in arms your men could have in such a time as this.

Having become acquainted with the enemy, let us now get to know the man he seeks to capture—for the more we understand his inner world and natural struggle, the better equipped we will be to encourage his resolve and draw him into true intimacy.

# SECTION III
## READING
## YOUR MAN'S MIND

## *Chapter Nine*

# THE GREAT SECRET:
# A MAN'S INNERMOST FEELINGS

*Men are risk takers ... but sharing feelings*
*presents a risk with a bottomless abyss.*
*—H. Norman Wright*

*The inward thought and the heart of a man are deep.*
*—Psalm 64:6*

Beneath the waters off the northern coast of Australia lies a secret world called the Great Barrier Reef. Though invisible to the naked eye from the surface, this vast system of coral reefs and underwater islands stretches for some two thousand miles and teems with hundreds of thousands of species of marine life. So stunning are its bedazzling colors and remarkable creatures that it has been called one of the seven natural wonders of the world.

In some ways we could say that a man is like the Great Barrier Reef. Hidden beneath his seemingly straightforward and usually calm surface lies another world—colorful, sometimes turbulent, and very much alive. This world of his true inner self—that core part of a man that experiences (but rarely reveals) the emotions of fear, anxiety, hurt, depression, insecurity, grief, even passion—tends to remain deeply submerged, sometimes hidden even to himself.

But men are no less emotional than women. There's a somewhat silly riddle that goes something like this: "Who chokes up at sappy movies? Who gets so swept up in excitement that they leap up and hug complete strangers?

Who falls apart when a relationship ends? The answer: men. That is … if the movie is *Field of Dreams*, the exuberance explodes in stadiums, and the breakup is not their idea."

One thing is certain. Men are deeply emotional creatures. Just as are women. Yet as we will see in a moment, it is an inescapable fact that men process and express emotions differently than women. In general, however, we should acknowledge that some men are more emotionally intact than others.

## In-built and Built-in

There are three factors that greatly affect a man's ease in identifying and expressing his emotions: personality (in-built), upbringing (built-in), and the cultural generation (built-in) in which he was raised. (This is true of women as well by the way.)

Some men are naturally more expressive in their *personalities*, more at ease with transparency, more able to identify their feelings, while other men are simply more reserved in their personalities, just as women are.

*Upbringing* also plays a huge factor. A boy's family deeply affects his emotional development. Some families are masterful at working through conflict. They welcome the sharing of feelings and work through them immediately, openly, and unashamedly. The boys who grow up in such families become men who are in touch with their feelings and able to process them in a healthy way. But you and I both know that such families are becoming increasingly rare.

Many families *ignore* feelings altogether. They stay busy and preoccupied, never going beneath the surface to discuss important inner feelings or to resolve family conflicts. A man who comes from such a family grows up emotionally uninformed and stunted. And since true intimacy always involves emotional transparency, he finds himself in completely uncharted territory. It is little wonder he is unable to be intimate, or tends to run from it when he needs it most.

Other families *squelch*, even *shut down* the expression of feelings, while still others live in outright *denial* (such as homes where parents are trapped in addiction and codependence). The damage to all of these children is inescapable. But boys are especially vulnerable. In their young male world where it isn't cool to express fear or anxiety, they are driven to put on a tough and smooth exterior and to present an image of having things totally together. Unlike girls, boys don't naturally seek out a male friend with whom to confide their feelings; and when the guys get together, it tends to be all about exploring and competing and conquering their world. So unless someone comes along who can get close to them and provide an environment of healing, these boys will grow up angry, confused, and emotionally destitute.

The greatest tragedy is that those unhealed wounds and unresolved emotions don't go away and die. They live on, encased like secret buried treasures deep inside a man's heart, behind carefully constructed protective walls. And like the giant walls of living corals, those walls continue to grow thicker and higher with every year that goes by. As the tides ebb and flow, those emotions live on—ever preserved, ever pulsing, and ever shaping the man, his choices in life, and his relationships in the world.

One woman shared with me the sad story of her husband's life-shaping childhood:

My husband has always run away from hard things. He ran away from his first wife and family. And he has left so many jobs during our marriage that I have lost count. He never let me close enough to see inside his heart, so for years I thought he simply didn't have emotions. Now he is divorcing me because he "doesn't love me anymore."

It wasn't until we recently went in for marital counseling that I learned why he is running. When he was ten years old, he accidentally shot his brother (who was his best friend) and killed him. Immediately following the accident, no one spoke to him of what had happened. He was sent away and not permitted to attend the funeral; when he returned home, all of his brother's pictures and things were completely gone. His parents never spoke of that brother or the tragic accident again; it was as if his brother had never lived.

As a result, my husband never grieved; he never cried once or talked about the terrible guilt he felt. The one time he returned to that house as an adult, he felt numb. But it has followed him all of his life.

Had his parents embraced him, acknowledged his grief, and worked through the pain with him, what a different outcome there could have been! Deep within the heart of many men lies some great sadness or grief of which the rest of the world is quite unaware.

Oftentimes it relates to their fathers. There is no doubt that the deepest hurt of a man's life occurs when he fails to receive sufficient intimacy and verification from his father. A father's character and love provides a rock upon which a young boy can build his own manhood. But when that is missing or betrayed, he is left to grieve and slug through life on his own, hungering for the father he never really had. When my husband speaks at men's conferences, he has observed that it is the "dad" talk during which strong men actually break down and cry. There is no more important love to a man than the love and blessing of his father.

The third area affecting a man's emotional life is the *generation into which he was born* and grew up. Consider your father or grandfather who were part of what has been called the Greatest Generation. These men were indelibly marked by two world wars and a depression. In such dire times, men must be exceptionally strong, for the survival of their nation and families depends upon it. Yet while sacrifice, honor, and courage became the great traits of those generations, there was also an emotional price to be paid. That price came in distant, emotionally unavailable dads who rarely opened up or engaged on an emotional level with their significant others—unless it was in the one socially acceptable emotion of anger.

I recently learned of a man who died after fifty good years of marriage. When his wife and grown children were going through his things, they discovered a World War II Medal of Honor. They were stunned. All those years he had spoken little of his wartime experience, and never once had he mentioned the act of valor that precipitated such a medal.

Dr. Ken Druck, who has studied men in the area of emotions for twenty-five years, writes,

> [We] men lead secret emotional lives, often hiding our deepest fears and insecurities, as well as our most cherished dreams, even from those we love and trust.... We block off entire areas of ourselves, stamp them "TOP SECRET" and file them away. And we keep their very existence a secret from wives, girlfriends, children and buddies.[1]

There's no question that today's generation of men has become more expressive than their fathers and grandfathers. But let us not be deceived. Generations X and Y have lived through the generational culture of divorce—a war of its own kind, with mortal wounds to the heart for which no medals of valor are given—and they are equally good at hiding those wounds.

Here is what a woman most needs to understand: No matter what his personality or background, the male sex tends to be *less emotionally available* than the female sex. Why is this?

## THE INHERENT DIFFERENCE IN MEN

Men are encoded from conception *to process their emotions in a fundamentally different way* than women. And this is by God's purposeful design. When a man's natural propensity is combined with a healthy ability to express and identify feelings, he becomes a powerful force for good in this world. His wiring becomes an asset and a *gift,* enabling him to rise to his manly calling and to accomplish the tasks that God has designed him to do.

Consider the blessing of God's innate wiring of our men:

- A man's wiring enables him to separate out his feelings.
- A man's role of protection and provision requires that he submerge his feelings.
- The sex act is itself an *emotional* expression for a man, and when he is healthy emotionally, it draws him into intimacy.

### A Man's Makeup: Wired to Separate Out Feelings

God has uniquely equipped our men *physiologically* and *psychologically* to set aside their emotions in order to better undertake the manly tasks they are inherently driven to accomplish.

Until recently, no one could have imagined just how different the male and female brains are in the area of emotional expression. Even though we have always observed these differences, groundbreaking research on the brain and complementary behavioral studies are uncovering what is at the root of those differences.

Men are designed by God to be action-oriented, aggressive, able to "take it." Even in childhood development, this inherent trait is obvious. Boys' large motor skills develop earlier than girls', while his verbal skills develop much later.[2] Even then, his earliest words tend to be action words. Give a third-grade boy an assignment to write about how he *felt* on his first day of school and he will be stumped; he wants to write about what he *did* on the way to school—like ramming his bike into a tree or tearing his pants on a high fence.

Here is the fascinating news about the brain. In the womb a boy's testosterone *slows the growth* of the brain's left hemisphere and *accelerates growth* of the right. In females, the "social brain" (a nerve circuitry dedicated to person perception) and language centers that lie in the left side of the brain tend to be far more developed. But in males, research shows that even *lack of eye contact* (inhibited by testosterone) and the *tendency to focus on objects rather than faces* are built into a boy's brain from birth.

Have you ever noticed the differences between the natural way men relate to men and women relate to women? Visit any Starbucks and you will notice how women tend to draw close, face one another, touch each other, and look into the eyes when they are talking, while men are more comfortable sitting side by side, looking off at the surrounding world. (Moms, this is an important difference when you think about talking to your boys about something hard and deep. If you go for a drive, or talk by phone, or sit by his side on the couch, he will more naturally engage you on an emotional level. Wives, you can look into your man's eyes and touch him when engaging him [please do], but there is something about sitting side by side or lying close beside him in bed—staring up at the ceiling [and occasionally at one another]—that enables a man to open up more readily.)

Men also have more white matter in their brains; white matter carries fibers that *inhibit* "information spread" in the cortex, *enabling compartmentalizing, single-mindedness* (required in spatial reasoning), and the ability to suppress activation of areas that could interfere with work. Women, on the other hand, have 15 to 20 percent more gray matter, carrying nerve cells and dendrites that *enable thought-linking*. Women also have a more concentrated corpus callosum (which links the brain's hemispheres), *enabling the right side of the brain to quickly access and interact with the left*. Since the "emotional brain" and the "word brain" use different codes,[3] the female brain, with its *greater capacity for "brain talk" between emotional signals and language*, has a more ready access to these codes and is better able to *contextualize*. Thus, our innate capacity for empathy.[4]

In his groundbreaking research on the differences between the male and female brain, Simon Baron-Cohen noticed how this was borne out in childhood play. The typical rough play of boys requires lower empathizing, while it feels insensitive to girls. Boys are shockingly more combative in their play. Young boys are fifty times *more competition-oriented* in their play, and girls are twenty times more apt to *turn-taking*, which requires sympathy. Little girls show more empathy and comfort for the distress of others, and are better at *decoding nonverbal communication*. They score high on the "Reading the Mind in the Eyes" test, while boys score higher on *systemizing and compartmentalizing*.[5]

A man's *compartmentalization* and a woman's *contextualizing* serve us well in our innate roles of life.

But it also lends itself to certain weaknesses: a man's need for greater emotional acuity, and a woman's need to separate out her emotions. This is why we need to value what each of us brings to the table, and learn from one another!

Sadly for boys growing up in a sinful world, toughness has become the single greatest virtue, and emotions (other than courage or anger) have come to be seen as weakness. And since natural masculine prowess wrongly insinuates that real men always have it together and are always fearless and in control, any revelation to the contrary tends to be shunned in a man's world. By adulthood, the majority of men simply don't speak in terms of emotions or feelings or *wounds* (if ever there was an unmasculine word, that is it)— even though they deeply feel these things. The exception is when a man is with a woman, and even then he has to be mature emotionally and feel very safe for that to happen.

I vividly remember an interaction I heard between my husband and a neighbor. The two men were only casually acquainted, and Steve was asking him about his recent long absence from home.

"Oh, my dad died, and I had to go back and take care of the finalizing of his affairs," he said.

"That's a big job to tackle," Steve replied, and they moved on matter-of-factly in their conversation. No mention of the grief or emotional difficulty of what this man had just gone through. Now, losing your father is an emotional milestone that affects men deeply even in the worst of relationships. And any socially adept woman (even with the most casual of acquaintances) would have at least expressed empathy and acknowledged the difficulty of losing a parent. But Steve intuitively knew he would be crossing a male boundary in that conversation if he had moved to the deeper emotional side. Had he been closer to this man, he would have surely handled it differently. But a man has to earn the right to enter into another man's world of emotions or even to *touch* upon it.

### A Man's Calling, and the Submerging of Feelings

A man's calling of protection and provision necessitates that he submerge his feelings. What a blessing, then, that his emotional makeup actually *enables him to rise up to his calling.* I find myself amazed at God's inimitable wisdom in so equipping our men.

In the spring of 1940, some 400,000 Allied soldiers (primarily British) became trapped on the beaches of Dunkirk, France, with no means of escape. They faced annihilation unless someone could get in close enough to rescue them. The British navy saw no hope for their rescue … until a nervy plan was devised. A call was put out to the everyday male citizens of England—to anyone at all who owned a boat. On the night of May 26, "Operation Dynamo" quietly went into effect. A quickly assembled volunteer army of 700 boats from all over England—fishing boats (ill-designed for the seas), pleasure craft, merchant marine boats—were assembled for a trek across the stormy channel into the enemy waters off Dunkirk. For nine long days those "Little Ships of Dunkirk" snuck into the foggy shore, endured the pounding of German aircraft and ground artillery, and evacuated 340,000 of those men to safety.

Wives waited at home with no word until their exhausted and starving husbands returned home at the end of the mission. Some men never did return. But the Germans were stunned at such a feat of ingenuity and sheer guts by England's everyday men.

Our men are called each day into their own Battle of Dunkirk, and they rise to that calling with ingenuity and guts. They not only protect the nation, but they also protect and provide for their homes and families. A woman needs to know that men thrive on this calling built into them by God. Even in a feminized world, *the majority of men still want to be the primary providers* of their home. Does this mean men don't appreciate a wife's skills in making a difference in the world or contributing to ease financial pressure? Surely not. But there is something emasculating to a man when a woman completely replaces him or outdoes him in this area.

In a recent survey of men of all ages, both single and married, religious and nonreligious, three out of four men said that even if their significant other earned enough to support the family, they would still feel a compulsion to provide for their families.[6] This drive is so deeply rooted that almost nothing can relieve that feeling of duty. Indeed, when a man is not inclined to provide, everyone knows he has lost a central component of his manhood somewhere along the way. The desire to provide is not some kind of need to control; on the contrary, it is a divine calling, and our men instinctively know it.

God spoke about this male calling in His curse of Adam after the Fall:

> *Cursed is the ground* because of you; in toil you will eat of it all the days of your life. Both thorns and thistles it shall grow for you; ... by the sweat of your face you will eat bread, till you return to the ground. (Gen. 3:17–19)

Isn't it interesting that the curse of the woman had to do with her relationship to her husband and children, while the curse of the man had to do with his relationship to the task of provision? When a woman finds herself in the position of "tilling the soil" and having to carry the burden of provision all alone, she experiences that same curse.

Therefore—even though a man's work is the most meaningful and fundamentally manly thing to do—our men enter into battle every time they step into it. Provision is filled with struggle, enormous pressure to succeed, and the continual threat of failure. In fact, this heavy burden a man carries is equaled only by the ever-lurking fear of *losing that burden*. As one man whose business was in a difficult season put it, "Every day, with every step I take, I feel like my skin is being flayed off."[7] It is little wonder that a man who loses his job tends to fall into a pit of depression.

Most of us don't really comprehend the kind of pressure our husbands live under, partially because our men don't often speak of it, and partially because most of us don't carry it in the same way they do. We are also unaware of *why* our men work. Men don't tell us this, but most men don't work only as a matter of self-fulfillment; they do it as a quiet but genuine expression of love.

Sadly, more than half of all men don't feel appreciated at work. Even worse, in their homes, one in four don't feel an active appreciation for the work they do, and an amazing 44 percent actually feel *un*appreciated.[8] When this is the case, a man is laying down his life in a thankless vacuum. It's a bit like the Vietnam vet who returned home to a thankless nation.

When you add to this pressure a man's second important call at home— to nurture his wife, to watch over/discipline/train up his children, and provide leadership for his family—you can see why there are times when a man can feel like he is pushing two rocks up a hill. It is true, God has designed a man for this role, and when he is displaced from it, he suffers another loss of identity. But our men feel especially inadequate to fulfill this particular role today. It takes great wisdom, energy, and focused time to be a good husband and dad, and if a man can look back on his own dad and emulate what he did, he has a template for stepping into this role. But too few men today have had such fathers; so they are left to make it up as they go. It is a risky, fragile place in which a man finds himself. In the uncharted waters of leading well at home, four out of five men feel very insecure, but don't want to show it.[9]

The bottom line is this: *A man's role of protection and provision requires that he submerge his emotions.* A man can no more reveal fear or anger or stress among his fellow workers than the pilots of those boats at Dunkirk. He has to lay aside these things in order to carry on and accomplish the task. And at home a man doesn't want to worry his wife or upset his children. If he lets on every time he is afraid or worried about finances or concerned about his job, what would that do to him? He is the "man," the strength and rock in his children's lives, the one his family looks to for security and stability. A man who withholds his feelings for the benefit of those he loves and necessarily submerges those feelings at work deserves genuine respect and appreciation.

Do his worries and concerns still emerge, sometimes in a harmful way?

Absolutely. And that's the downside for a man. This is where you are so important. You must skillfully enter his emotional world, draw him out, and be a catalyst for emotional growth. Never let "distance" enter and plague your marriage. Pursue intimacy, and persist until you are able to connect with him. So many times it has fallen to me to be the "distance" breaker in our marriage, but that is okay. Steve is a man, and he needs to be drawn out.

When our husbands walk in the door, we have to assume that they have been submerging certain emotions. And we also have to assume that they feel a certain fragility in their role of husband and father. A man whose wife often considers and appreciates this fact is a very blessed man.

### Sex and a Man's Emotions

Few women grasp the connection between sex and emotions in a man.

Sex is actually a means of emotional expression for a man. It is often the one place a man can find an outlet for his feelings.[10] In fact, *lack of sex is as emotionally serious to a man as his sudden silence or poor communication is to you.*

Sex *comforts*, *encourages*, and *gives confidence* to a man. It makes him feel loved. It actually *counteracts* his stress, his fears, his loneliness. And men are very aware if their wives are not fulfilled or engaged during sex. In one survey, 97 percent of men said that getting enough sex wasn't by itself enough. They want to feel wanted.[11]

We don't tend to know this about our men, because they don't tend to reveal this to us. The truth is that many men are not even conscious of the deep emotional connection they have with sex.

Emotionality in sex works differently in men and men. *Women tend to see sex as an* **expression** *of (or way of finding) emotional closeness. Men tend to view* **being emotionally close** *as sex.*[12] In fact, many men can tend to condense intimacy into the sex act. And an emotionally underdeveloped man may well view sex as the *only* way to be close, the *only* expression of intimacy. Is this healthy? Surely it isn't, and we must help them to discover that. But this difference helps to explain why sexual rejection hits a husband particularly hard.

Just as important, a man's physiology creates within him the desire for this closeness on a regular basis. *This is God's way of calling us to short accounts and a continual emotional intimacy in our marriages.* Sin has perverted that blessing, but it is a blessing nonetheless.

Here is what our men want us to know: Their desire for sex is not purely physiological. It is also highly emotional. And it is from God.

Therefore, especially in the case of the less emotionally developed man, it falls upon a woman (being the relational creature that she is) to build a bridge toward her husband—a relational/emotional bridge—if their sexual relationship is going to be healthy and meaningful.

Unfortunately women are often made to feel "weaker" and "lesser" for their propensity to identify and express emotions. Since our world tends to get this so very wrong, it is worthwhile to stop and look at a biblical view of emotions.

When we look into Scripture, we find something surprising. Emotions are a reflection of the very nature of our God, and they are part of our human makeup for very good reason.

## GOD IS EMOTIONAL

God *invented* emotions. They reflect His image. And they have been given to play a powerful role in our lives.

When God said within the Trinity, "Let Us make man in Our image, according to Our likeness" (Gen. 1:26), He was including that part of His Being that feels and expresses emotions. *Our God is an emotional God.*

When Jesus was asked to give the greatest commandment, He spoke of an emotion.

You shall *love* the Lord your God with all your heart, and with all your soul, and with all your mind. (Matt. 22:37)

I find this unexpected … and moving. He did not say, "Be holy." I would have expected this. But He commanded that first (and foremost), we are to use our minds, hearts, and souls to relate to God with the *heartfelt emotion* of love.

What matters most to our God is not that we *believe* with our minds, or *do* good deeds for His approval, but that we *love* Him from our hearts. God wants to be our Father, our Friend, our greatest Love. Abraham drew close in a loving relationship to God; thus he was called the "friend of God." The church is referred to as the bride of Christ. Is not a bride's uppermost emotion that of *love*? If we say we are Christians and do not love God, we are missing the whole point.

Is love a purely emotional trait? No, godly love is infused with an enduring commitment that weathers the tide of changing emotion. But in the end, if a person never *feels* love for his God, he cannot know the joy of being His child or the intense fulfillment of serving Him. "Rejoice in all things," said the apostle. But isn't joy a natural offshoot of love?

The Bible is clear. Our God is very emotional. And because His emotions emanate from His holy nature, they are completely untainted by sin. While love is His primary emotion ("For God *is* love," 1 John 4:8), an entire range of holy emotions is attributed to Him: sorrow, compassion, anger, jealousy, even hatred. Jesus, the God-man was deeply emotional. He loved His disciples, wept over the sins of Jerusalem, and grieved over death. He felt passion about the truth, compassion for the sick and diseased, anger at the hypocrites, and disappointment in selfishness. In the Garden of Gethsemane we find our Lord in great distress and angst. How many of us have stopped to consider that Jesus actually felt gut-wrenching anxiety? But did it make Him any less of a man? Clearly it did not. Jesus empathizes with our every emotion because He experienced them as the God-man (Heb. 4:15).

I remember as a child memorizing the shortest verse of Scripture, "Jesus wept." It never dawned on me in my childishness just how pregnant with meaning that simple statement is. But Max Lucado has captured it well in a chapter of his book *No Wonder They Call Him the Savior* titled "Miniature Messengers":

Tears.

Those tiny drops of humanity. Those round, wet balls of fluid that tumble from our eyes, creep down our cheeks, and splash on the floor of our hearts. They were there that day. They are always present at such times. They should be, that's their job. They are miniature messengers, on call twenty-four hours a day to substitute for crippled words. They drip, drop, and pour from the corner of our souls, carrying with them the deepest emotions we possess. They tumble down our faces with announcements that range from the most blissful joy to darkest despair.

The principle is simple; when words are most empty, tears are most apt.[13]

When we feel emotions, we are displaying the character of God.

## THE IMPORTANCE OF MALE EMOTIONS

Once, Steve and I went snorkeling near a coral reef. Because I am a light-weight (compared to my husband), my greatest challenge besides breathing was keeping myself from being thrown against the reef by the waves. Just as I would settle in, a giant wave would grab me and throw me against the coral, cutting my feet and legs. Finally I decided I would rather view this beautiful and dangerous world from a boat.

It wasn't until later that I learned that in the dark of each night, the hidden tentacles of those living corals quietly unfold to wage a ferocious battle, one against the other. They are vying for space, pushing up against one another, and fighting to the death with the weapons unique to their particular species. Then as the dawn returns, they recoil back into their unthreatening, placid beauty.

Our feelings are also powerful forces of life. One writer explains it this way:

Emotions are the motivating forces of our lives, driving us to go ahead, pushing us backward, stopping us completely.... *There is nothing in our lives that does not have the emotional factor as its main-spring.* It gives us power or makes us weak, operates for our benefit or to our detriment, for our happiness or confusion [italics mine].[14]

Dr. Gary Oliver, who has researched and written extensively on male emotions, writes this about men:

Our emotions are complex.... [They] involve sensory, skeletal, motor, autonomic, and cognitive aspects. Our emotions influence the spiritual, social, intellectual, and physical part of our lives.[15]

There are some two thousand words in our language that can complete the sentence "I feel _____." It is an array as varied as the species of living creatures in the reef.

Yet too often men view emotions as "something women have" and see tears as the epitome of emotions run amok. One writer of a well-known Christian book on marriage referred to tears as a woman's "sweat." (That writer not surprisingly is a man.)

Perhaps you are familiar with the Commandments for Men:

(1) Thou shalt not cry.

(2) Thou shalt not need affection, gentleness, or warmth.

(3) Thou shalt comfort but not desire comforting.

(4) Thou shalt be needed but not need.

(5) Thou shall touch but not be touched.

(6) Thou shalt be steel, not flesh and blood.

(7) Thou shalt be inviolate in your manhood.

(8) Thou shalt stand alone.[16]

I had to look up that word *inviolate*; it means to be uncontaminated or uncompromised. Since this makes up only eight commandments, I took the liberty to add two more, bringing the complete list to ten:

(9) Thou shalt never know real love.

(10) Thou shalt die of a hardening of the emotional arteries.

But strong men *do* cry. And the more grounded and secure a man is, the more he is able to allow himself to feel pain and allow others in on his pain. A healthy man is a *tender* warrior (as Stu Weber explains in his book by that title). If a man does not care deeply enough to weep, then he is merely a warrior—only half a real man, so to speak.

William Wallace cried. Abraham Lincoln cried. And Jesus cried.

Men don't realize that in those moments they endear themselves to the women in their lives and elicit our greatest respect. I feel closer to my men when they cry than at any other time (and I tell them so). When a man becomes transparent about his fears, his burdens, his frustrations, his hurts, he is saying, "I am weak; I don't have it all together. I love you enough to risk exposure. I need someone else in my life to understand and encourage me." The expression of emotions moves a man out of the lonely hiding places of the reef and into the sunlight of warm relationship. There is nothing that bonds a woman more to a man than when he is transparent with her.

G. Gordon Liddy was wrong when he said, "To be strong a man must be able to stand utterly alone, able to meet and deal with life relying solely upon his own inner resources." That sounds very macho, but it is a completely unbiblical concept. (I seem to recall that Liddy broke the law, lied to the nation, and did time in prison for his acts.)

Men need other good men, not as strong and silent islands floating alongside each other, but as intimate friends who become like iron sharpening iron. They also need emotional intimacy with their wives and their God. Of course men need to learn to stand alone against the current of evil around them. So do women. But the toughest man on earth needs other people. The New Testament is filled with admonishments that we need one another in this world.

Liddy also said, "Once I held my hand in the flame of a candle—just to see how tough I was." But I would propose that opening your soul to those who love you and reaching out in humble weakness for the strong hand of God takes far more nerve than holding your hand over a candle flame.

## EIGHT THINGS EMOTIONS DO

Dr. Ken Druck writes, "Feelings make up about one-third of our potential awareness. Feelings are guideposts through life—emotional impulses sent out to signal our basic psychological needs for protection, support, nurturance, and boundaries."[17]

Why did God give us the gift of emotions?

(1) *They motivate us.* Emotions actually stimulate us; they light a fire in us and provide creative juice.

(2) *They connect us to people.* We are told in Psalm 17:10 that the wicked are unfeeling; to be *un*feeling is a disastrous thing. Our emotions equip us to empathize and discern the needs of others; they enable us to cooperate and relate well socially. An emotionally healthy person will be more naturally generous and sensitive to people.[18]

(3) *They drive our choices.* We choose what we desire, and our desires—or "affections," as the great theologian John Owen called them—are shaped by our emotions. That's why St. Augustine was able to say, "Love God and do what you desire." If you truly *love* the Almighty with your whole being, you can't help but want to please Him.

Our emotions feed our choices. A woman who stays in an abusive relationship inevitably does so because she is *more fearful* of some greater injury or loss if she leaves. A man who obsessively works himself to the bone twelve to sixteen hours a day (especially when it is unnecessary) does so because it is *less painful* than going home, or because he is *fearful* of turning out like his unsuccessful father, or because his *insecurity* drives him to find his worth in success, status, and a financial portfolio. If you look beneath the choices we make day in and day out, you will find an underlying emotion.

(4) *They assist our reasoning.* Now this goes against the male grain. But emotions are crucial to our reasoning. They inform us about life, about ourselves and people and situations around us, and they bring greater acuity of judgment. While reasoning certainly processes fact, emotions are part of the factual information that enters into and informs our perceptions and judgment. Many men who consider themselves to be ruled solely by reason are actually profoundly influenced in their reasoning by unconscious emotions.

(5) *They enliven and enrich our lives.* Imagine life without music, or dancing, or recreational play. Imagine a world without laughter and the animated interaction of people. Imagine the only literature being a newspaper—no fantasy, poetry, drama, or suspense. Imagine eating and sleeping and working with people with whom you only discuss weather and statistics. That is a world without emotions.

(6) *They affect our health.* For example, tears release toxins, and in so doing they promote health just as much as laughter does. We have known for centuries that emotions play a large role in our health. But today a critical mass of solid, sophisticated scientific research documents the strong connection between emotions and health.

Are you concerned about your "interleukins"? You should be. New imaging technology is now documenting that emotions weaken our body's defense and cause disease; they also lead to health.

> Interleukins, neurotransmitters, and hormones … send signals to each other and make people sick or well. Strong, painful emotions trigger these chemical messengers in ways that tip the balance toward disease. Good health represents a different molecular balance. Laughter may thus actually be, as the saying goes, "the best medicine."[19]

Research shows an intricate interconnection between brain-based emotions and the functioning of the neuroendocrine and immune systems. It turns out that the physiological "cross-talk" between emotions and our body significantly affects our health.[20] The bottom line is that a man who is healthy emotionally will be a much healthier man in general.

(7) *They protect us.* This is huge. Emotions truly do protect us in every part of life. No emotion is inherently good or bad; every emotion is God-given and plays a beneficial role in a fallen world. Let me give two examples.

Anger is a healthy human emotion, which, when used well, has great potential for good ("Be angry and yet do not sin," Eph. 4:26). A man or woman who never feels anger is either indifferent or far too passive to be worth his or her salt in a relationship. Righteous anger is holiness, love, and a sense of justice all wrapped up together. If we do not allow ourselves to feel it, and feel it to its full extent, we cannot fight for what is good or against what is bad. A world without the purging light of righteous anger is a dark and destructive world.

Fear is equally good ("Tremble [or be anxious, agitated, quiver, quake], and do not sin," Ps. 4:4). Fear alerts us to flight or fight. A person who does not fear is a dangerous, foolish man. Recently our firefighter/paramedic son was called to an apartment complex in a nearby city. A twenty-four-year-old man was partying and drinking, and, having lost all inhibitions, he climbed up on the roof and dived into the pool below. He survived, but is now paralyzed from the neck down. "No fear" is extremely unhealthy.

A mature emotional life protects us from the ravages of sin. But our human tendency is to become unbalanced and go to extremes: to overcontrol ("stuff" our feelings) or to undercontrol (let our feelings run wild). Too much anger (an anger that takes the wheel and drives you into the ditch) or too much fear (a fear that slams on the brakes and becomes paralyzed in traffic) can kill.

This is the challenge in maturing emotionally—to value our emotions, capture them, and use them for the purpose they were intended. Grief is actually very healing unless it is allowed to turn into bitterness. Sacrificial love bears rich fruit, unless it is allowed to rule your life in an unhealthy way—making you too soft, too easily manipulated, and unable to draw boundaries or risk necessary conflict.

Jesus showed us how to live emotionally mature lives. While He experienced all of the emotions, He did so with great balance and control. In his classic *The Person and Work of Christ*, B. B. Warfield speaks of the complex emotions of Jesus—how varied and yet how harmonious they were. He writes,

> Various as they are, they do not inhibit one another; compassion and indignation rise together in his soul; joy and sorrow meet in his heart.… Strong as they are—not mere joy but exultation, not mere irritated annoyance but raging indignation, not mere passing pity but the deepest movements of compassion and love, not mere surface distress but an exceeding sorrow even unto death—they never overmaster him. He remains ever in control.[21]

Our Lord not only *felt* strongly, but He also knew what to do with His feelings. He was their master. That is the great challenge in our emotional journey: to feel, and then to use what we feel with wisdom and self-control.

(8) *They connect us to God.* Psalms is a book of emotions, a sort of "male journal," in most cases between David and God. David admits to an astonishing range of emotions of which the following are a sampling. He felt …

| | | |
|---|---|---|
| terror and distress (18:4, 6) | joy and gladness (16:9, 11) | comfort (86:17) |
| crushed in spirit (34:18) | alarm (31:22) | revived (71:20) |
| hope (39:7) | exultation and thankfulness (28:7) | brokenhearted (34:18) |
| loneliness and affliction (25:16) | sorrow (13:2; 31:10) | love (31:23) |
| delight (40:8) | despair and mourning (42:5) | fear (56:3) |
| happiness (1:1ff.) | dismay (6:2–3) | hurt and betrayed (41:7, 9) |
| anxiety (139:11) | | rest (37:7) |
| | | satisfaction (17:15) |

Christian men find great relief in reading the Psalms, for David is a man's man. Sometimes his vivid revelation of male vulnerability and weaknesses takes your breath away:

My heart is like wax; it is melted within me. (22:14)

I dissolve my couch with my tears. (6:6)

My soul refused to be comforted…. You have held my eyelids open;
   I am so troubled that I cannot speak. (77:2, 4)

I am weary with my crying; my throat is parched. (69:3)

I am pining away; … for my bones are dismayed. (6:2)

Yet in the end, David turned his heart to God.

[God,] You are my hiding place. (32:7)

His song will be with me in the night. (42:8)

God is our refuge and strength, a very present help in trouble. (46:1)

Hope in God. (42:5)

Blessed be the Lord, who daily bears our burden. (68:19)

Oh, give thanks to the LORD, for He is good, for His lovingkindness
   is everlasting. (107:1)

Emotions were meant to lead us into intimacy with God.

## TRUTH ANCHORS EMOTIONS

I have found it very interesting that oftentimes those who are least in touch with their emotions are most controlled by them. On the other hand, the more adept we are at recognizing and processing our emotions, the better able we are to grow into emotional maturity.

Perhaps the greatest sign of emotional maturity is when a person understands the role God *never* intended for emotions to play.

*Emotions were never intended to be central.*

They are never to be the rock, the focus, the tether of our lives. Left by themselves, emotions can shift like the wind. They can blind and confuse, as a violent storm in the night or a whiteout blizzard in the day. An emotion-driven faith is unbalanced at the very least, and easily deceived at its worst. We must put emotions in their place.

*Truth is to be central.*

Trouble and anguish have come upon me, yet Your commandments are my delight. (Ps. 119:143)

God's truth is to be the rock and the tether of our emotions. He gave it to us to help us sort out our emotions and discover what to do with them. Truth taps into emotions, stabilizes them, leads them, interprets them, and captures them for the glory of God. And when that happens, people discover life abundant (John 10:10).

However, without emotions, truth is dead and lifeless. Infused with godly emotion, truth takes the world by storm. Truth and emotions are meant to work together, making us whole people. And whole people are set free to grow into emotional intimacy and "oneness." Do you wish to be emotionally intimate with your husband? In our last section, From Reading to Connecting, we will learn the skill of drawing out our man from the safe and secret places of the reef.

But now let us consider a second area of natural separation in the inner world of our men.

## THE GREAT DISCONNECT:
## LOVE AND SEX

*[Sex is] more conspicuously than anywhere else, the place where the angel*
*and the animal in man meet face to face, and engage in mortal struggle.*
*One of them must die.*
—Mike Mason

Certain things are inevitably true:

- Day follows night.
- Summer follows spring.
- Birds fly and fish swim.
- The tide rolls in and the tide rolls out.
- Sex and love go together in marriage.

All of the above are true except one, depending on whom you talk to.

Sex and love are *not* inextricably linked together for a man, which is unthinkable for a woman.

How is it that a man can move from an unresolved fight in the kitchen (or car or restaurant or, say, even a church parking lot) to initiating sex in the bedroom? If sex does indeed involve a certain emotional expression in a man (which we have just said in the last chapter), it is difficult to comprehend the male ability to bypass relational/emotional *non*intimacy and move right into physical intimacy.

It's downright startling.

I don't mean to say that good men don't wish for them to be linked.

Rather, a man's innate wiring doesn't *require* them to be linked. While some women may view this as a character flaw, it actually arises out of the innate male design, which we will examine in a moment. But women need to know: Relationship does not necessarily affect a man's desire for or even his ability to enjoy sex.

In Dr. Archibald Hart's nationwide study of men who ascribed to be conservative Christians, 81 percent said that they believed it was physically possible for them to have sex with someone they didn't love. They didn't say they would, and many emphasized that based on their moral value system they would not. Yet in all his years of counseling, he never had a female of similar beliefs who agreed with this idea.[1] Experience teaches us that this is true.

So there it is. While a relationally healthy man highly values communication and connection and close affection, every man possesses the innate *ability* to disconnect. That is where we find the fundamental difference.

On the other hand, for women sex and love *are* inextricably linked. It's a part of our being that we may attempt to ignore, but we simply cannot deny. Even the "queen of eros," Erica Jong, said in the later years of her life, "Sex with someone who doesn't love you is totally meaningless and it's not pleasurable."[2] It's a sad fact that those women most prone to emotional disconnection are typically the ones who are deeply wounded and abused.[3]

It is equally sad that on college campuses in our country, intimacy has become something quite disposable. "There's always been a lot of sex in college," says Harvard University psychologist Mark O'Connell. "It's the quality of sex that has changed. It's incredibly disconnected."[4] Yet the modern college woman who is "hooking up" in what Dr. Laura Sessions Stepp calls the "un-relationship" (no *feelings*, no *expectations*, no *relationship*—before, during, or after sex, just a series of "pleasurable" liaisons for the fun of it) finds she cannot quite escape her innate need to connect. Dr. Sessions writes, "Our need to be connected intimately to others is as central to our well-being as food and shelter."[5] Author Wendy Shalit, who interviewed hundreds of college women for her book *Girls Gone Mild*, echoes that idea: "The only real way to remove emotions," she says, "is if you are buried six feet under."[6]

In other words, for healthy, normal women sex is an expression, an extension, a communication of an already existing emotion or relationship. How we feel about our relationship profoundly affects our desire for and ability to enjoy sex. We can't help ourselves, for this is how God has designed us. A woman is physiologically and psychologically wired to experience sex in the context of a loving relationship. And that is a great thing.

To use the old line, "What was God thinking?"

Nothing separates men and women more than this single difference.

But we can't let it throw us. Rather, the better we understand and appreciate this difference, the richer and deeper our marriages can become. God knew what He was doing.

As I ventured out on the high wire of this chapter, I was painfully mindful of the balance pole I carried. One tip either way, and one of us—man or woman—would be misunderstood, even injured. It is a delicate relational life-and-death thing, this matter of sex and love and their dual demand for connection. Without connection we perish. Love is maligned and sex is empty. Disconnection kills a marriage. Connection is its lifeblood. By the same token, sex is integral to marriage, and without it our men perish and marriage is maligned. A sexless marriage is a loveless marriage.

So we must understand the hidden blessing and curse behind our innate male and female design. To err by looking at only one side or the other is to fall off the wire.

There are two basic things to be said about the *natural male disconnect* between love and sex:

(1) It is understandable, and in its rightful place, even helpful.

(2) Ultimately, when misused, it is unacceptable.

There are also two basic things to be said about the *natural female connection* between love and sex:

(1) It is a good, healthy, and necessary part of the sexual relationship.

(2) Ultimately it should never be used as a tool for self-centered evasion, manipulation, or punishment.

## WHAT CAUSES THE MALE DISCONNECT

We have been gradually drawing a composite of the male inner world. We have said that men are different in their sex drive, and we have also said that they possess a unique ability to compartmentalize. Put these two together, and you have a natural disconnect. Since this is so foreign to the typical woman, let's try to get to the bottom of this.

We know that men carry a cyclical, aggressive sex drive, driven by testosterone, which creates a need to release. But in our oversexed culture many women are in the dark as to what is "normal." Physiologically in a marriage where sex is able to thrive, this can easily occur every forty-eight hours. The average married guy in his prime may initiate sex two to three times a week.

But don't assume this is true of all men. It isn't. Variation exists among the most normal of men. Some men have a higher touch need than others. And as men grow older, frequency tends to decrease—but not always. However, a man who feels the need for sex *every* day is considered "hypersexual," and his drive has most likely been fed through an oversexed adolescence (or early manhood) and fueled by an obsession that is unhealthy for him (and exhausting to his wife). Such a man has to learn how to control this obsession, which he truly can.

On the other hand, a man who feels the need for sex, say, only once a month, or for even longer intervals, is considered "hyposexual." Hyposexuality is becoming more common largely because of lower testosterone levels (which is greatly affected by stress and a man's general state of health). A 2003 study showed that one in five men was hyposexual, and those numbers are rising.[7] There are cases in which a man's lack of desire for sex in his marriage has nothing to do with his health, but rather stems from the fact that he is satisfying his sexual appetite apart from his wife. But whatever the case, hyposexuality is not normal or healthy for a man or for his marriage.

## *The Fallout from Low Testosterone*

If the issue *is* low testosterone, there are serious repercussions to a man's health. Men with low levels of testosterone are more likely to die young (33 percent more likely),[8] they are more vulnerable to depression (271 percent more likely to display clinical signs of depression)[9] as well as mood swings, and they are at greater risk of obesity, higher cholesterol and blood pressure, weaker muscles, and osteoporosis.[10] Low levels can actually double a man's risk of bone fracture[11] and even mask the presence of prostate cancer.[12]

I'm not trying to frighten you here … but this really is nothing to sneeze at. If your husband is not interested in sex, the first step is for him to get a full physical. Women have told me, "I wondered if my husband didn't love me; it was a relief to discover that his lack of sexual interest had less to do with me than to do with his excessively low testosterone."

Some men resist medical help (no surprise to most women), but if a man wants to be around to see his grandchildren, a simple blood test is the least he can do. One husband was so resistant to seeing a doctor, his wife finally told him she was considering taking out a larger life insurance policy on him. Then when he still resisted—out of concern for him more than anything else—that's exactly what she did. It was only then that he succumbed to the physical. The good news is that low testosterone can be addressed and reversed, and thankfully, in his case it has been.

But it's not just a man's health that is at risk. A man's lack of interest creates a physical distance in marriage, which in turn promotes an emotional and relational distance. While some women are relieved that their husbands "couldn't care less," you need to know that it is ultimately very unhealthy for your marriage. Regular sexual intimacy, when it is mutually shared, has a way of stimulating relational intimacy and very short accounts, and that forces people to grow and marriages to become stronger.

The sad truth is that there are increasing cases of uninterested men who are actually getting their sexual needs met elsewhere. I recently learned of a beautiful woman who felt otherwise happy in her marriage to a solid

Christian man, but was absolutely mystified by his lack of interest in sex ...
until she happened to discover he was regularly looking at pornography. It is
something that they are now working through together.

In the end, however, most godly men with normal levels of testosterone
have a healthy sex drive that is directed toward their wives.

### Stepping into a Man's Shoes

Let us step into the body of such men for a moment.

I have a female friend who unexpectedly did this. She was given a high-
level testosterone treatment for a health problem, but once it kicked in, she
couldn't believe herself. She found herself thinking about sex all the time,
looking for books on sex at the bookstore, and initiating sex even when there
was significant relational disconnect with her husband.

Her comment was, "I had no idea! I thought I had a pretty strong drive,
but this is on a whole new level." Frankly, she could hardly wait to get back
to her normal self. Although most of us can't walk a mile in our man's sexual
shoes, we can still catch a glimpse.

A man's drive for sexual release is as insistent and natural as the turning
of the earth on its axis. It is a reality he deals with regularly, and it is always in
the recesses of his mind. You could compare it to our drive for hunger. None
of us is hungry all the time. But at fairly regular intervals, we become hungry
and need to eat. The longer we don't eat, the stronger and more urgent our
hunger for food becomes. When left to languish in marriage, it is not surprising when this drive builds up within a man like a volcano—strong, urgent,
and impatient.

### Ego versus Fragility

We say it once again: Sex is the great joy and pleasure for men in
marriage. It's number one. It's at the top. But as we have also said, it is a
great source of vulnerability. When a man initiates sex, he is going out on
a limb ... every time.

When I was growing up, I would often hear about a phenomenon called "male ego." I remember wondering, what about "female ego"? Are we saying that men have more pride and ego than women? We all know this isn't true or biblical. I eventually realized that what is at the heart of this idea is really a unique *fragility* inherent to manhood.

*Men* are the ones who are called to daily step out and take risks. They are called to lead, protect, provide, and oversee—all tasks that require a willingness to step up to the plate and risk striking out. And there is no greater risk to a man than in the vulnerable area of sex. As we said in chapter 3, a man's stronger drive for sex and his natural desire to initiate puts him in a fragile place. I have come to see that *what we have often referred to as "male ego" is really "male fragility," forced upon a man by the sheer nature of his calling.* A woman should honor that fragile position in which a man continually finds himself, recognize it for what it truly is, and handle it gently.

Think for a moment about the natural hunger for food. A man can satisfy his hunger any number of ways; he can pull quickly into a drive-through or sit down at a nice restaurant. But sex is a one man/one woman affair, intended for marriage alone. While this is God's good design, it places a godly man in a very dependent, risky place. If a wife doesn't get this about her man and coldly turns her back on him, he is basically up a creek. And his fragility leads to a kind of shattering in his soul. But as we will see in a few chapters, a wife who does get this is like medicine to a man's soul and a most powerful weapon in his fight against sexual sin.

## MALE/FEMALE DIFFERENCES IN SEXUAL INTERCOURSE

In sex, a woman is so very different from her man that it is almost stupefying.

As Mike Mason puts it, "We are each a hand and a foot, attempting to coordinate in reaching the same goal." But let's put the microscope on this and see it up close:

(1) We know a man is assertive by nature, while a woman is receptive. The sheer physicality of how our bodies are designed displays this difference.

(2) Men are driven toward orgasm (they have semen to release); therefore, *for a man, touching and physical affection are usually connected to sex* (which is why men feel awkward hugging other men). In general, women have lower libido (due to different hormones and cycles) and are not as driven toward orgasm (since there is no semen to release). For women, *physical affection can be enjoyed completely in and of itself.*

(3) A man's need for sex actually cycles *two to three times faster* than that of a woman.[13] So the most virile of women tend to lag behind the most virile of men.

(4) More hidden is the fact that *men and women experience touch very differently* throughout the day, creating a difference in need. Men can go an entire day without touching another human being, except with a handshake. Women, on the other hand, are far more affectionate with one another, and mothers of young children are hugging and kissing and lugging little ones around all day long. As a man's "word quota" is often used up when he arrives home from work, so a woman's "affection quota" can also be used up. Once the door is locked and the kids are asleep, she either wants to lie in bed and talk (not having had a normal conversation with another adult all day) or just roll over and sleep. He wants—oftentimes *needs*—to touch. Somebody has to sacrifice here.

Many men honestly feel that their wives save only the crumbs for them, that they are last on their wife's list of priorities. And to tell the truth, that is often the case. We can alter that perception by being *intentional* occasionally, by doing something (not every day, but once in a blue moon) that tells him "I'm thinking of you right now" or "I'm looking forward to spending some time alone with you tonight."

We can also put the shoe on the other foot by occasionally leaving the children with our husband for a weekend. Try it; it really works. Don't worry if the children will survive (they will!) or if he might not do things the way you do them (he won't!). Don't call home every hour or lay out everything perfectly for him. Just let go of them for a weekend and allow reality to do its wonderful work. Your man can live for a long time on an evening of your planned thoughtfulness toward him, and one weekend alone with the children can go miles toward building his empathy toward you.

(5) Men are also *immediately ready*. On the other hand, women naturally need *warm-up time*, transition, a release from the worries and burdens of the day (much as a man needs a transition from his day into the area of verbal and emotional connection). As one woman said, "It's like trying to stop a cruise ship that's going full steam ahead and making it turn on a dime. I can't quite turn off the day and do an about-face in the blink of an eye like he can."[14]

I like to refer to it as the difference between dial-up and DSL (for you computer people). Another woman described her dilemma: "For guys it seems, sex provides relief or escape from exhaustion. For women, we have to pull ourselves out of exhaustion in order to want to have sex."[15] She's right. Sex tends to be energizing for men, while there are times it can be energy-draining for women.

(6) Healthy men *rarely have difficulty achieving orgasm*. But it is not unusual for a woman to *have more difficulty in discovering how to achieve orgasm* (a fact too many young brides are never told), and there are many things that can physically affect a woman in this area (such as exhaustion, physical or emotional trauma, childbirth, monthly hormonal cycles, or menopause).

(7) Finally, a man's ability to *compartmentalize* enables him to separate himself from his surrounding world and *hyperfocus* on sex. The argument in the kitchen is filed into one compartment, sex in another. It's not that he doesn't feel the distance; he does. Rather, that feeling does not diminish his drive. If the disagreement has been intense, it may diminish his desire to pursue his wife, but the drive lives on, having a life of its own.

A woman, however, is *greatly affected by nonsexual aspects* of life and relationships (no surprise to us). We can be distracted by, as one man put it, "the crickets outside the window, the unlocked door and dirty dishes in the sink, or whether the children are really truly asleep." Of course we are also affected by much deeper things—events of our day, anxiety over problems unsolved, and, yes, scars and wounds from our past.

We already know the greatest turnoff for a woman is when she has been treated in an unloving manner by her husband. Degrading words, excessive impatience, lack of empathy, miscommunication, unresolved conflict—in short, a relational breakdown with our husbands—are all complete nonstarters for a woman. These things are not readily dropped at the door of the bedroom, nor should they be! For us, all of life *resides in the same compartment as sex*. Intuitively, we take "intercourse" to mean just that—an intimate form of "communication."

### A Bridge and a River

In short, sex is a continuation of a day for a woman. It is also a continuation of a conversation or a relationship with our husbands. For men—and this is important—sex is a recreational break from the day, and it can be an entirely separate conversation with us all its own.

For some men who fear intimacy, sex can become their only avenue of resolving marital conflict.

But let me lay that idea to rest.

Sex never resolves conflict.

It may bypass it or put it on the back burner, but if sex is the primary means of "making up," your marriage is in trouble. Like the child of an alcoholic who copes through denial, you or your husband may be using sex as a coping method of denial. Meanwhile, the dysfunction lives on and things only get worse.

For women, sex is like a bridge that crosses from one riverbank to another. Each riverbank is a marriage partner, and the bridge is the connection. For men, sex is more like a cool dip in the river below, to be enjoyed for its sheer fun and invigoration. Of course a woman can be drawn into that cool river, but she needs to know that her dignity and emotional health won't drown in the process. In the end, a woman has to feel loved to truly enjoy sex, whereas in an inverted manner, by enjoying sex, a man feels loved.

Because we are so different, we have to explain ourselves to our men. We can't expect them to read our minds. Men struggle with our seeming complexity (though they are equally complex sexually). One man saw it this way: "If something is so much fun and it is free, why don't women want to do it more often?" They may not verbalize it, but our men tend to view our lack of quick response as a rejection of them, when it may be nothing of the kind. Another man said that the area of sex is "the only time a guy's guard is completely down with the woman he loves. So she can pierce his heart like no one else."[16] If the rejection is often, the sense that his wife doesn't desire him can tend to lead a man into darker waters.

## THE DOWNSIDE OF DISCONNECTION

Disconnection is ultimately unacceptable to God. God never intended for sex to be separated from love.

Mike Mason says, "Without love the greatest prowess and technical success in lovemaking will procure about as much true satisfaction as a mouthful of sawdust."[17]

God has made it clear: Sex and love are to be intimately connected:

Husbands, *love your wives,* just as Christ also loved the church and gave Himself up for her. (Eph. 5:25)

Husbands, … *live with your wives in an understanding way* … and show her honor. (1 Peter 3:7)

This is why a good woman should never settle for less.

Indeed, *a woman's natural emphasis on relational connection may well be the greatest gift she brings to the sexual table.*

As Paul urged Timothy not to "neglect the spiritual gift within you" (1 Tim. 4:14), may I encourage you in the same way? Never abandon this gift for connection with which you have been endowed! *Hone it, learn to use it well, but never abandon it.* I have known far too many women who have done just that, and I have yet to see it prove anything but damaging to their marriages.

A woman has to learn which battles are important and which ones are not. Each one of us has to learn to read our particular man and to understand his particular inner world—his unique vulnerabilities and tendencies and needs. Your husband is different than mine. But every man has an inner script. Sometimes a man's outer anger is an expression of an inner anxiety. Sometimes his silence is the result of too much introspection and self-doubt. Step back before you step in, and rather than flaring up and taking his actions and words personally, find out first what lies beneath.

In our home, nine times out of ten, my guys are struggling more within themselves than they are with me. Women can be remarkably skillful at reading their men if they can *momentarily step to the side of a personal offense and learn what's really at the root.* When a man feels understood, he is much more likely to let down his guard and let you get even closer.

## Saying No with Grace

The question women often raise is this: "Is it appropriate for a wife to ever say no to sex?" Of course it is. But that brief answer is not adequate.

In an ideal relationship …

- *a woman would never have to say no,* because her husband would be sensitive to *her needs*; and when there has been a communication breakdown, he would work for understanding and reconciliation first.
- a woman would be so tuned in to her husband's needs that she would know when her intentional "yes" is precisely *what he needs* most.
- *both partners* would be more than willing to talk through an issue for as long as it takes, admit their faults, and get it resolved.

*In other words, in an ideal marriage, "yes" would be "yes" for both.*

But unfortunately, most women don't live in such a marriage. Sometimes our answer has to be "no, not yet," especially when there has been a serious breach of trust or a violation of the boundaries of dignity and respect.

Consider the case of a breach of trust. If a partner has gotten into an affair or some other sexual sin, he (or she) must first restore trust. *Trust is the most crucial boundary of all.* This takes time—lots and lots of time. It means that the offending partner will intentionally and sacrificially build up a deposit of trust in the marital account before sex is reintroduced. So whatever length of time it takes (and the level and seriousness of the betrayal usually fits the amount of time), that must be the length of time the offending partner is willing to wait. But a willingness to wait is actually a clear indication of true repentance. Constancy of changed behavior for a necessary time is the only way to restore trust. There must be "a long obedience in the right direction," or true reconciliation will never occur.

In the case of major communication breakdown, a woman must have a sense of self-dignity that calls forth respect and draws a man into relational restoration. And she must draw boundaries. Boundaries are biblical; they are necessary for each partner to feel safe and for love to flourish. However, when it comes to drawing those important boundaries, you and I must be willing to walk *all the way through the process*—starting with honesty, moving through the fire of conflict, and ending at mutual understanding and trust. It doesn't help your man if you bail out midway through. It takes a certain willingness on the part of a woman to risk in this way. This is *our* area of fragility.

In the last two chapters of this book we will cover this subject of healthy boundary-setting. But for now, you should know that if you use your "no" option wisely, you could actually end up bringing your sexual relationship closer and closer to the ideal.

Is it necessary for two people to completely agree? No. But in a healthy relationship both husband and wife need to *feel that they have been heard and that their viewpoints and feelings have been validated.* And that takes a great deal of listening and humility and owning up—by both.

If this has not happened and boundaries have been disregarded, here are three biblical guidelines for saying no to sex:

(1) A biblical "no" is *concerned about the man*, the marriage, and the children. (Children are highly intuitive and deeply affected by a loveless marriage in which two people go on as if all is well. Don't do that. Sometimes you must say no, not only for your own well-being but also for your children's and your man's.)

(2) A biblical "no" is also *kind*. It says, "I *want* to give to you, I *want* to meet your sexual needs. But until this is resolved, my heart will not be in it. It would be an empty and untruthful act on my part, and in the end, *I realize that wouldn't meet your needs at all*." This is how we must always say no.

(3) A biblical "no" should be *more rare than common*; it should not go on for months and years. It *pursues short accounts and resolution, and it refuses to allow distance to persist*. If the problems persist, for the sake of all, get help. Don't carry on in a place of physical distance indefinitely. Couples who abstain for long periods (unless there is physical illness or a forced physical distance) are leaving themselves wide open to the enemy (1 Cor. 7:5). And, frankly, that would be just as bad as having no boundaries at all.

Men are extremely reluctant to discuss sexual problems with their wives. In his nationwide study in which H. Norman Wright asked Christian men what subjects they hesitated most in bringing up or discussing with women, sex was number one on the list.[18] May I make a suggestion? Get him a copy of Jeff and Shaunti Feldhahn's little book *For Men Only,* and ask him to read the section on women and sex. Or if he is open, give him portions of this book to read. Tell him it will help the two of you to have more sex. (I'll eat my hat if he doesn't read it.) When a man begins to understand what you need and why, it can be the tipping point for you both.

There is one more pressing question: Do our men have control over their sex drive, or are they completely at its mercy? What about single men, or situations in which sex is not possible in a marriage—such as illness, physical separation, or times of complete communication breakdown? Such times are a reality of life.

Does a man perish without sex?

## THE THORNY ISSUE OF MASTURBATION

Today, single men are marrying late into their twenties, even early thirties. This means that at the point of a young man's sexual prime, he is asked by God to abstain. Virginity is God's call upon him. What then is he to do with his innate drive?

Before we dive into this subject, let me make one important clarification. There is a time during adolescence in which a boy's sexuality awakens and he discovers how his male body works through the early experience of masturbation. As Dr. James Dobson explains, this is a completely innocent and "normal part of adolescence"[19]—as normal as any young girl's entrance into womanhood when her monthly cycles begin. It is also a time when a father's wise input is as important for his son as a mother's input is for her daughter. A boy needs to know what to expect from this newly emerging sexual drive, why God has given him such a marvelous and pleasurable ability and how it was intended to be used for good in his life. But it isn't long before he reaches the *postdiscovery period* in which he consciously begins to decide how he will handle this drive God has put within him. From this point forward, he will choose a path of indulgence or abstinence. And it is this postdiscovery, lifelong period of which we now speak.

Are our men slaves to their sexual urges?

Here is where the hunger analogy completely breaks down. While a man cannot live without food or water, he is able to live without sex. And when it is necessary to do so, he truly can. Men are not mere animals. They are able to control their thoughts. And interestingly, because of their ability to compartmentalize, they can develop a healthy defense against temptation.

Is it easy?

No, in this culture it is *war*.

For many single men, it will be the greatest challenge of their lives. But it is entirely within their grasp. Don't let our jaded, sex-obsessed world deceive you. As we will see in chapter 12, single men are able to sublimate their sexual drive. If professional athletes can train their bodies to perform at practically superhuman levels in a sport, why should we assume that those very same men are a pile of putty, mere slaves to their bodily sexual desires? They are not. Listen to the words of Paul:

> For many walk, of whom I often told you, and now tell you even weeping, that they are enemies of the cross of Christ, whose end is destruction, *whose god is their appetite,* and whose glory is in their shame, who set their minds on earthly things. (Phil. 3:18–19)

> Therefore I run in such a way, as not without aim; I box in such a way, as not beating the air; but *I discipline my body and make it my slave,* so that, after I have preached to others, I myself will not be disqualified. (1 Cor. 9:26–27)

Paul wept over those whose god had become their appetite, and he taught that we need not be so enslaved. "You are no longer a slave, but a son.... For you were called to freedom, brethren; only do not turn your freedom into an opportunity for the flesh" (Gal. 4:7; 5:13). What's more, God has provided a way of escape:

> No temptation has overtaken you but such as is common to man; and God is faithful, who *will not allow you to be tempted beyond what you are able,* but with the temptation will *provide the way of escape* also. (1 Cor. 10:13)

There are times when a man awakens from the misery of enslavement and newly desires to walk with God. Are we to say that it is too late for him? God forbid. Many a man has walked away from years of a total disconnect between sex and genuine, sacrificial love. But it always begins with a change of heart.

## From Slavery to Connection

I have just finished the biography of John Newton. Known for his hymn "Amazing Grace," Newton is one of the most unusual men ever to grace the pages of history. Like his predecessor St. Augustine, who lived in slavery to sexual sin before his conversion many centuries earlier, Newton also was addicted to sexual sin as a young man. Though he had fallen into debauchery as a lad at sea in the British navy, his sexual sin spiraled out of control when he began working aboard slave ships. He gave himself over to the raping of black slave women, letting his "lust run unchecked … without any restraint…. I not only sinned with a high hand myself but made it my study to tempt and seduce others upon every occasion."

In the end, his involvement in slavery actually ended up enslaving him. Even when his life became unbearable (at one time he was made a slave himself while on the coast of Africa), nothing seemed to penetrate his hard heart.

One evening aboard a homebound ship caught up in the throes of a terrible storm, he picked up the book *The Imitation of Christ* by Thomas à Kempis. He was struck by his own mortality and the wickedness of his heart. Then the teachings of Scripture from his mother in his boyhood began to flood back into his mind. Fearing his own judgment for what he now realized was grievous sin, he began reading the New Testament. On March 21, 1748, he came upon the story of the prodigal son. Seeing himself in the prodigal, he realized there was hope, and he fell to his knees. "I see no reason why the Lord singled me out for mercy … unless it was to show, by one astonishing instance, that with Him 'nothing is impossible.'"[20]

Perhaps one of the most redemptive blessings of his life was Polly, the exceptional woman who became his wife. Polly not only loved him unconditionally, but was the love of his life. He once wrote to her at a time of separation, "I am always a little awkward without you. It is not a humble servant who says this, but a husband, and he says it, not in what is called the honeymoon, but in the twenty-third year of marriage." Years later he wrote,

"The blessing of the Lord has in the course of thirty-five years ripened the passion of love into a solid and inexpressibly tender friendship. I shall never find words fully to tell you how much I owe you, how truly I love you, nor the one half of what my heart means when I subscribe myself."

Polly was sick for an estimated one quarter of their marriage before she died. Yet there is never a hint of an iota of deviation in John's faithfulness to her. Here was a man once hopelessly enslaved and disconnected, now set free to connect in true sacrificial love.[21]

God's grace is extended to men who, because of early perpetual sin, wage a particularly difficult battle; however, it is not grace but *license* that says that the battle need not be waged at all or that it cannot be won. The human will is central to this divine battle, and it must be brought under submission to Christ. But what joy to the man whose will is committed to following such a Savior!

### A Hidden Provision

Many women are unaware of a hidden provision by God. There is a natural release that occurs during sleep (called "wet dreams") that enables men's semen to discharge. A man who refuses to feed on sexual images and masturbate (which feeds his sex drive) will find that these natural releases not only occur, but in time they actually occur on a far less frequent basis. While masturbation is natural in the very early development of a boy, no mature man needs to masturbate, whether married or unmarried. This comes, by the way, from very wise and sexually healthy men, some of whom have at one time gone the route of permissiveness and come out the other side.

It may surprise you to know that St. Augustine actually wrote about this in the fourth century. Augustine's father was a pagan drunkard, while his mother was a godly believer. She taught her son the Scriptures in his early years, and when he went astray at age sixteen, she did not cease praying for him until he came to Christ many years later.

His early years as a young man were characterized by a passionate pursuit of every form of hedonistic pleasure; he prided himself in being first at everything—including evil. He drank, had sex, hung out with the biggest rabble-rousers of the town, all the while excelling as a literary scholar and brilliant mind. Then he began to live with a woman who bore him an illegitimate son (who died at a young age), and she remained his concubine for fifteen long years.[22] Eventually he abandoned the woman, and in an attempt to overcome his sexual sin, became engaged to marry a woman of repute. But before the marriage took place, he had already taken up with another woman.[23] His internal guilt and hopelessness only mounted, and the marriage never took place.

Then Augustine underwent a life-altering experience in which he was converted and transformed in his heart. He writes prolifically of this in his own autobiography, *The Confessions*—written in the style of a conversation between himself and God. There he writes of his postconversion commitment to abstinence, reserving sex for marriage only. But he writes of how in his sleep, against his conscious will, dream-memories would rush into his mind and he would experience sleep-orgasm. He struggled over this until he realized that this *involuntary nocturnal emission was actually a gift* from God.

Now this is good stuff. Augustine writes,

> Yet there is at least this much difference: that when it happens otherwise in dreams, when we wake up, we return to peace of conscience. And it is by this difference between sleeping and waking that we discover that it was not we who did it.... Is not thy hand, O Almighty God, able to heal all the diseases of my soul and, by thy more and more abundant grace, to quench even the lascivious motions of my sleep? Thou wilt increase thy gifts in me more and more, O Lord, that my soul may follow me to thee, wrenched free from the sticky glue of lust.[24]

How good is our God to give our men such a gift that relieves without leading inherently into sexual sin!

### Blind Men in New York City

Here is the remarkable thing. A single man's subjugated sex drive can actually go into something akin to hibernation (except that he is not in a cave). His drive is still very much alive and must still be reckoned with, but temptation becomes far less demanding.

Take it from countless men who have discovered this to be true. This is God's reward to a man who is willing to wage war. It is actually possible for a man in a room full of sexy women to be like a blind man in the middle of New York City. Should he put himself there? No. But if he finds himself in such a situation, the blinders can be moved into place and the mental habits of his life will begin to pay off. Now that doesn't happen overnight, but it truly can become the pattern of a man's life.

Maybe you're shocked at what I have just said. And no doubt there are some in the Christian world who would take issue with my suggestions about masturbation. There are some who worry that by suggesting abstinence to a man struggling with masturbation, we produce undue and counter-productive guilt. This is confused thinking. Masturbation produces guilt already! Suggesting abstinence may highlight that guilt, but why would any-one ever compromise teaching a truth that in the end sets a man free?

Abstinence in any form, when explained clearly and in love, is *freeing*. And it should always be accompanied by an *equal emphasis on grace in the midst of failure*. No one can walk out of a sinful pattern flawlessly. Failure is part of the process of moving to freedom! Most men will fail, time and time again. But when a toddler falls over and over while he is learning to walk, do we reprimand or spank him? No! We are delighted when he is successful. And we know if he just keeps at it, he *will* eventually walk without falling on his face. A young boy needs to feel, know, and be constantly reminded by his dad that failure is a part of growing and getting better at anything worth-while. Any man who wants to become free has to embrace the *continual amazing grace* of God, even in the midst of failure.

Contrary to the idea that "You can't handle the truth!" (Jack Nicholson's infamous line in the movie *A Few Good Men*), our men can totally handle it.

Let us think clearly here. If we are counseling a young couple who have just come to Christ but are presently living together, we would not hesitate to help them draw some very clear boundaries. How else will they escape the lifestyle they are now living? How else will they experience true love and commitment to fidelity in their marriage? If they come back for further counsel and we find them still living together, would we wink or turn a blind eye so as not to "inflict guilt"? No, we would lovingly hold them accountable, leading them before God's throne of grace to seek His forgiveness and His power to make the hard decisions that will set them free. We would do the same for an alcoholic or drug addict.

Why should we handle masturbation any differently? Masturbation is not just a little hiccup. It is the gateway to sexual sin. It is enslaving. It *disconnects* sex and love. It makes sex *a self-centered act*, reducing it to a means of self-satisfaction. The *path of masturbation leads to lust* (which is not only a sin but a complete disconnect from love), and—let's be real here—*more often than not, it will move a man toward involvement with pornography.* From there can come a tragic downward spiral.

No one can refute the harm that accrues to the path of compromise, nor deny the great benefit that accrues to the path of abstinence. He who embraces the value of waiting will be a much better husband, for *he will have learned how to connect sex and love.*

## A WORD TO SINGLE WOMEN

We have seen a man's natural drive and *holistic approach to physical intimacy.* That's why for the male sex, passionate physical intimacy is "foreplay," with its natural driving destination being consummation. Many single women don't realize this powerful fact. When we do, it changes everything. God designed our men this way; He intended that foreplay be the first course in the banquet of intercourse. And men instinctively know this. Foreplay causes a man to fantasize over and be *driven toward intercourse.* Women are vulnerable here as well but not nearly as vulnerable as men. Don't be angry with a man who pushes toward intercourse when there has been heavy petting. He is acting out of his natural wiring. Instead, let every woman who "has ears to hear" take heed to care about your men. When you lead a man on with foreplay, *it creates in his mind the drive toward and fantasy of intercourse.* It isn't fair to him.

When asked about what physical boundaries dating couples should set for themselves, my husband simply replies, "NB." No breasts, not even at Chick-fil-A. That should help. Steve knows guys. He knows what a man can handle. And single guys concur when they hear this boundary (even though they may sometimes do it begrudgingly).

The next chapter adds to our composite of the inner male world: the world of the eye-gate, and this all-important issue of fantasy.

## Chapter Eleven

# THE GREAT TURN-ON: VISUAL IMAGE

*A man falls in love through his eyes, a woman through her ears.*
*—Woodruff Wyatt*

Allow me to state the obvious:

*Men are highly visual.*

That statement doesn't seem adequate. Let me back up and take another run at it.

*Men are exceedingly, astonishingly, irresistibly riveted by visual image.*

That's closer.

The most visual of women cannot truly comprehend the power of the visual upon a man. So if you happen to find yourself turned on by a visual image, multiply that many times over when you think of your man.

A man doesn't need to see a naked body to be turned on. He doesn't need to see cleavage or legs. Any woman with a great body—even an attractively dressed woman in a business suit—is an "eye magnet" for a man. The feeling of just looking at her is a deeply powerful pleasure against which few things can compete.

In the book *Every Heart Restored*, Fred Stoeker says that men are visual until the day they die.

We [men] have a visual ignition switch when it comes to the female anatomy, and it takes very little to flip it on. Women very seldom understand this, because they aren't naturally stimulated in the same way.... The ignition switch for women is tied to touch and relationship.[1]

So while men are triggered by *sight*, women are triggered by *loving, relational connection*. (How many times have we already said this? Yet it comes back to us again.) Do women like a square-jawed, lean but muscular, "sexy" man? Well, if we didn't, all the James Dean/Brad Pitt types in Hollywoodland would be looking for other jobs. Are we physically attracted to a good-looking man who dresses with class and smells good and carries himself with a strong and easy masculine stride? I've never met a woman who wasn't.

But when you get right down to it, the thing that really turns us on is when a man looks deeply into our eyes and connects with our souls. The most powerful thing a man can do to attract a woman to him is to treat her with a manly tenderness and pursue her intentionally through conversation and relational intimacy. That's why it is not unusual to hear about a woman that has walked *away* from a good-looking husband who never connected with her relationally, and *into* an affair with a man who is less outwardly attractive but focused on her inner soul and connected to her relationally.

Even the oversexed (sexually obsessed) woman cannot get around this innate female wiring. In her article "Being Single, Seeing Double," Iris Krasnow of the *Washington Post* comments on the HBO blockbuster *Sex and the City*:

> I'm looking at the recent *Time* magazine cover that pictures the four buffed stars of HBO's *Sex and the City*, women who talk dirtier and have more sex than anyone I have ever met. Front and center is Sarah Jessica Parker, with her tumbles of long locks, perfectly highlighted and curled, falling to breasts encased in a white strapless gown. Her lips are glossed into an iridescent purple pout; the look in her cat-green eyes says, "Take me now." ...

They are clearly stunning on the outside, but they do not exude real joy from within, and any single woman who has been dating too long and too much can tell you why: Sex in the city feels good for fleeting moments; it's no ticket to a satisfaction that endures.... Most women don't want intimacy on the fly with a carousel of lovers. Most women want to finally find a partner *who looks beyond* the bottle-gold fibers of highlighted hair, and *into the fiber of their being* [italics mine].[2]

What is most remarkable is this: While the "ears" have it for women and the "eyes" have it for men, God actually planned it that way! Once again, there is a rhyme to our Creator's reasoning, an inherent goodness, a great wisdom in His male/female different-but-complementary design.

So giving God the benefit of the doubt for the moment, let's plunge in.

## SEEING THROUGH A MAN'S EYES

Our wired differences are so great in this area that it requires a great stretching of our female minds and the forming of a new paradigm. We must begin to see the world through the eyes of our men if we are to exercise *philandros*, speak the male language, and grasp their innate needs and vulnerabilities.

We know about the power of pornography. But consider sources that are less obvious, such as magazines, popular movies, and TV. As one man put it,

I believe that women do not understand the full impact of visual stimulation upon men.... [In fact] I believe wives would remove the televisions from their homes if they fully understood how great a battle is waged by the TV for the minds and imaginations of their husbands. While men do not necessarily understand the negative impact of romantic novels upon their wives, so women seem to fail to identify the real impact of television (and most feature films).[3]

Of course, removing the television from our homes would be as untenable as prohibition was in the early 1900s. Wisdom says that Christians must learn how to *handle* the world around them, rather than attempting to become monks in our own self-made monastery.

Should families block out certain channels? Of course.

Should parents implement certain "locks" that prevent children from viewing objectionable material? That goes without saying.

Are certain programs off limits? Absolutely.

It is foolish to put a TV in your child's bedroom for his own selective viewing. A family TV is enough, don't you think? The eye-gate of television is as powerful as the eye-gate of cyberspace porn. During their college years, our sons actually asked us to block out MTV (and like channels), so as not to have the temptation of looking at what has now become pornographic material. If a company refuses to block certain channels, switch companies or pick another package that excludes these channels.

All of this is fairly obvious.

But unfortunately for our children, there is always the neighbor's and friend's house. And for all of us, exposure is unavoidable. Recently our family was gathered to watch the NBA Slam-Dunk Contest, a highlight for men of all ages across America. Suddenly a commercial for *Sports Illustrated*'s swimsuit issue splashed across the screen. The effect of seeing moving images of virtually naked women stretched out on some remote and beautiful beach … well, let's just say it produced the shock and intrigue that was intended. It also summarily dismissed one of our most valuable freedoms: "viewer's choice."

The reality is that "safe" TV is safe no more. It is laced with powerful sexual images, just as movies rated PG and PG-13 have become daringly explicit. What's more, TV and movies are only two of a plethora of tributaries entering the vast river of daily images flowing your man's way. Our men see them everywhere they turn.

### Everywhere, All the Time

A man has to stop at a red light. He can't prevent a sexy woman from walking across the street in front of him. He cannot help standing in the checkout line of Home Depot behind a blonde in her short shorts, holding her little pint of paint. These women are in grocery stores and filling stations and restaurants and malls. Their images are on billboards and in every newspaper and virtually every magazine.

Think about your adolescent son. What about the mass of adolescent girls who are wearing suggestive halter tops, low-cut jeans, and thong underwear (peeking out suggestively)? What is your budding young male supposed to do with that? How about the world of music and the mental images conjured through the explicit lyrics of the songs? These songs make their way to our kids, one way or another. "Sexy" is everywhere.

The point here is this: We women must understand that when you and I are seeing things, our men are *seeing* things (with a capital S) and being inadvertently aroused by them. The effect of those images is more riveting and arousing than we, the XXs of the world, will ever comprehend.

I remember when one of my sons was teaching me about the world of MySpace. When we first logged on to his account, a close-cropped, video-stream image instantly popped up in the top right-hand corner. It was a freshman-type, all-American college girl dressed in a form-fitting top and skirt, casually sitting on her dorm-room bed. Then she got up and, turning her back to the camera, reached down suggestively to pick up a few things off the floor. As if on cue, she casually turned to face the camera, and leaning over just enough for you to see cleavage, she paused her mindless activity and gazed shyly and longingly into the camera. Beneath her was a box for you to click if you wanted to see more of her.

I said immediately, "That girl looks like an idiot. I mean, really, how much sillier can it get?"

I was totally turned off by her. (It's rare for me to speak in this manner to my boys, but this particular son had been happily alerting me to certain male "eye-catchers" that I would never think of as a woman, and I felt very free.)

He agreed. Then as an afterthought I said, "Is that what guys think when they see that?"

"Mom," he said, "I wish we did. You're right. That girl *is* an idiot. But when guys look at that, we are affected. That's all it takes to get a guy's mind going. In a strange way it is a turn-on for a guy. I hate it that MySpace puts these ads up. I've sent them numerous e-mails asking them to remove them."

"Have they replied?" I asked.

"Oh sure," he said. "They always just say something like, 'Sorry, but we are a business and we have to make a living,' and that's the end of it."

"How do you cope with that video always up there?"

"I purposefully ignore it and shut it out," he answered.

But how many young guys have been mentored in the art of diverting the eyes and mind? This is a *learned* skill, as we will see in the next chapter. (He has since then decided to switch over to Facebook, which as of this writing doesn't allow such ads.)

So this is the situation for our men.

Image is everywhere. And it powerfully affects them. Once an image enters a man's eye-gate and is transferred in that mere nanosecond to the brain, it falls upon him as to what he will do with it—and that decision is very important. But our men cannot alter the fact that *visual image is the single most powerful trigger of male sexual arousal.*

If this bothers us as women, we need to "get over it," as Joan Rivers used to say. This arousal through the eye-gate is not a result of sin. It is sourced in God. He built it into man *before sin ever entered the world.* Why? Because He intended for men to be the natural initiators in male-female relationships. To facilitate that, He not only gave them a strong sex drive, but He also wired them to be vastly pleasured by the sight of the female body. When He finished His wonderful design of man, our Creator stepped back and called it good.

## INSPIRED "EYE-GATE" LITERATURE

Lest there be any question as to God's blessing upon a man's arousal through the visual, consider that tiny little book that completes the wisdom trilogy of Proverbs, Ecclesiastes, and Song of Solomon. I don't personally know any parents who have ever read Song of Solomon to their young children (wisely so), and I have heard few pastors, save a few hardy souls (God bless them!) who have dared to preach from its pages and to expound its vivid contrast between the exceeding pleasure God intended in sex and the banal pleasure that surrounds us in our culture.

Because this piece of inspired literature is so graphically sexual and so euphorically expressed, we tend to urge people to … well, just be sure and go read it! Yet there it is in living color, right in the center of the Bible—a treatise on romance, love, and sex. And shock of all shocks. What do we find there but a man's intense pleasure at the *sight* of a woman's naked body—openly described and celebrated without abandon!

Some years ago on a trip to Israel, I remember seeing the numerous neatly frocked Hasidic Jewish men, ringlets dangling, upright and stoic, skittering about their important business in downtown Jerusalem. And I distinctly remember smiling to myself on the inside. These Jews treasure the Holy Scriptures wherein we find Song of Solomon, and though they are all strictness on the outside, you have to know that behind closed doors, when the black hats and frocks come off, they, too, glory in the sight of their wives' naked bodies—as much as any man in Jerusalem, or London, or Paris, or LA. In fact, in certain Jewish sects, the reading of Song of Solomon is withheld from a child until he "comes of age"; then it is opened to him (or her) as a treasured rite of passage upon entering adulthood.

So let us read for a moment from Song of Solomon. Consider this required reading for this chapter! (Such delightful required reading I would like to have had in school.) Notice the importance of the visual to the husband/

lover. In chapter 4, he is gazing upon his bride and describing her inebriating visual power over him:

> How beautiful you are, my darling, how beautiful you are!
> Your eyes are like doves behind your veil;
> Your hair is like a flock of goats that have descended from
>     Mount Gilead.

These were exquisitely coated goats, unlike some of the scruffy ones you may have seen.

> Your teeth are like a flock of newly shorn ewes
> Which have come up from their washing....
> Your lips are like a scarlet thread,
> And your mouth is lovely. (Song 4:1–3)

This passage continues on in its rapturous description, but for the sake of brevity, let us pick up our reading again in chapter 7 (vv. 1–9), where the bride's veil and clothing have been removed and the two are lying upon the marriage bed:

> How beautiful are your feet in sandals ...

Evidently her delicate sandals were the only item of clothing not yet removed.

> The curves of your hips are like jewels,
> The work of the hands of an artist.
> Your navel is like a round goblet
> Which never lacks mixed wine;
> Your belly is like a heap of wheat fenced about with lilies.

It may not sound like it, but this is a compliment referring to the enticing curves at her waist.

Your two breasts are like two fawns,
Twins of a gazelle.
Your neck is like a tower of ivory,
Your eyes like the pools in Heshbon …
Your nose is like the tower of Lebanon …

This refers to the elegant shape and alabaster color of this well-known mountain in Israel; the Old Testament speaks of the "glory of Lebanon" (Isa. 35:2).

Your head crowns you like Carmel …

Carmel was a prominent wooded mountain in northern Israel; the "majesty of Carmel" is also praised in the Bible (Isa. 35:2).

And the flowing locks of your head are like purple threads;
The king is captivated by your tresses.
How beautiful and how delightful you are,
My love, with all your charms!
Your stature is like a palm tree,
And your breasts are like its clusters.
I said, "I will climb the palm tree,
I will take hold of its fruit stalks." …

Ah. We know where this is going.

Oh, may your breasts be like clusters of the vine,
And the fragrance of your breath like apples,
And your mouth like the best wine!

Virtually every part of the female anatomy—from head to toe—appears in these pages, save the most secret part, which is deftly insinuated in the image "a garden locked ... a spring sealed up" (4:12).

We get it. The female body is meant by God to be a turn-on.

Let us never decry this great gift given by God to our men. Let us simply understand it, appreciate it, and be realistic about its downside.

Consider this question: Why is it that men are the ones who are typically cautioned in Scripture not to sin in their looking? That is because women do not naturally look at a man and undress him. It is a man's innate nature to do so. And apart from the tainting of sin, it is a glorious thing.

Unfortunately, because of the Fall and the sin nature we are each born with, there are two innate downsides to the power of visual image upon our men:

(1) Every man's gift for visual *memory* is now easily turned against him.

(2) Every man now possesses a sinful inclination toward adulterous *fantasy and lust.*

Let's tackle the memory downside first.

## A Man's Inner Computer

Think of your man's brain as a computer that is always on, has unlimited megabytes, and no "trash" function.

Once visual images are input and downloaded, they are burned into the hard drive of a man's mind, stored away (not always willfully) to pop up (sometimes completely unsolicited) at the most vulnerable, unsuspected moment. It's as if a man's brain is constantly "online." And a man need never worry about punching in "save." It *will* be saved. Worse yet, putting those images in the "trash" is virtually impossible. Once downloaded in the brain, an image is permanently imprinted.[4] This is shocking to most women.

A man's visual memory is not only long, but it is also vivid and remarkably accessible—whether it was downloaded three minutes ago or three decades ago. The earlier and the more erotic the image, the more vivid the memory. (As we have said before, the young mind is not developmentally equipped to process such images in a mature way.) But any image will do, whenever, wherever.

Does this mean that our men are doomed to a life of sexual sin? Far from it. God has provided a way for a man to defend himself and avoid that pit. But what it *does* mean is that our men are doomed to a life of sexual *temptation*—a temptation that hits them not only from the *outside* through the eye-gate, but also from the *inside*, through the ever-lurking, readily available images already burned and stored in the brain. Because this is so, every man falls at some point.

Do you love sugar? Do you know how bad it is for your body? Do you break down and eat it knowing these things? Even the most disciplined among us would have to say yes. Now, eating sugar and lusting after a woman are on two vastly different levels. I am only using this as an example to help you understand the difficult situation our men are continually faced with.

If you are questioning this, ask your man. While every man is different in his personality, upbringing, and level of maturity, it is an issue all men must struggle with in a way women do not. Some men have arrived at a point where the temptation to lust is more of a nuisance. But these men are becoming increasingly rare in our world. For most men, visual temptation *is* more of a stumbling block. And in some cases—because of an obsessive personality or a background of pain or early exposure—it is an arduous war a man initially finds himself waging. But the man who is willing to fight those battles *can* find victory, and what a sweet victory it is. Does he have to stay alert? Always, as does every man in this ongoing war. But life can take a new turn, and old patterns can die.

How does a man's long-term memory of the visual affect him? Once an image enters a man's mind and is downloaded, it is unconsciously cataloged and able to appear again at any time in the form of powerful temptation.

In essence, it becomes a "mental time bomb."[5]

Let me put it this way: A man may have refrained from looking at pornography for years. Then out of the blue, an old image can pop up. Men tell me it can happen unsolicited at the smell of a particular scent, driving down a country road listening to classical music, or right in the middle of prayer.

The memory of a sexual image is unlike remembering a name or face. Sexual images leave sharp, clear imprints; it's like memory in HD, as indelible as the imprint of a bloody battlefield in the memory of a soldier. But, as we have already said in our chapter on pornography, sexual images are different from war images because they tap in to the pleasure center of the brain, much like alcohol and cocaine. So they become as *appealing* as they are powerful, bringing addictive factors into play. This is why it is better for a young man never even to start looking and lusting in the first place—unless he is looking at his wife!

You should know that there is a difference between inadvertent input, and intentional input and download. But we will get to that in a moment.

## Can the Mind Be Healed?

Are we saying that memory of sexual images is not erasable?

Let me come at this from the perspective of a sex addict.

Can the mind of a sex addict be healed? Yes. But while his healing involves learning how to handle his thoughts, *it does not erase his memory.* This helps us to understand why walking out of sexual addiction is such a deep struggle for men. If a man could shut down the computer, it would help. But he can't. So he must learn how to build a robust defense system—something like inputting a software program that detects computer viruses. Building a defense system is very doable, as we will see in the next chapter.

Before we leave this subject of memory behind, however, let me use an illustration a woman can relate to. I know of women who were abused sexually as young girls. Can they be healed from the wounds of those memories? Yes! Are their memories completely erased? No. Not in this lifetime. The day is coming when the Lord will return for His children and "create new heavens and a new earth; and the former things will not be remembered or come to mind" (Isa. 65:17), and "the Lord GOD will wipe tears away from all faces" (Isa. 25:8). What a great day that will be.

Until then, here is the good news: The *power* that our memories hold over us can be broken. This is not just good news. It is great news! So even though a woman cannot erase her memory bank, her mind can be renewed and made healthy. And the more a woman thinks rightly and becomes freed from her sad past, the less power those memories will have upon her. And the less she will even think of them. *They will recede, as it were, into a place that holds no power over her.*

The same is true for our men. The more a man learns how to repent from destructive lustful thinking and implement a defense that will loosen the bonds of slavery, the less power those stored images will have upon him. And *the less he will be apt to even think of them.*

But what about the other downside—that of a man's natural inclination toward fantasy and lust?

## FROM IMAGE TO LUST AND FANTASY

Visual images for men move quickly from a mere thought—to lust and fantasy. Being *inadvertently aroused* by an image (the thought), and *pondering* that image (lust and fantasy) really is the difference between temptation and sin.

The thought is the *temptation*.

Fantasy (and the lust it begets) steps over the line into *sin*.

A man can't always control what enters his eyes and therefore his mind. But he can *decide* whether he will fantasize and lust.

There is a very thin line, a brief moment of decision between temptation and sin, between the introduction of an image and the *decision* to really look and ponder upon that image. Using the illustration of the computer, this is the difference between input and download. When an image inadvertently enters through the eye-gate, a man can refuse to download that image into his hard drive.

Many women wonder, "What exactly *is* lust?" (For we women lust too.)

Lust occurs when a man moves from seeing, noticing, and innocently appreciating the beauty of his neighbor's wife to fantasizing over and coveting his neighbor's wife (Ex. 20:17). This line (where heavy battle is waged) can be so thin, so easily crossed over, that an image need only be caught with one eye ("If your right eye makes you stumble, tear it out," Matt. 5:29) to become a powerful temptation to step into lust.

There is, by the way, a *holy lust* in which a man fantasizes about his wife. When your husband is driving home from work and fantasizing about you, do you think he is visualizing hugging and snuggling with you on the couch? No, he is thinking about foreplay and consummation. This is healthy and holy.

But in Matthew 5, Jesus speaks of an *unholy lust* that fantasizes over any woman who is not a man's own wife.

By the way, have you ever considered that Jesus was tempted to lust? It may startle you to ponder this idea, but if indeed Jesus was fully a human man (which He was), and if He was "tempted in all things as we are, yet without sin" (which He was, Heb. 4:15), then Jesus was tempted to lust. He could speak to men out of His own human experience as a man. *Jesus fully grasped the intense battle that occurs in a man's mind at the point of mental arousal.* And He was very clear that when those thoughts were dwelt upon and fantasized over, they became sin.

A man *decides* what he will do with images. Will he turn his back and flee these thoughts mentally, or will he fantasize and lust? You've heard the old adage: You can't keep a bird from flying into your tree, but you can keep it from nesting there. Jesus warned that the conscious choice to mentally lust takes the mind over the line from temptation (which is not sin) into sin. Here is what He said:

> You have heard that it was said, "You shall not commit adultery"; but I say to you that everyone who *looks* at a woman with lust for her has already committed adultery with her in his heart. (Matt. 5:27–28)

Lustful thought is more than a precursor to the sin of adultery; it *is* adultery. Wow. But there it is, from the lips of our Lord.

Let us contrast this unholy lust to holy thinking—that life-giving response commanded by a life-giving God:

- *Lust* is a conscious choice to entertain the idea of sexual pleasure apart from one's own spouse. *Holiness* is the conscious choice to turn away from those thoughts.
- *Lust* objectifies a woman, undressing her and fantasizing over her. *Holiness* looks at a woman as a human being, deserving of dignity and godly compassion.
- *Lust* lingers on the image and mentally indulges in sexual thoughts. *Holiness* does not linger; it has learned the art of fleeing in the opposite direction.
- *Lust* feeds on erotic/tempting material. *Holiness* feeds on material that stimulates faithfulness and incites godly pleasure within marriage.

We could go on, but you get the gist.

In a 2008 survey of one hundred of the best divorce lawyers in the country, the question was asked, "What are the top ten causes of divorce?" The top cause was that couples married too young. (In other words, they flung themselves into a lifelong relationship without maturity or wisdom.) The runner-up to the top cause was that *one partner was having "virtual affairs" via pornography, thus separating the couple and disabling their loving connection.*[6]

If divorce lawyers can call sexual fantasy an "affair," then we should certainly be able to call it an affair. Sexual fantasy over someone other than my spouse is an affair of the mind. And if these lawyers acknowledge the damage, why don't we?

Do women lust? Yes, we do.

In fact, if we look upon another man and desire him over our husband, if we fantasize over him, long for him, regret that he is not ours, linger lustfully over past memories of another man other than our husband, we are committing *relational adultery* already in our hearts, and we are breaking the tenth commandment. Just as God calls our husbands to turn their thoughts and hearts toward us, He calls us to turn our thoughts and hearts toward our husbands and refuse to let the enemy entice us into looking for greener grass.

## HOW WOMEN CAN MAKE A DIFFERENCE

Our men want us to understand them in the area of the visual and not to judge them for their attraction to womanly beauty. They need for us to care enough to be part of the solution rather than the problem. How do we do this?

(1) We must look at the world *through a man's eyes*.

(2) We must *appreciate our man's innate attraction to beauty* and the female body.

(3) We must consciously *choose not to be a stumbling block* in our dress and actions.

(4) We must *become a vital part of our man's robust defense*.

Read any book by a man on men and you can't miss this point: Attractiveness in a woman is inherently important to men. Years ago Dr. Willard Harley brought this to the light of day in his research book titled *His Needs, Her Needs*. Physical attractiveness was number *three* on the list of the needs of men in marriage—behind sexual fulfillment and recreational companionship.[7] Is this fair? We must realize that it has nothing to do with fairness and everything to do with a man's natural wiring.

Can an emphasis on beauty get completely out of balance with a man? In a fallen world, of course it can. But if a man expects his wife to always look as if she were twenty—tight, skinny, and ravishingly beautiful, perhaps he should stop and take a look at himself. (You were hoping I would say that, weren't you?) A man who compares his wife to airbrushed images that are far from life's reality has something fundamentally wrong at his core. Chances are that he is feeding on (or has fed upon in the past) those objectified, highly sexual images that create a shallow overemphasis on the external. This can be a red flag of a deeper problem in your man. But in any case, it's an unhealthy and harmful approach to you, the woman who lives with him day in and day out, who bears and cares for his children, and who covers a million bases in the real world.

Most men, however, don't think in terms of such unrealistic perfection. They understand the realities of life. Their only desire is that their wives would make it a priority to attempt to stay attractive and care for their bodies. This *does* matter to a man, though he will rarely say it.

Before you toss this book across the room, I hope you'll take a moment to hear me out. It could make a difference in your ability to find peace in this area of your life.

In a real sense, a woman represents her man in public. He chose her, and when she attempts to stay attractive, she is telling the world that he is a man of good taste. That he is a man worth looking good for. The more a woman recognizes how fundamentally important this is to her man, the more palpable is the joy she gives him.

Does she need to be drop-dead gorgeous? God save us all from such a thought! *Good men want a wife who cares enough to be as attractive as she can.* And that is all. Every woman can be attractive, and when we care enough to try, our men are thrilled! (That includes our boys. Boys care that their mother tries to stay attractive. It boosts their spirits and gives them great respect for her.) More on this in a moment.

As to the issue of becoming a stumbling block to men, that's easy enough to deal with. It needs only a certain awareness and sensitivity to men in the way we dress. I have watched many attractive women figure this out by tuning in to the temptations of men and changing the way they dress and act. If you're wondering if something you are wearing is too revealing, ask your man. My men have no problem letting me know. And here is a most interesting thing: A woman who dresses attractively and modestly has become a classier and *much* more appealing woman. That kind of woman is the kind that a man can ride the river with. This is what good men tell me.

Ultimately the best way to help our men is by gaining a *biblical* view of beauty. We need a breath of fresh air. A new paradigm. We need to look through the eyes of our Creator and find out what true beauty is.

## BEAUTIFUL WOMAN

In a recent interview, actress Julianne Moore bemoaned the fact that the new ideal in Hollywood is size 0. She is a size 4, four sizes smaller than the national average size among women. Marilyn Monroe (a size 12) would have a tough time getting a part in a Hollywood film today. "All actresses are hungry all the time," Moore said.[8] I spoke to a Hollywood writer who reiterated the unhealthy state of affairs on Hollywood's back lots. "You should see in person those women who act in weekly sitcoms," he said. "Honestly, it is so unappealing. They are skin and bones, like something straight out of a prison camp." As one article put it, "They are whittled within an inch of their lives."[9]

How do they do it? They barely eat enough to stay alive, and far too many of them take drugs, use laxatives, chain-smoke, and/or live a beastly regimen of working out and spending a fortune on every conceivable beauty treatment known to man.[10] No normal woman in her right mind could live this way … nor should she. But how many try!

Are you completely and totally happy with your body? If you answered yes, I'd like to meet you. Dissatisfaction with our bodies is as common as breathing among women today. If it isn't our genetic profile, it's the size and shape of something, or the inevitable wear and tear of growing old.

There, I said it. Growing *old*.

Whatever happened to growing old with dignity and grace? There is nothing more beautiful in this world than a woman who has done just that. Harriet Beecher Stowe once said, "So much has been said and sung of beautiful young girls, why doesn't somebody wake up to the beauty of old women?"

Well, God has done that. How old do you think the "Proverbs 31

Woman" was? This we know: Her children were old enough to rise up and call her blessed. That's getting down the road a piece. Yet we find that she possessed a genuine beauty, the "real article," an inside-out kind of beauty that comes from a beautiful heart and an outer strength and grace:

> She makes coverings for herself; her clothing is fine linen and purple....
> Strength and dignity are her clothing, and she smiles at the future....
> Charm is deceitful and beauty is vain, but a woman who fears the LORD, she shall be praised. (Prov. 31:22, 25, 30)

This woman has a beauty that emanates from the inside out; it exudes from every pore; it shines through her eyes and face; it characterizes her spirit as well as her outward appearance.

Unlike this woman, there are two very unhealthy views of beauty today that have hijacked the thinking of too many women. The first is the idea that attractiveness is of *ultimate* importance. When we adopt this view, we obsessively scrutinize ourselves and determine to jump through every hoop the world sets before us. We will not be happy or content until we look like those sexually alluring images foisted in our faces every single day. Even worse, we regularly question—even repute—God's wisdom in shaping us the way He did in our mother's womb. We detest His design. We say, "If I can be different, I will be happy." But when we are different, we *still* aren't happy.

Body obsession has created the runaway rise in eating disorders among Christian women. If you are plagued by such a disorder, you have objectified beauty in the same way that many men have today, and you are paying a terrible price. Bodily obsession consumes the mind, distorts life, and keeps a woman from growing into spiritual health. *There is a direct connection between the explosion of pornography and the explosion of eating disorders among women.* One sickness feeds the other. But you can be healed from this struggle. The next chapter will help you greatly, for the same path that sets our men free also sets *us* free.

The second unhealthy view is that physical attractiveness doesn't matter at all. There is a mind-set among certain groups of Christian women that sees any thoughts about external beauty as selfish and, yes, even sinful. Beauty is worldly, and concern with makeup or dressing attractively and stylishly is "earthly minded." As a result, they couldn't care less about their weight or how their men feel in public with them; they are busy about the Lord's work, and any man who expects more from them needs to get over it.

While these women are not the norm, this attitude *can* actually filter into the thinking of any woman who struggles with weight (which is about 95 percent of us) and is far too busy about the business of "life" to spend hours on her beauty. Those of us in that category find ourselves caught between wanting to please our men and finding it the greatest challenge of our lives. And we resent being judged on the basis of that empty external factor, rather than on the basis of the inner person—mind, heart, and soul. We need to be saved from such a mind-set.

It is entirely possible for *every* woman to be beautiful and to be an eye magnet to her man! Consider the following three elements of biblical beauty and make them your own.

## HEART, HEALTH, AND HAPPINESS

True beauty emanates from the *heart*.

This is the first and primary focus of beauty. Beauty begins in the heart. If you want to be beautiful, work on your heart, your character, your inner spirit, your genuineness, your love for the God who made you, your passion for His kingdom. A woman of God who begins to take on the characteristics of her heavenly Father is stunningly beautiful! There is a regal, exquisite nature about such a woman who rises above the muck and mud that surrounds her.

Do you want your daughter to feel beautiful? Draw attention to her character, praise her, tell her how beautiful her innate gifts are; tell her what a treasure she is in her personality and uniqueness; tell her how glad you are that God gave her to you. And tell her how she is physically beautiful (for every girl is). Refuse to ever point out what the world might lead her to think of as genetic "misfortunes." For heaven's sake, don't tell her she needs to lose a few pounds. (And please don't let your husband do that either; it is devastating.) She's highly aware of her weight; she is reminded of it every time she turns around. Encourage good health instead. And when she pursues outward beauty, make sure it is out of a healthy desire to be attractive (undergirded by an inner positive self-esteem) rather than an empty need for attention from the world. By all means, take her with you to pick out makeup and clothes that look great on both of you. She can help you become more attractive if you listen.

An outwardly gorgeous woman whose heart is ugly eventually loses her appeal to any man, even the reprobates among us. But a beautiful heart draws a man, and it makes every part of a woman's being beautiful. Women with beautiful hearts know how to reach out unselfishly, how to make people feel loved and encouraged and uniquely important. A man feels wanted and adored by such a woman. Do you know how absolutely appealing that is? Character is *always* at the heart of great and enduring beauty!

True beauty also sees the body as a temple, something to be nourished and kept in physical *health* … for the glory of God.

> Or do you not know that your body is a temple of the Holy Spirit who is in you, whom you have from God, and that you are not your own? For you have been bought with a price: therefore *glorify God in your body*. (1 Cor. 6:19–20)

Living an intentionally healthy life glorifies God! This should be our greatest underlying motivation for taking care of our bodies.

Do you trash your body by what you eat? Do you ignore your body's need for movement and exercise? We all know that physical health is paramount to feeling good in every way—emotionally, spiritually, even sexually. A healthy woman has energy and stamina and is less prone to depression. And sex becomes far more enjoyable. A woman who takes care of her body brings honor to God.

She also owes it to herself—and all of those she loves—to make her health a priority. One young woman who suffered a heart attack and flatlined but was brought back to life in a hospital emergency room wrote this: "It changed my life. I said to myself, 'You've been taking care of everyone else. It's time you took care of yourself.'"

Taking care of yourself is not only biblical, but it is also the expression of true love. When you exercise and eat nutritiously, you are expressing love to your husband and kids.

Does this take discipline?

Anything good in life takes discipline!

But when you go the extra mile to work at being healthy and fit, you are telling everyone you love that you care enough about them to be healthy for them. That kind of love speaks volumes! Do you struggle with pounds that refuse to melt away? Don't hate yourself for that. Just work at being healthy, and if they come off, be thankful. If they don't, carry on. Do what you can and be grateful for the health with which you are blessed.

Many women say they honestly don't have time to exercise. In the scheme of hectic family life, that is the plight of most women who truly care about their families. Ask your husband what he would be willing to do in order for you to get healthy. You might be surprised. Most guys (even the stingy ones who balk at putting out money for a romantic dinner out on the town) will foot the bill for a health-club membership or a treadmill. And they will babysit for as long as necessary if it means you're getting healthy. Men aren't dumb. They know healthy women enjoy sex a whole lot more than unhealthy women. But it doesn't take any money to eat right and put the baby in a backpack or stroller and go for a brisk walk. If need be, take all the kids with you and get them involved in exercise; and by all means *get your husband off the couch and take him with you.* The positive endorphins alone that are produced in such a minimal routine make the effort worthwhile!

Then there is *happiness.* I'm speaking of a happiness that is deeply joyful, takes a positive approach to life, pursues godly contentment, and suffers with endurance. A happy woman is absolutely beautiful. She possesses a spirit about her that is a magnet to the world. People want to be around her. They want to know her secret. They feel better for having been with her. They think she is beautiful. On the other hand, a constantly discontented, anxious, miserable, or bitter woman can be a total knockout, but she will never be truly beautiful.

I sat across the aisle from just such a genuinely beautiful woman on an overseas flight. Her husband had been assigned to the seat beside me, and while she peacefully slept across the aisle in the long hours of the flight, he told me their story.

Her first husband had died after a long bout with a horrific illness. She had nursed him and cared for him until the day of his death. She had gone on to raise their boys—each of them now emotionally very strong men, despite the loss of their dad. And when it became necessary to provide for them, she did so without bitterness. She decided to use the opportunity to grow, and after finishing her doctorate, went on to teach college. She came to enjoy outside sports and even learned to cross-country ski.

He had worked under two presidents (overseeing the "Star Wars" technology of the 1980s as well as other progressive areas of national defense) and now in his seventies was presiding over a national think tank. His first wife had died of cancer, and he never imagined meeting another woman who could captivate him as she had.

Then in their late sixties, they found one another.

Often as he spoke, he would look over cherishingly at her and when she awoke, I was no longer in the picture. What did she look like? She had beautiful gray-white hair, bright brown eyes, a mesmerizing smile, and brilliant skin adorned with the kind of endearing wrinkles that denote a life well lived.

I will never forget his statement as we were about to land. My magazine had fallen open to a picture of a fiftyish woman peddling cosmetic surgery. "Don't these people get it? Whatever happened to growing old with dignity and grace?"

Well said, my friend.

God agrees.

# Chapter Twelve

## THE GREAT CHALLENGE: BUILDING A DEFENSE

*"I can fight," cried young William Wallace.*
*"I know. I know you can fight. But it's our wits that make us men,"*
*said Malcolm Wallace, his father.*

—Braveheart

George Washington led the fight in two great wars. In both he won some battles and lost some battles. In both he was ultimately victorious. The first was the very public Revolutionary War. The second was a private war within himself.

Washington fought against sexual temptation as fiercely as he fought against the British. What made him great was his enduring ability to stay in the battle and conquer the enemy. It made him great not only in his home and family, but as the first leader of our nation.

When Washington was a sixteen-year-old, his friends saw him more as a potential womanizer than as a potential man of character and leadership. As Marvin Olasky reveals in his enlightening research on the man, he "could readily have become a rake":

They called him the "stallion of the Potomac" and expected him to run wild. His mentor, Lord Fairfax, warned the young ladies of Virginia, "George Washington is beginning to feel the sap rising, being in the spring of life, and is getting ready to be the prey of your sex, wherefore may the Lord help him."[1]

The Lord did indeed help him. But it took some doing for Washington to come to grips with his need for a strong defense against his own natural sexual impulses:

> The sap was rising, but Washington over the next decade worked hard on self-control. As a teenager he wrote a sonnet to one young lady.… But when she did not surrender, he desisted. Later he courted Mary Eliza Philips, whom he called "deep-bosomed." She rejected him. Washington in his early 20s admired passionately a young married woman, Sally Fairfax, and wrote to her that she had drawn him, "or rather I have drawn myself, into an honest confession of a single fact": that she was "the object of my Love."[2]

Some historians believe that Sally was unmarried when she became the object of Washington's affections, and that once she married, he ceased to pursue her. But whatever the case, Washington ended this courtship and eventually married the young widow Martha Custis, taking as his own her four-year-old son and two-year-old daughter.

Their marriage lasted forty years. In the years that followed, Washington became known "not for his passionlessness but for refusing to give in to his passions."[3] And it was this quality that gave his troops unfailing respect for him and a willingness to follow him through horrific defeat and deprivation. It is doubtful we would have won the war were it not for this man who, by sheer character and determination, led our poorly equipped, underfinanced, and outnumbered motley crew of soldiers to victory.

Just as Washington had to muster a wise strategy of defense, so does every man.

## NO INNATE DEFENSE

When it comes to sexual temptation, men lack an innate defense system. Dr. Archibald Hart has stated the crux of the matter well: "Men don't have an innate defense against sexual arousal, so they have to construct it for themselves."[4]

In Eden, of course, man didn't need such a defense. But sin's curse means that every man must now consciously develop a system of defense. In one survey, men were asked which marriage vow was the hardest to keep: 19 percent said "in sickness and in health"; 19 percent said "for richer or poorer"; 60 percent said the toughest part was "to forsake all others."[5] Given what we have learned about the male design and wiring, this should come as no surprise.

Every man is born to the internal war to gain control over his passions. Every man is challenged to develop a battle plan. And every man can be a victor against the temptation to give in to sexual sin. He may lose a few battles. He *will* lose some battles. In some cases, he may even lose many of them. But victory is within the grasp of any man who is willing to wage the fight.

I interviewed numerous men who had at least one time in their lives fallen deeply into sexual sin, to their great humiliation and sad self-destruction. At their lowest point it appeared humanly impossible for them to walk out. But by the grace of God and their own willingness to follow His clear battle plan, they did. And God has blessed them beyond their wildest hopes.

In Section II we saw the battlefronts as they are today.

In another twenty to thirty years, the enemy's frontline strategy will have evolved—for he is relentlessly inventive. He has no intention of letting up.

But here's the good news: Satan's *fundamental* strategy has always been predictably, consistently, and inevitably the same. And God's plan to trounce and defeat him has always been precisely the same.

Let me ask a question: Whom are we fighting? Are we fighting the culture of sex and divorce and porn-profiteering companies? There is no question we are. But Paul sheds light on the *unseen* essence of this war:

Our struggle is not against flesh and blood, but against the rulers, against the powers, against the world forces of this darkness, *against the spiritual forces of wickedness* in the heavenly places. (Eph. 6:12)

The real enemy is Satan and his unseen demonic forces. And the real General on our side is the Almighty Lord. Was Daniel up against the lions in that den? From a human perspective, you bet he was. But Daniel was really up against the unseen enemy—Satan. And God alone could shut the mouths of the lions.

This is a spiritual war. We must fight it with the armor of God (Eph. 6:13). With that in mind, let us look at the six-step strategy Satan uses to draw a man (or woman) into sexual sin.

## SIX STEPS TO THE GALLOWS

The scene opens in Proverbs 7:6–23.

King Solomon looks down from his upper lattice window and sees a young man in the streets below. He is being "led to the slaughter" by a harlot.

The whole thing unfolds in a matter of moments.

### Step One: The victim has a naive, open mind.

I saw among the naive ... a young man lacking sense. (v. 7)

This young man is dangerously *predisposed* to fall. Why? Because he is unwary of sin's traps. The word *naive* means "simple," and its root word means "an open door." He is not only open but he is also foolish, "lacking sense." He lacks the resolve that comes through mature, clear thinking. He has been warned, but he's not sure he believes what he has been told.

He is intrigued. Curious. Considering his options. He may be "open" because of an unmet need, a poor role model, or perhaps a permissive culture that has softened his resolve. He may have peers—men at work, friends he hangs with—who are making immoral choices. Whatever the case, there is a soft spot in his armor, an *opening* through which the enemy can attack.

Sexual immorality always begins with an unwary, open, "I can handle this" attitude of the heart.

### Step Two: The victim steps toward the temptation.

Passing through the street near her corner ... he takes the way to her house. (v. 8)

He makes one simple decision. It is a mere step. Innocuous. "Innocent." All he wants to do is check her out. But in so doing, he is *tempting temptation*. Why else would he choose to take the road that passes by her house? It's no mystery that he knows where she lives. Everyone knows where she lives. He convinces himself there can be no harm in walking in her direction.

### Step Three: Temptation hotly pursues.

Now that he's opened his heart and made his move, temptation grabs him by the throat. Like a gang of thugs, it pursues him, surrounds him, and pins him to the wall. How does temptation pursue him? First *visually*, then *verbally*, then through *overt sexual aggression,* and finally through *promises*—so many promises.

The temptress starts with his eye-gate. She makes sure that he *sees* her; she is "now in the squares, and lurks by every corner" (v. 12). She draws his attention to her body, being "dressed as a harlot" (v. 10) and acting "boisterous and rebellious" (v. 11).

Then she *boldly pursues, through verbal persuasion and aggressive kisses.* She "comes to meet him" (v. 10) and, knowing he is aroused, she "seizes him and kisses him" (v. 13).

A man who is seized and passionately kissed tends to melt like butter in a microwave.

Then she tells him that there is more ... and he can have it all. His arousal can be fulfilled in euphoric pleasure. This is the perfect time, and she will take him to the perfect place. She compels him to come to her bed of fine linen, sprinkled with wonderful scents (vv. 16–17). What an enticing image: Picture a honeymoon suite on a beautiful, remote island ... minus the wedding.

Then she *promises the best sex* he could ever imagine and throws in "love" along with it. They will make "love until morning" (v. 18). Think of it. Lovemaking all night!

She has pursued him through his senses of sight, hearing, and smell, and then directly through shocking aggressiveness and promises of heavenly pleasure. He is intensely aroused. He thirsts for the fulfillment. This is the kind of sex a man can only dream of.

*Step Four: All is secretive.*

The element of secrecy is key. It is tantalizing. And no one will ever know.

> Come, let us drink our fill of love until morning; let us delight our-
> selves with caresses. For my husband is not at home, he has gone on
> a long journey; he has taken a bag of money with him, at the full
> moon he will come home. (vv. 18–20)

Before him lies an evening of *secret bliss* ... they cannot be found out. Her husband is gone on a long journey. Besides, it is growing dark and no one will ever see him (vv. 9, 16–20). He'll be able to sneak out just before dawn, grab a shower, and even have time to stop for a cup of Starbucks on his way to work.

*Step Five: There is an accompanying rationale.*

> With a brazen face she says to him: "I was due to offer peace offerings;
> today I have paid my vows. Therefore I have come out to meet you, to
> seek your presence earnestly, and I have found you." (vv. 13–15)

Now she's moving in for the kill.

Like a bait with a sharp hook, she implants a rationale. She declares she has just come from church—yes, you read that right. She has been worship-ping God and offering a peace offering. She really is a good woman at heart. Now—alas!—she must fulfill the Levitical law by eating the remaining meat before the evening is out (Lev. 7:11–18). He must come and sup with her! Why not join her in fulfilling God's law?

Unbelievable.

"Come help me fulfill God's ceremonial law—*while we break His moral law*," she is basically saying. What nerve for her to suggest that God might approve of this liaison.

Yet do we not rationalize in the same way? "Surely God understands. Surely He knows how hellishly miserable I am. Surely more than any-thing, God wants me to be happy. Isn't that what the preacher said this morning at church? I'm sure of it. Besides, doesn't God want me to be myself, to be in touch with my inner consciousness, my natural inclina-tions and hungers? Wouldn't it actually be *repressive* if I denied these? Surely what I feel so passionately couldn't be 'evil.' It could be the very thing I need."

You probably think I got that from an afternoon talk show or psychology book or some romantic movie. The "feel good" rationale is everywhere. But let me assure you, it's right out of Proverbs 7.

Initially, at least, there is always an effort to placate the conscience by justifying the immoral act.

### Step Six: There is a promise of pleasure without consequences.

Let us drink our fill of love…. Let us delight ourselves with caresses. (v. 18)

Is her promise of pleasurable "love" and "delight" fulfilled?
We must be truthful. It is.
There is initial pleasure in sexual sin … for "stolen water is sweet." But

it will soon make him sick, for it contains a poison. The Bible says that sin brings "passing pleasures" (Heb. 11:25), yet it proves to be an empty "striving after wind" (Eccl. 2:10–11), eventually leading to "death" (James 1:15).

There may be no immediate consequences on the horizon—except for guilt and shame, the necessity of lying, the possibility of venereal disease and pregnancy, and the haunting emptiness that fills the void after the act. (How interesting that these are rarely if ever mentioned in romance movies or novels.) As one writer put it, we live in a generation that has the "visual long-sightedness of a gnat." Like Scarlett O'Hara in *Gone with the Wind*, we will worry about consequences tomorrow.

Nevertheless, long-term consequences *immediately* begin to move into play, and they start to take their toll. Eventually they will indeed bring down a man or woman who continues on this path:

> Suddenly he follows her as an ox goes to the slaughter, or as one in fetters to the discipline of a fool, until an arrow pierces through his liver; as a bird hastens to the snare, so *he does not know that it will cost him his life.* (vv. 22–23)

Like Eve, who looked at the forbidden fruit and "saw that the tree was good for food and that it was a delight to the eyes, and that the tree was desirable to make one wise" (Gen. 3:6), this young man is rendered foolish by the promise of pleasure without the consequence of death.

For centuries, these six steps have led men and women down the surprisingly short path into sexual sin:

(1) An open mind

(2) A small decision to walk toward the temptation

(3) The plague of temptation's ensuing hot pursuit

(4) The attraction of secrecy

(5) A rationale to make it morally palatable

(6) The promise of pleasure without consequences

How long did it take for this chain of events in Proverbs 7 to reach its unhappy conclusion? My guess is, not long.

These were the observations of a busy king looking momentarily out of his palace window. Time is not the thing. Satan will grab a kid in his (or her) naive youth, or he will wait years until a Christian leader has become sufficiently softened and vulnerable. It matters not to Satan. He has been known to wait for decades to spring the perfect trap.

## THE "OTHER WOMAN"

How does a man head off the enemy at the pass, so to speak? He must pursue *another* woman. The very next chapter, Proverbs 8, tells who the "other woman" is.

She is called Wisdom:

Does not wisdom call? ...
Where the *paths* meet, she takes her stand;
Beside the *gates*, at the opening to the city,
At the *entrance of the doors*, she cries out:
"To you, O men, I call....
O naive ones ... O fools....
Listen, for I will speak noble things."
(Prov. 8:1–6)

Wisdom is the "other woman" who will save a fool from destruction. Wisdom stands at the crucial point of decision, where ...
* the *path* splits in two different directions (one to death and one to life);
* two *gates* are ready to be swung wide (one toward ultimate misery and the other toward genuine fulfillment); and
* two *doors* wait to be opened (one to foolish entrapment, the other to freedom).

She cries out, "Don't follow the harlot and the path of death. Follow me! Enter the gate of life and the door of salvation." And she also makes promises:

> My fruit is better than gold, …
> And my yield better than choicest silver.…
> Blessed is the man who listens to me.…
> For he who finds me finds life
> And obtains favor from the LORD. (8:19, 34–35)

"Come, eat of *my* food, and drink of the wine *I* have mixed," says Wisdom (9:5). "Sup with *me*!" she invites. For the delicious food and wine of Wisdom is far better than the wafers and cheap drink of the harlot. We cannot conceive of true pleasure, rejoicing, and unalloyed delight until we have walked the path of Wisdom, says the writer of Proverbs 8 and 9.

Who is this mysterious Wisdom?

She is God's wise counsel, revealed in His Word. She was present at the forming of the foundations of the world (8:23–30), and advises us throughout the pages of Scripture.

How does Wisdom counsel us to encounter and beat the enemy? We can put it in six steps as well.

## SIX STEPS TO VICTORY OVER THE ENEMY

God's Word gives us a strategy that inevitably spells defeat for Satan. And it can be summed up in these six steps:

(1) *Assuming* a fighting spirit

(2) *Assessing* innate vulnerabilities

(3) *Killing temptation*—by starving it and fleeing from it

(4) *Feeding* upon good things—the wise words and counsel of God

(5) *Locking arms* with transparent, like-minded friends

(6) *Using healthy sex* in marriage as a weapon against Satan

I will speak in terms of our men. But remember, the same is true of us women.

### Step One: Assuming a Fighting Spirit

Instead of opening himself to sin, this man has decided to fight the good fight. He is not passively naive. He is ready to fight.

How does such a fighting spirit develop in a man?

First he has become convinced that this fight is a worthy fight! He "hungers for righteousness," and in its pursuit, he realizes that the enemy must be engaged and brought down. A man with a fighting spirit possesses a "linebacker mentality" (as my husband calls it). Linebackers are tough. They have a "killer" mind-set. And they never quit. Come what may—even if they just got nailed—they get up after every play, position themselves anew, and tackle the enemy head-on. Teams that are characterized by this kind of mentality always possess the winning edge.

What's more, this man has come to see sexual sin for what it is: destructive and repulsive. He realizes that entering into sexual immorality is like taking "fire in your bosom" or walking "on hot coals" (Prov. 6:26–28). You can't do those things without getting burned. He recognizes the deadly lie behind the allure. And that discernment *solidifies his will to fight.*

The man who has already been burned in that fire, or is living in the midst of it at this moment, must take a first step. He can gain a fighting spirit by walking through the *gate of genuine repentance.*

What is genuine repentance? It is more than sorrow; it is a heartfelt sickness over sin and an equally heartfelt choice to *reverse* course and walk in the opposite direction. Thomas Watson described true repentance as the "vomiting of a man's soul." My young male interviewees of the first chapter concur: Sexual sin must make you so sick in your gut that you really want to vomit. Charles Spurgeon said that a man's repentance is evident only when it is as great as the sin he has committed. For the man who is deep into sexual sin and addiction, repentance involves a no-more-secrets, face-to-the-ground, gut-wrenching kind of repentance. Such humility does something remarkable in a man's heart. It imbues him with a will to fight and a passionate desire for victory.

There is a kind of halfhearted, false repentance that has no staying power; it is driven by the desire to change public opinion rather than a desire to change the inner core of the heart. With false repentance, there is no true conviction and humility before God, no real sense of shame. This person is sorry for having been *caught* and wishes to avoid certain consequences. On the surface it is initially convincing. But since it is about damage control, when the damage *is* controlled and "normalcy" has returned, the sinful thinking of the heart remains intact. And tragically, nothing has really changed.

True repentance is very different. It is characterized by a no-holds-barred, transparent admission of sin (a full disclosure, if you will) to all of the significant people in that person's life. It is forthcoming, palpably ashamed and openly humble, willing to accept the consequences, and committed *to doing whatever is necessary for change and restoration.* True repentance is evidenced by a very obvious and open walking away from sin. Does this mean that henceforth the repentant one is flawless? Every person who truly repents experiences setbacks. But those setbacks are just that—setbacks. And even in failure, the *desire to pursue holiness persists.* As John Piper explains, true repentance does not produce "a *perfect flawlessness* in this life … it produces a *persevering fight.*"[6]

But the will to fight needs something beyond a hunger for righteousness and a genuine repentance.

It also needs a *huge dose of God's grace.*

Satan hates repentance. He tries to discourage a truly repentant heart. He accuses and accuses. He is *the* great accuser of the brethren (Rev. 12:10). He wants us to struggle day and night, not live in the peace and hope of God's goodness and grace.

Think on this. God forgives a genuinely repentant person. He forgives *completely* and *forever.* Those sins are no longer held against us. Amazing. They have been removed "as far as the east is from the west" (Ps. 103:12). This amazing grace is life-changing. What do we tend to do when we blow it ... when we see the sin, and hate what we see? We tend to condemn ourselves and despair. We begin to live under a dark cloud of self-condemnation (Rom. 7:24). But we need to remember that condemnation is not from God (Rom. 8:1). It is from the enemy. And it crushes our spirit and saps all our hope. When self-condemnation rules the day, we lose heart and end up going right back to doing "the very thing I do not want to do" (Rom. 7:16). On the other hand, when God's amazing grace floods the soul, and we remember it in those accusing moments, we are moved from *humiliation* to *humility*. Humility says, "Yes, I am flawed. But God's goodness and grace are far greater than my sin. And God will complete the work He has begun" (Rom. 8:37–39; Phil. 1:6). Humility can rest—rather than struggle, for there is a sure hope in *His* transforming work.

### Step Two: Assessing Innate Vulnerabilities

Theologian John Owen used to say that the two most important matters of the soul are first, "to know thyself," and second, "to know thy God."

A man must know himself. He must discover his trigger points—what trips him up and causes him to stumble. He needs to get dead serious about this.

How many times are we simply unaware of what trips us up? So we just keep doing the same thing over and over, and we go right on falling into the same old pit. A person must get to know his unique vulnerabilities, the things that seem to take him down every time.

Is it a hotel room where TV porn awaits? Is it a woman at the office? Is it a dark parked car or an apartment? Is it a computer or certain movies or music? Is it trouble in your marriage? (A man is very vulnerable when he is feeling continually unappreciated, unloved, put down by his wife. At such times he should not be silent on that score; he needs to express what that is doing to him. And you and I should listen.)

A guy can figure out pretty easily where he is vulnerable.

But a woman must also get to know her man. The more aware you are of his vulnerable times and innate weaknesses, the better partner in arms you can be in this war. Think with me about some of the things that give Satan an opening:

- Does your man have an addictive, painful, or sexually active background?
- Is he fearful of intimacy?
- Is he deeply disappointed in your marriage?
- Is there a silent distance or much arguing and high drama between you?
- Do you have a troubled child who is tearing you apart in your marriage?
- Is he sexually unsatisfied or starved in your marriage?
- Is he greatly stressed in his work?
- Is there a woman in his office who understands him or connects with him better than you do?
- Does he keep secrets or have areas of his life you cannot be privy to?

All of these make a man more vulnerable to the enemy.

If you don't know the answers to these questions, you need to know. In chapter 14, we will delve into the art of getting inside your man's heart. Every man needs a woman who understands his vulnerabilities.

### Step Three: Killing Temptation—by Starving It and Fleeing from It

*Starving* and *fleeing* are really two sides of the same sword.

One kills the temptation by starving it to death. The other runs like mad whenever temptation rears its ugly head. Let's look at starvation first.

(1) *We are to "put to death" the fleshly temptation that would consume us and kill us.*

> For if you are living according to the flesh, you must [are about to] die; but if by the Spirit you are *putting to death* the deeds of the body, you will live. (Rom. 8:13)

This is another way of saying that we are to starve our fleshly desires. If we don't feed them, they die.

After John Newton married, you may be surprised to learn that he continued as a slave-ship captain during the early years of his marriage. It was a gradual process for Newton's new spiritual eyes to be fully opened to the evil of slavery; but once opened, he fought fiercely alongside men like William Wilberforce for its abolition. He did however become immediately concerned for the well-being of his slaves and sensitive to their needs, feeding them well and treating them with kindness and dignity.

Yet while the scales were still falling from his eyes on the issue of slavery, his sight was astonishingly clear when it came to the depravity of sexual immorality. His conviction in this area was full and complete. Newton knew that being away from his wife, Polly, aboard ships for long periods of time would put him at risk. This was where the old temptations to indulge in sexual free-for-alls (which most captains regarded as their right aboard ship) would come back to devour him. If he was going to avoid falling back into the old patterns of drunkenness and sexual immorality, he had to come up with a plan. Biographer Jonathan Aitken writes,

> One of Newton's self-disciplinary defenses against the power of his own libido was *a strict diet of water and vegetables that commenced as soon as his ship was sailing away from the coast.* He admitted this in later life to his close friend and contemporary Richard Cecil (1748–1810), who recorded the conversation in a footnote to his own writings about Newton:
>
> "I have heard Mr. Newton observe that as the commander of a slave ship he had a number of women under his absolute authority: and knowing the danger of his situation on that account *he resolved to abstain from flesh in his food and to drink nothing stronger than water during the voyage; that by abstemiousness he might subdue every improper emotion: and that upon his setting sail the sight of a certain*

*point of land was the signal for his beginning a rule that he was enabled
to keep"* [italics mine].[7]

This plan worked for Newton. By changing his diet and completely
abstaining from alcohol, he was able to succeed. In essence, Newton figured
out how to starve and kill the temptation before it could even get to him.
Every man has to find a way to starve and kill the temptation that assails
him. Unfed temptation will perish.

(2) *We are also to "flee" sexual temptation.*

Now flee from youthful lusts and pursue righteousness, faith, love
and peace, with those who call on the Lord from a pure heart.
(2 Tim. 2:22)

It is not cowardice to flee. It is wise fear. Fleeing actually takes the powerful legs of character that can run well when the moment calls for it. And
we have to develop those muscles on a regular basis.

Joseph fled when his youthful hormones were raging and Predator (the
name of Potiphar's wife, christened by my husband) was coming on to him,
enticingly, persistently, day after day. On that fateful day that she grabbed
his coat in passion, begging him once again, "Lie with me!" Joseph resolutely
answered, "How can I do this great evil and sin against God?" Then he fled
like the wind.

Now there's a young man who had character. Character is what you are
when your boss or your wife or your kids or your Christian friends or the
members of your congregation are not around. Character answers to God.
Our men need the conviction that Someone else is watching, that the "eyes
of God" are looking about the earth, seeing all and calling all into account.
They need to know that He judges what we do in secret.

How does a man flee today? Let me give a few illustrations.

*A man can avert his eyes.*

Our boys used to watch their dad like a hawk. They wanted to see if he averted his gaze. They would notice a sexy woman at the mall, then they would look at their dad. Sure enough, he took note of her and immediately looked away. He did not allow himself to dwell. They would stop in the car with him at a light and see some chick crossing the street in front of the car. They would look at their dad, and his eyes did not follow her. It amazed them. They wanted to know how to do that. So this is basically what he explained to them.

"It's like dribbling with your left hand. You know how it is easy for you to bounce the basketball with your right hand? And you know how I used to make you bounce it with your left hand when we were shooting hoops in the backyard? You hated that, but soon you got good at it. The reason I was teaching you to dribble with the left hand is because even though it isn't natural, you can learn to do it with practice. And if you can get as good with your left as with your right, you will beat your opponent. He never knows which way you're going to go on the court.

"It takes practice to learn how to avert your eyes. But the more you practice it, the better you get, until it almost becomes unconscious. You don't want to stop practicing, though, because it is a skill you can lose if you neglect it for long."

*A man can avoid/remove those things that trip him up.*

Sometimes this means drastic measures. I know of one newly married young man who confessed his addiction to pornography to his innocent young bride. At first she was devastated. But when she saw how tortured he was and how much he wanted to change that, she agreed to become his accountability partner.

The greatest temptation for him was when he traveled, which he did constantly. He made a pact with her that he would do something drastic. He would have the TV removed from his hotel room every time he traveled. Then he would call her and let her know that he had implemented the plan. Guess what? Hotels will remove your TV if you ask. Drastic? Yes. Sometimes it takes drastic measures to remove the stumbling block.

I know of men who routinely unplug the TV the minute they walk into a hotel room alone.

When he was a pastor, Steve decided not to counsel any woman long term. (Male counselors who do work with women have to build special boundaries into their lives.) Now that he travels, he restricts himself to ESPN and the news when watching TV. In mixed conferences, he has boundaries with women. He has had women come up to him after a talk at a conference and say, "Can I just hug you?" In reply, Steve will graciously smile and say, "Well, actually, no. There's only one woman who gets to hug me," and of course everyone laughs. But he is serious.

We used to get *Sports Illustrated*. When the swimsuit issue first came out, Steve called and requested an exemption from that issue; otherwise, he would have to cancel his subscription. The magazine said they couldn't do that. So every year he canceled the period of months in which that issue came out. That made an indelible impression on our boys.

When sexy commercials appeared during programming, Steve immediately changed the channel. Our boys picked up on that so fast that it became habitual to them very early on. Men like to change channels anyway!

Becoming intentional can even involve something as severe as changing jobs. But is not a marriage far more valuable than any job for any amount of money on the planet? God provides for such a man. I know one man who became involved in an affair with a woman at work; but he decided his wife and family were more important than that particular job, and he walked away. It was the hardest thing he had ever done, but it saved his marriage.

I know another man who was very careful about whom he hired as his secretary; if a woman posed a ready temptation, he simply did not hire her. He knew himself and his vulnerabilities too well. Discrimination? You bet. Wise and discerning discrimination.

A man has to do whatever is necessary to flee. If he's a single guy in love, as one man I know, he will stop taking his girlfriend back to an empty apartment and make sure that the two of them make a point of spending time together with other people.

There is always a way. And if a man hears a voice in his ear saying, "There's no way around this temptation, you're trapped," then he can easily identify that as the voice of the enemy. No matter the temptation, "God is faithful ... [and He] will provide the way of escape" (1 Cor. 10:13).

Do you want to talk about drastic? The words of Jesus are drastic:

> If your right eye makes you stumble, tear it out and throw it from you.... If your right hand makes you stumble cut it off, and throw it from you. (Matt. 5:29–30)

The severity of the action must match the seriousness of the temptation at hand. We can't fool around with Satan. If there are "Fifty Ways to Leave Your Lover," as singer Paul Simon claims, there are a million ways to flee sexual temptation. A man can and must find a way to flee. And he who flees cuts that temptation right off at the head.

### Step Four: Feeding upon Good, Healthy Mental Food

Jesus told the parable of a man who was demon possessed. The unclean spirit in him was thrown out and wandered about seeking a place to rest. Finding none, the spirit said to himself, "I think I'll go back and see if that house is available." When he returned, he discovered it to be empty (though now it was swept and put in order!), so he went and called his friends (seven other spirits more evil than himself), and they all came over and had a huge party (I am paraphrasing of course), and then they all set up residence there. "And the last state of that man becomes worse than the first," He said (see Luke 11:24–26).

In other words, it's not enough to clean house by running from temptation (for temptation will return again and again). We have to fill that same house with something good. Fleeing is only half the battle. We must feed our minds vitamins and organic fruits and vegetables and protein—all things that are good and pure and of good repute (Phil. 4:8). Otherwise we leave ourselves open for future attack.

The simple truth is this: *Something* is going to fill our minds. We decide every day what that something will be. If we spend hours feeding at the trough of the world, what are we to expect? If we let the empty noise around us drown out the quiet truth of God's words, who will end up shaping our choices? When we don't fill our minds with truth, we become like kids taking a biology test in school without ever having gone to class or opening the book. Do we think that the process of cellular respiration and replication will just magically appear in our minds?

*What our mind feeds upon is what we become.* Plain and simple. It shapes our worldview, our reasoning, our desires, and ultimately our decision-making. "Abide in Me, *and My words*," says the Lord (John 15:7). "I am the Vine, you are the branches; he who *abides in Me* and I in him, he bears much fruit, for *apart from Me you can do nothing*" (John 15:5).

Today I spoke with a young woman who struggles with an eating disorder. Food addiction shares many similarities with sexual addiction. Her problem had started all the way back in her adolescence when her father left.

Now that she knows Christ, she is realizing that the root of her struggle began with a feeling of never really being good enough. If her dad didn't love her enough to stay, why should anyone? And if the world says that thinness is what makes you appealing and lovable, you'd better get that right. When she became a Christ follower, she realized that her Creator had not only come to earth and died for her but also that He would never leave her. She began to dwell on the fact that He could be trusted, that He loved her immeasurably more than any man would ever be able to love her. The more she fed on the truth, the more she saw His handiwork in her life, and the healthier she became emotionally.

But she has also noticed something very interesting. When she stops feeding on Scripture for any great length of time, the obsession over her body and food tends to creep back in.

God's Word is our "air," our "lifeblood," our "food and water," keeping us strong and enabling us to live victoriously.

These first four steps to victory are personal decisions men (or women) primarily make for themselves. But the last two steps are where a woman becomes a key player, coming alongside as a partner with her man.

### Step Five: Locking Arms with Good Friends

In football, we call this "special teams." But another word for this among believers is *accountability*. Accountability has been a buzzword in Christian circles over the last few decades. But to be honest, an accountability group is only as good as the people in it. What is true accountability? True accountability is a humble willingness to explain yourself openly and transparently, for the sake of repentance and healing. We all need some form of accountability. This is why the church is called a living body, for the body has different members who supply what the other body parts need (Eph. 4:16), and one way we do this is by laying aside falsehood and speaking truth to one another (v. 15).

We would be crazy to think that any of us can go it alone. We need others who are like-minded, who are struggling with sin and fighting the same good fight shoulder to shoulder with us.

Here is where a good marriage comes in. Marriage can become a place of safety, a place of rebuilding and shoring up defenses. It can become a place of healthy accountability, each partner with the other. A wife who is her husband's friend is his closest partner in arms.

What is a true friend? Proverbs tells us:

A friend loves at all times. (17:17)

There is a friend who sticks closer than a brother. (18:24)

Faithful are the wounds of a friend. (27:6)

Oil and perfume make the heart glad,
So a man's counsel is sweet to his friend.
Do not forsake your own friend. (27:9–10)

Loving at all times. Sticking very close. Kind wounds. Sweet counsel. Never forsaking.

Such friends are a rare treasure.

If you are a single woman, pray for such a friend, and *be* such a friend.

If you are married, be such a friend to your husband. And when it comes to his inner world, never think, *I wonder if my husband struggles with sexual temptation.* You should *assume that he struggles.* Ask him in love, "How do you handle the temptation that hits you every day?" and if he feels safe with you, it is likely he will open up. When he admits to struggling, don't get upset. Appreciate that. The sheer act of admission is a major part of building a strong defense. Steve once told me it was his greatest deterrent. At times when the temptation to keep looking was unusually powerful, he found himself thinking, *I don't want to have to confess this to Mary later.* How much trust is built between a man and woman when that kind of accountability is present!

### Step Six: Using Healthy Sex in Marriage as a Weapon against Satan

What is "healthy sex"?

It is sex in a marriage where two people are expressing freely and sacrificially their love for one another in a setting of transparency and communication.

Okay, I admit it. That's a mouthful. But if you remove any part of that sentence, you have an unhealthy sexual relationship in marriage:

- "Expressing freely" = individuality and choice
- "Expressing sacrificially" = unselfishness
- "Transparency" = openness and accountability
- "Communication" = listening, speaking, and mutual understanding

When these are present, your sexual relationship is healthy. And the more healthy the sex in your marriage, the stronger the defense will be against sexual sin. It is a remarkable phenomenon.

Healthy sex in marriage is a mighty weapon against the enemy. Let me quote once again from John Piper:

If it is the joy of each to make the other happy, a hundred problems will be solved.…

Faith wields the weapon of sexual intercourse against Satan. A married couple gives a severe blow to the head of that ancient serpent when they aim to give as much sexual satisfaction to each other as possible. It makes me just want to praise the Lord when I think that on top of all the joy that the sexual side of marriage brings, it also proves to be a fearsome weapon against our ancient foe.[8]

Well said.

So the better you get at healthy intimacy and sexually pleasing one another, the less Satan can get a word in edgewise. No man who is well content and decidedly happy sexually with his wife is going to be easily tempted by some vacuous slinky babe at work. Believe me, she can't even hold a candle.

## WHEN YOU THINK SOMETHING IS VERY WRONG

Though this is not a book on addiction, it behooves a woman to know the red flags of sexual addiction. While it is true that the step from temptation into sin is a short one, the steps into a sinful lifestyle and addiction are many.

All sin is addictive. If left unchecked, sexual sin can easily carry a person into an addictive cycle. In simple terms, that cycle is (1) *sinning*, followed by (2) *a feeling of simultaneous pleasure and guilt*, (3) *a rationalizing or denying of the sinfulness* of the action, (4) *a feeling of being unsatisfied, empty, "hungry" again* (since the person's real need has not been met), and (5) *a returning again to the same sin* for the temporary relief, escape, or pleasure. The cycle then repeats itself, taking a person deeper and deeper.

When does sin turn into addiction? In a single sentence, it is *when that sin becomes a person's primary way of handling his or her emotional need or pain.* We can become addicted to work or constant activity that brings us strokes. We can become addicted to chocolate or buying things. Anything that numbs our emotional pain can become addictive. We turn to that for our comfort and escape. But it doesn't last. The comfort is brief. The escape is temporary. And the pain that remains only gets worse.

So it is with sexual addiction. In the case of sex, an addiction can be well hidden and very hard to detect. But there are usually some red flags if your spouse is in trouble in this area. I interviewed numerous counselors and wives of sex addicts to gather the following red flags, but each one expressed that there are times when a sex addiction is so well hidden that there are no red flags at all. You have to do the best you can with what is before you, and ask God to bring to light what is hidden in the dark. Consider these questions:

- Do you *sense something isn't right*? Don't ignore those inner warning signals, especially when you become aware of a very real change in your man.
- Is he is *viewing pornography* at home? If so, you can be sure there *is* a problem.
- Has your husband become *more withdrawn and distant*, relationally and spiritually?
- Is he spending *large, unaccounted-for periods of time away* from home or excessive time at the office for which there is no good explanation?
- Is there a *growing sexual dysfunction* in your marriage? Has he become more demanding, or is he exhibiting an unusual increase in appetite? Has he had a complete loss in sexual appetite? Is he sexually "not there" most of the time, or initiating strange things sexually with which you are uncomfortable?
- Is he *sealing you off* from certain aspects of your finances or clearly excluding you from access to certain phone and credit-card records?
- Does he become *defensive when you ask questions* about any of these things?
- Does he *deny even the most obvious problems* in your marriage?
- Does he *refuse to go with you for counseling*?

If the answer to any of these questions is yes, don't go about your life in quiet angst. Be willing to ask your husband the hard questions. If you suspect an affair, ask him. One man who had an affair advised this: "Tell women that they need to *just ask*. Don't wait for the sky to fall. Ask him. He just might answer. And that could be the beginning of something good in his life. Not every man will come clean, but it is definitely the place to start."

If there is only one red flag, the issue may be brought to light and honestly worked through together. But when there are many (and always if pornography is part of the equation), it is most likely a sign of something deeper and more serious. Never decide to just "let these things go." Not even one red flag.

Some men are so good at hiding that their wives never suspect a thing. But more often than not, there are signs. If this is the case for you, refuse to be passive. Address it openly and honestly. Love him enough to pursue the truth. And get all the help you can from mentors who are wise in the counsel of the Lord.

## FIGHTING THE GOOD FIGHT

Part of your calling as the woman in your man's life is to fight the good fight with him. This means building a strong wall of defense together with your man.

Martha Washington was only five feet tall, dark haired, and gentle mannered. But she was a fighter, just like her husband. She had a hard time with the formality of being the president's wife, disliking "formal compliments and empty ceremonies," preferring instead "what comes from the heart." Abigail Adams (who often sat at her right in parties and receptions) called her "one of the most unassuming characters which create Love and Esteem."

During the war, however, Martha actually went to the front lines. In the winter of 1775, she traveled to her husband's camp and stayed by his side for six months. Nine months later, when the army was camped at Morristown, Washington became ill, and she went to his side to nurse him back to health.

And when the army was camped at Valley Forge, she spent that entire infamous winter of deprivation there with the troops, seeking to raise the morale among the officers and enlisted troops. She became so greatly loved by them that they called her "Lady Washington."[9]

Perhaps there is indeed something to the old saying that behind every great man is a very good woman.

# SECTION IV
## FROM READING
## to CONNECTING

*Chapter Thirteen*

# GROUNDED

*For your husband is your Maker, Whose name is the LORD of hosts;*
*And your Redeemer is the Holy One of Israel,*
*Who is called the God of all the earth.*
*—Isaiah 54:5*

We began our book in free fall.

As we draw toward the end, it's fitting to wrap up with our feet firmly on the ground. This chapter is about the necessity of being firmly grounded in order to have great connection with our men.

Great connection is crucial to healthy sexuality.

*When a man and a woman connect deeply, great things happen.* Men find true intimacy, women know deep love, and our children are inwardly delighted. They grow up wanting this same kind of love that we, their parents, have labored to achieve.

This is why we must embrace our feminine gift for connection and our innate drive toward connection. God created us for this. Our men need this. A woman can be the "glue," the "binding tie," the "change factor" that alters a man or boy's world and makes him all the better for it.

Why, then, are we beginning a section on connection by talking about our own hearts? The answer is that if a woman desires to truly connect with her husband in a deep and healthy love, something must first happen in her heart.

She must become *grounded*.

What does it mean to be grounded?

It means that you have found a firm foundation, a deep inner core of security (which does not primarily depend on your husband or children or job or circumstances in life), and that you have developed the ability to "separate" without "severing" yourself from your husband. This is the first step toward strong feminine connection.

*Women who are grounded are able to become outstanding connectors.*

I recently asked this question of a wise and seasoned marriage counselor: "What would you say to a woman who is trying to connect with her husband, especially when communication hits a wall?"

"That's an easy one," he replied. "Men don't want weepy women. They dismiss them. They don't want drama. And they really don't want mothers."

That made sense.

"What *do* they want?" I asked.

"They want space. Not 'distance.' Not a self-willed 'independence.' But a healthy 'space.' Men need *inter*dependence in a relationship—*a healthy separateness and individuality in the context of continual connectedness.* They definitely need a woman who is real and says what she thinks and doesn't let them get away with murder. But they also want a woman who listens, who 'gets' what is really going on with them and doesn't take things too personally."

That was helpful. But his last statement is what hit home.

"Ultimately," he said, "men need a woman who is grounded in something other than her husband and her marriage. They need a thinking, grounded woman who *converses within herself and with God—before she converses with her husband.*"

Well that lays it out there, doesn't it? Interdependent. Separate, yet connected. Thinking and self-possessed. Grounded.

Such a woman is not a clinging, climbing weed. Nor is she a carnivorous Venus flytrap. She is more like a well-rooted tree.

Grounded women are a rare treasure these days. When you find them, you want to soak in all you can from them. Why are they so rare? Because, just like our men, we have lost our way. Our template for womanhood has become so marred that confusion has settled in upon us like a pea-soup fog. We need a template, just like our men.

## Wanted: A Feminine Template

What template did you have growing up? Most of us were taught that a strong woman is independent, accomplished, capable of doing whatever a man can do. It was ingrained in us that we are equals (which we *are*) and that we should therefore pursue a life of independence and self-reliance, unhindered by our man's career or the needs of anyone else. Above all things, we are never to depend upon a man.

At the same time we were fed another relentless message—the message that our identities are connected to having a great body and personality appeal. We were encouraged to obsessively focus on ourselves and our bodies and made to feel that to be accepted and admired and loved in this world, we must succeed on every count—including being physically beautiful and sexually appealing. So we have found ourselves in this schizophrenic state: living on a philosophy of *complete independence from* the male sex, all the while desperately *needing their approval and love*. It's pretty much a killer.

Within the church we have yet another form of confusion. We are all over the map on the idea of biblical womanhood and the role of "submission" (a word I rarely use because of its modern misguided, negative connotations). So, even though male leadership is taught throughout the New Testament, we fear that this idea will squelch our womanly self-expression and hinder our giftedness—even though this was *never* the plan of God. (We will answer this concern, by the way, in the last chapter of this book.)

I am meeting more and more women today who are starving for a mentor, someone to show them what it looks like to be a real woman. They are searching for a healthy template for biblical, "strong femininity."

Let me tell you of one such treasure who lived in the last century. Her name was Joy Davidman.

## An Unlikely Template

"The Lord really is my Shepherd, by gum!" Joy wrote to a friend from England in 1953 at the lowest time in her life. Her alcoholic, philandering husband had divorced her and left her to raise their two adolescent boys. They were living in a tiny two-room apartment in London, subsisting on his unreliable alimony checks and her equally unreliable royalty checks from freelance writing.

But Joy was also an unlikely woman of faith. Once a card-carrying Communist and atheist, this brilliant Jewish writer-poet had come to the end of herself at a crisis point in her marriage. Realizing she was not the "master of her fate" or the "captain of her soul," her heart began to change. "I must say, I was the world's most surprised atheist," she said of that moment of her conversion to belief in God. Immediately she began to consume the Bible, where she met her Redeemer. "When I read the New Testament, I recognized Him. He was Jesus."[1]

Little did Joy know that she was destined to become the wife of C. S. Lewis—Christian thinker and writer, most popularly known today for The Chronicles of Narnia series—with whom she would share three of the most remarkable years of marriage before dying of bone cancer. Lewis tells the story of their unusual marriage in his book *A Grief Observed*. In her last days of illness, it was Joy who kept Lewis going. "I am ashamed ... to tell you that it is Joy who supports me, rather than I her," he wrote.[2]

After the boyhood loss of his mother, the only other woman in Lewis's life had been Janie Moore. Janie was an engaging mother of a dear friend to Lewis who had died in the war, and for whom Lewis had vowed to care in the event of his friend's death. She was a staunch atheist who became very influential in Lewis's early years at Oxford. She showed him compassion and friendship, but her love was a needy, draining kind of love.[3] Oftentimes she enveloped his life completely. When she died, it was as if a weight had been lifted off his shoulders.

Joy, on the other hand, possessed a certain healthy disconnect; she was not ultimately dependent on Lewis for her happiness, which is why she was able to love him so well. Their friendship and eventual marriage is a lesson in healthy connection. Lewis spoke of her as "my trusty comrade, friend, shipmate, fellow-soldier. My mistress, but at the same time all that any man friend has ever been to me."[4]

This is what our men need: a woman who is *grounded in something deeper and greater than herself*, a woman whose lifeline is not primarily sourced in the *people* around her or the certainty of a *particular outcome*.

(By the way, we women also need this in our men, do we not?)

The question is this: How did Joy arrive at such a place? Such women don't fall from outer space. They are born with weakness. And out of their weakness arises an inner strength, a strength that has come from a certain shaping and chiseling and hard-knocks experience. Along the way they have discovered a template, a tutor, a voice of reason to lead them through this chaotic world. Even the most skillful connector among us *needs such a tutor* ("Older women are to … encourage [or tutor] the young women," Titus 2:3–4).

Her memoirs make it clear that Joy got her template from immersing herself in Scripture. If, like Joy, you did not grow up with a good template in your mother or grandmother, don't despair. There are worthy templates throughout the pages of Scripture. There is Abigail—discerning wife of an unbelieving drunkard—who saved David from disastrous vengeance. There is Deborah—godly sage in the dark period of the judges— who used her strong femininity to encourage Barak's weak male leadership. There is Mary—single woman and sister to a very busy Martha—who stepped away from her hectic world to sit rapt at the feet of Jesus. And there is the other Mary, named Magdalene—repentant ex-prostitute—who washed His feet with her tears and was among the first to declare His tomb empty. Strong feminine women of great faith can be found from every background and at every turn of biblical history: Ruth, Esther, Lydia, Priscilla, and so many more. Much can be learned from each of these women.

But there is no greater template in the annals of Scripture than the "unnamed" woman we will study next. Many a woman has been awakened to her strong feminine calling by becoming acquainted with this remarkable individual.

## THE WOMAN WITH NO NAME

This most famous woman in biblical history has no name.

Yet her fame has preceded her for some twenty-five hundred years. She is the "virtuous gentlewoman" (as one theologian calls her), the strong *counterpart* to the "virtuous gentleman" we learned of in an earlier part of this book. She is the womanly version of the godly man so poignantly described in Job 29:12–25 and 31:1 ("I put on righteousness, and it clothed me"; "I was eyes to the blind … a father to the needy"; "I broke the jaws of the wicked and snatched the prey from his teeth"; "I have made a covenant with my eyes").

In modern days we have come to know her as the "Proverbs 31 Woman." We think of her as "ideal," and when you look at her character, she is:

- She is completely on her husband's team ("She does [her husband] good … all the days of her life," 31:12).
- She is disciplined, hardworking, and uses her skills industriously.
- She has well-thought-out priorities. In the midst of her many endeavors, one gets the distinct impression that her husband and family are her primary focus—which is why they rise up and praise her (31:28–29).
- She is a woman of peace (rather than anxiety), joy (rather than negativity), kindness and generosity (always with her hands held out), physical and emotional strength, and seasoned wisdom.
- And she is a woman of beauty—not a fleeting beauty but a lasting kind of beauty, which emanates from the inside out and ages with grace.

It is natural to be awed by such a woman. The clear intent of the writer was to raise a very high bar. Was she a real woman? I would contend that she was indeed. (Many of her "daughters" are alive today.) But one thing is certain: She was not born this way. She was a fallen creature who lived in a fallen world, and she had her fair share of shortcomings and problems.

How did she come to be such a woman? Hidden away in this passage is her secret. This "daughter" (31:29) *feared the Lord*, and ...

A woman who fears the LORD, she shall be praised. (v. 30)

Her fear was not an angst or dread of God. It was a calming kind of fear that actually quelled earthly fear ("She smiles at the future," Prov. 31:25)! It was a heart attitude that stabilized her life, a revolutionary worldview that shaped her thinking and choices. How did she come to possess this sapient, calming fear?

How blessed is the man [or woman] who *fears the LORD*,
Who greatly *delights in His commandments*. (Ps. 112:1)

The fear of the Lord comes from *delighting in the words of the Lord*. Somewhere in the course of her life, the Proverbs 31 Woman had discovered the amazing secret of living—let us say, *thriving*—upon God's words.

To put it another way, before she became the Proverbs 31 Woman, she was first a "Psalm 1 Woman."

What—or who—is a Psalm 1 Woman? She is the treelike woman from whom we will learn our most important lessons in this chapter.

Now this is the great news. While the Proverbs 31 Woman is an intimidating figure, the Psalm 1 Woman is not. She is immediately needy, a woman who requires emotional nourishment and counsel on a regular basis. She is no giant of the faith or some theological wonder; she's just trying to figure out how to make it through life. She is a regular woman who has grabbed hold of a most fundamental idea, and—this is important—has *implemented* it into her life. *Any* woman—regardless of her upbringing, her sins and failures, or her present difficulties— can become a Psalm 1 Woman.

## The Treelike Woman of Psalm 1

Trees inspire. Like rugged oceanic coastlines and snow-crested mountains, great trees calm our souls and call us away from the congested din of humanity. They awe, renew, and inspire us. One ancient poet wrote, "They are beautiful in their peace, they are wise in their silence. They will stand after we are dust. They teach us."[5] Ralph Waldo Emerson wisely noted that "in the woods, we return to reason and faith."

Do you remember the childlike poem penned by Joyce Kilmer?

> I think that I shall never see
> A poem as lovely as a tree.
> A tree whose hungry mouth is pressed
> Against the earth's sweet flowing breast;
> A tree that looks at God all day,
> And lifts her leafy arms to pray ...

Kilmer's tree is a tiny glimpse of the tree we are about to study. Yet I would propose that no greater poem has ever been written about a tree than that of Psalm 1.

The Psalm 1 tree is a strong, deeply rooted tree situated by a bubbling stream. Those who walk beneath her bows are renewed; they are quietly hushed and stilled; they are drawn to think upon the majesty of the One who made her; and they enjoy the fruit of her branches.

But the greatness of this tree is not her outer strength and beauty. Rather it is the underlying secret that keeps her alive. Let us look into this psalm and get at the root of her secret, literally.

### Five Traits of the Psalm 1 Woman

C. H. Spurgeon once said that Psalm 1 was the "text upon which the whole book of Psalms became the sermon."[6] It has been called the Psalm of Psalms, or the Preface Psalm,[7] (its "branches and leaves" therefore becoming the remaining 149 psalms). In many early Hebrew manuscripts this psalm wasn't even numbered. Psalm 2 was numbered Psalm 1, while this opening psalm formed the foundational introduction to the entire book of Psalms.[8]

Permit me to speak in the feminine as we study this psalm, for it is entirely applicable to man, woman, or child. The first verse opens with an immediate description of our treelike woman:

(1) She is *exceedingly* blessed.

This woman is more than happy. She is "blessed."

*Blessed* is the woman. (v. 1)

"Happiness" comes and goes with the wind. "Blessedness" is a deeper, more abiding state. To be "blessed" is to enjoy God's special favor and grace.[9] And this particular Hebrew word is plural; it means "multiple blessednesses"!

(2) She is *set apart* from the world.

She does not walk in the counsel of the wicked, nor stand in the path of sinners, nor sit in the seat of scoffers! (v. 1)

In other words, this woman doesn't get her cues from this world. Rather, she walks to another drumbeat. She listens to a different voice. But what drumbeat? Whose voice? (The text will soon tell us.)

(3) She is an *evergreen, fruit-bearing* tree.

She is like a tree firmly planted by streams of water, which yields its fruit in its season, and its leaf does not wither. (v. 3)

Are there such trees that are both evergreen *and* fruit-bearing? Yet here she stands—evergreen ("its leaf does not wither") and bearing fruit in her season. She is planted (or literally "transplanted") by streams of water. In Israel, such streams came and went with the seasons, being irrigated in summer and filled by rains during the wet times of year. This stream (with its many tributaries) is different. Its source is ongoing and endless. How did she come to be transplanted in this place? At the moment of her spiritual birth, God took her from her desert home and transplanted her here, giving her a new life with fertile soil and an eternal source of water.

(4) She bears fruit *in her season*.

> … which yields its fruit in its season … in whatever she does, she prospers. (v. 3)

So firmly rooted is this treelike woman that whatever life flings at her—whether it be the harsh cold of winter, the floods and howling winds of spring, or the heat and drought of summer—she remains standing, ever fruitful in her season. "In its season" literally means "in its time." So while this woman is sustained through times of joy as well as times of long-endured adversity, at the right moment, *at the time of God's choosing*, she bears much fruit.[10]

Does she feel the harshness and heat? She does. She weeps and grieves and hurts like any woman. She wonders sometimes if God is there. But in the worst of times, when hopes are dashed and life is most unfair, she is sustained and kept alive.

Let this encourage you!

There are times when God's work is an *inner, unseen work,* producing unseen, hidden character and endurance. There are other times when His work is *outward and visible,* bearing bountiful fruit. Mothers, take heart. Your thankless sacrifices are now rarely seen; but the fruit of them will eventually come; you can count on it. Single women, take heart. Your standard of feminine character may feel that all is for naught; but think it not! God will bless and bring forth delicious fruit from such a life. Wives, take heart.

Even when you may be presently facing what seems to be insurmountable distance from your husband, and when you wonder if God is working at all, know this: God is always at work, in surprising and unseen ways. Your plight is fully in His sights, He knows exactly what you are going through, and He hears your pleas.

A miserable, blustery, frigid day in winter *feels* unproductive and interminable. But "the eyes of the LORD move to and fro throughout the earth that He may strongly support those whose heart is completely His" (2 Chron. 16:9). A woman who remains deeply rooted can look forward to seeing fruit—in her season, set by God.

The fruit will arrive. The page will turn.

Now we come to this treelike woman's secret, and the crux of Psalm 1.

(5) Her lifeline is the *eternal spring of God's words.*

Her delight is in the law of the LORD, and in His law she meditates day and night. (v. 2)

Her secret lies in her continual, regular feasting upon the words of the Lord. As her roots reach down into the living water of the "law of the LORD," she drinks and drinks—regularly, often, in every season. It is this "law of the LORD" that is the "other voice," the "other drumbeat," the source from whence she receives her cues and which sets her apart.

What is this "law of the LORD"? It is certainly the law of Moses (those first five books of the Bible called the Pentateuch). But it is also the full revelation of God in Scripture.[11] The "law of the LORD" means "instruction" or "revelation"[12] and is synonymous with the "word of the LORD" (Ps. 119:1, 9–16). Jesus made this clear when He said, "It is written, 'Man shall not live on bread alone, but on *every word that proceeds out of the mouth of God*'" (Matt. 4:4).

In other words, *the law of the Lord is the Word of the Lord.*[13]

The Psalm 1 Woman *delights* in this Word and *meditates* upon it. Feasting on that Word is what keeps her alive.

## Delighting and Meditating

That word *delight* conjures up all kinds of images. The image of a bright-eyed little child, with his laughter and his little arms and legs running all which-away, creates carefree delight. The presence of a true and dear friend with whom you can always laugh and cry and in whose company you are continually encouraged brings refreshing delight.

When you "delight" in something, you enjoy, love, treasure, relish, savor, revel in, *feast* upon it. The picture of a Thanksgiving meal—with turkey and dressing and all the trappings—comes to mind. It takes hours, sometimes days, to cook such a meal and only minutes to eat. But what a glorious few minutes! This woman regularly feasts at the table of the Lord. She may have a million things to do, but she has come to the stark realization that she won't be able to do them well—sometimes she won't be able to do them at all—if she hasn't eaten. It is God's words that keep her alive.

As Psalm 119 teaches (a psalm of some 176 verses, which I refer to as "The Psalm on God's Word"), the words of God give counsel (v. 24), strength (v. 28), answers to questions (v. 42), hope (v. 49), comfort (v. 50), perspective in affliction (v. 71), protection (vv. 86–87), instruction and wisdom (vv. 98–100), a hiding place and shield (v. 114), mercy and life (v. 156), and peace (v. 165) … only to mention a few. One quick reading of this psalm reveals at least fifty things God's Word does for us.

Looking back on that list, we realize that God's words are the means by which He imparts *Himself* to us. This is profound. Do you wish to be close to God? Draw close to His Word.

## Meditation versus Bulimia

The Psalm 1 Woman not only eats but she also *digests* (or "meditates" upon) God's words. We will look at the how-to momentarily, but for now, consider this: She is neither spiritually anorexic nor bulimic. Rather than eating and regurgitating (forgive my frankness), as is most often what tends to happen when we read Scripture, this woman *digests* what she eats. She not only reads but she also *thinks* on what she is reading, *considers* what it means to her, *ponders* (and often writes down) the questions it raises, and *prays* over it all. In short, she interacts *within herself* and *with God* as she eats from His Word. In that quiet time of nourishment, her perspective is altered, her heart is changed, and her path becomes one of life.

Is this time always rich or earthshaking? Surely not. Sometimes she goes through passages that appear to have no real relevance to her at all. Not every meal we eat is Thanksgiving. But we still need to eat. For instance, what could it possibly matter if God told the prophet Jeremiah to go buy a clay jar, shatter it publicly before the elders, and then bury its broken pieces in a field (as I happened to read a few days ago in Jeremiah 19)? I mean, really? But then, if you keep reading, you start to understand. The meaning does usually begins to come clear in such readings. There are hard passages in every book of Scripture, but there are also equally profound, life-giving, *wonderful* passages buried in those same books!

Sometimes we enter dry seasons; but we go on eating, knowing that this is what it is, a season. The corner will turn and richness will return. I know many Psalm 1 Women who journal their thoughts and questions and prayers. Months later they are able to look back over that journal and realize just how many prayers and personal struggles have been answered and resolved. It is abundantly encouraging.

I remember as a single woman writing down a list of specifics that I realized I needed in a man. I began praying for that man. Many years later God brought him to me. After I was married, I came across that list (prayed over time and again), and I was struck at how God had so fully and specifically answered. Never have I been so aware of the existence of the Almighty One than at that moment.

There have also been those prayers that have remained unanswered. But a Psalm 1 Woman has learned to think "big picture." She has discovered that God's ways and times are not ours, that He is doing a unique work in our lives, and that He delights in our persistent petitions (Matt. 7:7–11).

In the end, a Psalm 1 Woman develops an "umbilical cord" that is dependent first and foremost on God. Just as a strong tree depends upon a well-established root system, she finds herself developing *a strong inner core* rooted in greater and greater dependence *on God*. She discovers that feminine strength is not about independence from a man nor is it about dependence on a man's approval. Real feminine strength is all about dependence on God and finding your ultimate provision and self-worth and stability and hope in *Him*.

The Psalm 1 Woman also finds herself less vulnerable to deception. As I write, the counterfeit of the moment is Eckhart Tolle's *A New Earth*. It is being read round the world and lauded as a pinnacle of spiritual wisdom (largely because of its promotion by a famous modern-day talk-show host). What kind of shelf life will it have? Not much, because tomorrow the hubbub will be transferred to a new fleeting deception. But the Psalm 1 Woman sees past these emotionally touching yet *partial* truths (which are Satan's trademark tactics of deception). As in the case of Tolle, she immediately recognizes the cunning perversion of the Bible and corrupt conclusions (such as the fact that we are "God")[14] because she is acquainted with the truth firsthand.

### *Life Beside the Stream*

Once the Psalm 1 Woman eats and digests, she rises to go about life. As her life unfolds, God's words are percolating; they are on the back burner. She is busy, totally focused on the task at hand. Yet God's words are still there, stored up in her heart. Then a problem arises or an event or a conversation.

Let's just say, "Life happens."

And that's when all this regular nourishment and prayer begins to pay off; the truth rises to the surface at the moment of need. God's presence is prescient. He calms. He brings perspective and wisdom. He instructs and encourages. He enables this treelike woman to stand and keep her wits about her.

When she becomes overly obsessed with her body, she remembers that she was wonderfully woven in her mother's womb (Ps. 139), that she is *His workmanship* created in Christ for good works (Eph. 2). Who is she to question His wisdom? When she feels alone, she takes comfort in the fact that she is never ever all alone, for "Lo, I am with you always" (Matt. 28). When she feels excessive pressure to perform, that pressure loses its grip, because "man looks at the outward appearance, but the LORD looks at the heart" (1 Sam. 16). When she is struggling with sin, she realizes that even Paul struggled (Rom. 7), and that in every struggle, God is at work within us (Eph. 2) to do His good will. When life crushes her, she is reminded that even in these moments God is at work for our good and for His glory (Rom. 8), and *nothing* will separate her from His love. Nothing.

In the quiet of those times of feeding on Him—amid the loud clamor and confusion of her world—she discovers that "He is there and He is not silent." He speaks to her. And she becomes grounded. Then as life twists and turns, she finds she has a rock upon which to stand, a shelter in the worst of storms, a word of counsel in the most confusing of times.

At this point, you may be saying, "But how? And *when*?" If faith and Scripture are new to you, you may be thinking, *I honestly don't know how to do this one-on-one thing with God!* Join the club of most women. In this crazy busy world in which the Bible is no longer integrated into the seams of our lives, we have to fight for that time. And we definitely need a plan.

## A MODERN-DAY TEMPLATE

Do you know someone who is a Psalm 1 Woman? If so, get some time with her and find out how she does it.

There have been many women in my life who have been exceptional templates for me. I'd like to introduce you to one with whom I have been close for several years. I decided to interview her by way of teaching the means to becoming a Psalm 1 Woman, for this woman grew from a tiny seedling in her own self-made desert to a giant Psalm 1 tree. Hers is an example any woman could follow. But to best learn from her, you need to know a little of her personal story.

Cheryl Scruggs was once what we might call a "walk-away woman." She and her husband, Jeff, write of their amazing journey in their book *I Do*

*Again*—a must-read that you won't want to put down.[15] But for the sake of brevity, I will give you the condensed version of her story here.

We will begin with the divorce.

Seventeen years ago, Cheryl divorced her husband and ended the stable home life of their four-year-old twin girls after becoming involved in an affair with another man. On the very day the gavel dropped and the longed-for divorce was final, she knew she had made a serious mistake. But the deed had been done; there was no turning back. Soon after, she not only ended the affair, but also came to the end of herself.

One Sunday, she attended a church and in what she now calls a "Damascus road" experience, she felt the strong tugging of God to give her life to Him. Immediately she began to read the Bible and spend time with God. And the more she read, the more the pieces of her life began to add up.

What started as a nagging little thought in the back of her soul grew to a humbling but unshakable conviction: The fundamental problem in her marriage had not been Jeff. It had been the lack of Christ's truth and presence in their lives. She began to see the great deception under which she had been living and the immeasurable value of what she had thrown away.

Although Jeff had received Christ as a child, he had left the faith for many years. Simultaneously (and unbeknownst to her), Jeff came back to Christ and began meeting with a group of guys and studying Scripture. The entire group started praying that God would meet Jeff's needs in a wife who would love him and be faithful to him. Meanwhile, God began to convict Cheryl of His desire for them to reconcile. Her conviction became so strong that she finally expressed her heart to Jeff. But his response couldn't have been more discouraging or final. He was understandably hurt and angry, and he was simply unable to forgive. She had betrayed him and he would never be able to trust her again. In his mind, that door was closed forever. At that time, the girls, now being shuffled between them, were playing "parent trap" every time they turned around.

For the next seven years this walk-away woman turned and walked toward God. On the surface those years appeared to be leading nowhere. But they were not. Underneath the surface they were the most productive years in her life. Cheryl was becoming a Psalm 1 Woman.

Oftentimes the *end* of a thing can be the *beginning* of something else.

In Cheryl's case, this was the beginning of growing from a tiny transplanted sprig into a firmly rooted tree. She tapped her roots into the living Stream and waited.

I asked her to describe her mind-set during that time. This is her answer:

It became clear to me that the only real happiness in life is *the happiness that emerges from a life grounded upon God.*

I realized my life, my children, my future—whether it be reconciliation with Jeff or not—everything was all in God's hands. If He willed it, Jeff would come around. If not—and that was a real possibility—God would provide for me and give me a work to do.

In Jeff's mind, reconciliation would never happen. So humanly speaking, it was a hopeless situation. God would have to change his heart on that score. It was out of my hands. Though it took some time to come to this conclusion, I quietly decided that if Jeff and I never reconciled, I would simply not remarry. This was what God wanted for me.

I'm not saying this is what every woman should do. It was just that I realized this was what God wanted *me* to do.

In those years of going one-on-one with God, He pursued me, changed me, matured me, molded me, and was my sole Lover.

I will tell you the end of her story; but first, let's glean from her experience. Cheryl was green to Christianity and the Bible. It was all new to her.

"If you were to tell a woman where to begin, what would you say?" I asked.

"Well," she said, "I'll tell you how it looked for me. My *procedure* is not so much the thing, but rather the *principles*. You are you, and I am me. I think the principles of the 'how' can still work very well, no matter who you are or where you are in life."

Cheryl went on to describe a few essentials she discovered in her journey with God. Let me give them to you as she expressed them in my interview with her.

## The Basics, in Cheryl's Words

Q: *When* were you able to find time to spend with God?

A: I had to come up with a *regular time and place* that worked at this stage of life. I'm a morning person. And I didn't have little children. So I decided to get up every day at 5:00 a.m. to be alone with God. It was a daily discipline that I soon found I could not get along without. As for the place, I have a favorite chair in the corner of a sunny room in my home that I love to sit in.

Q: Well, personally, I could never pull off the 5:00 a.m. thing! But it seems like you discovered that no matter what time a person chooses, it takes a certain discipline. Is that right?

A: Right! Initially it's tough, because it isn't a habit. But soon it becomes the best part of the day!

Q: So, what did you have with you? What were your *essential tools*?

A: Well, coffee was number one! Then I had a journal, a favorite pen, and the Bible. Those were my basic tools. *The key for me was starting with the right Bible.* I started with the *Life Application NIV* Bible, and when I needed help in understanding a passage, I would read from *The Message*. Since then I have been reading from the new *English Standard Version Study Bible,* not only because of its accuracy and readability, but its great study notes and maps. I needed something readable and clear at the start, with notes that helped me in tough places. At times I would also use other substantive resources to stimulate my thinking, like the excellent study *Experiencing God* by Henry Blackaby, or the classic book *Knowing God* by J. I. Packer, or even a good sermon series, like Tommy Nelson's Song of Solomon series.[16]

Q: What did you do to *connect* with God?

A: I discovered certain patterns that helped me to connect with God. I found it helped to begin by greeting God. It is always easier when I write down my prayers. So I would write down the specific things I was concerned about: thoughts I'd been thinking, decisions to be made, things Jeff or my kids were going through, things I was thankful for, and things I was worried about.

So I would start out basically talking to Him about these things. Then I would read Scripture and ask God to speak to me. I would take a particular book (like Deuteronomy or Ruth in the Old Testament or one of the gospels or Ephesians in the New Testament) and once I learned something about the book in the opening notations of my Bible, I would read a section. Sometimes it would be a few paragraphs. Sometimes a chapter. The main thing was to get the flow, the main idea the author was getting at. Context was everything. I began to realize that many verses I had seen on plaques and coffee mugs had been completely taken out of context. I realized occasionally that some teaching I had been taught was off base, out of context. I mean, if I were writing to someone, I would want them to read the whole letter so as not to misunderstand a particular sentence out of context. I began to see that God wants us to give Him the same courtesy.

Q: Is there anything else important that you learned along the way?

A: Yes, there's one more thing. I discovered that this time with God needed to be something *habitual* and *nonnegotiable*. Which meant that I needed to hang in there even when I didn't really feel like it. One reason was because I found that *when I departed from it, I drifted* and lost my perspective in the whole of life.

As a result, I have to say that this time every day became like my umbilical cord, my lifeline. It became unquestionably the most valuable thing I did in those seven years alone. *And it still is to this day.*

### Cheryl's Unexpected Fruit-bearing Season

Eventually the day came when Jeff realized the woman God had been preparing for him all along was Cheryl. But before he could pop the question, he asked, "How can I know you won't ever do the same thing again?"

Cheryl gave a great answer: "Well, Jeff, the truth is that this isn't about you. It's about God. I never want to disappoint God again." So they were remarried, with one daughter on each side of them beaming ear to ear.

The last nine years have been years of learning how to do what they had never done in their first marriage—deeply connect and love one another well. They have learned that in *any* marriage, both partners carry a level of responsibility for the problems they encounter. It's tough for the "victim" to realize that in his own way, he has also been a "perpetrator." Each one of us has something to learn.

Today they counsel couples in trouble, couples who have lost all hope and are ready to throw in the towel. Their message is this: When two people bow to the Lord, there is always, *always* hope.

## THE INGENIOUS REBEL TREE

It takes a *rebel* to become such a tree, to stand against the culture and *refuse to let it dictate your life*. It takes true grit to *feed your own soul*.

But women have always been great rebels, have we not?

How rare is such a woman today who stands against the norm, who says "No!" to the life-eating, mind-numbing, thought-killing rat race that swirls around her. Is she busy? Yes! Her children may be going a hundred directions, she may have a job that asks her lifeblood, she may be barely keeping her head above water at home, she may have e-mails and text messages and friends and meetings and—well, you get the idea.

She wakes up every morning with more to do than she could possibly do. But she will not—*absolutely not*—give way. This woman has made a firm decision to feed on the Lord's words at some point in her day. And though there will always be days when she cannot make it happen, that's okay. She refuses to give up *looking for ways to feed*, for she has learned that her feeding is not a duty or "rabbit's foot." It is literally her lifeline. It is a habit, built into her life by her own choice and self-discipline—no matter what season of her life she is in.

Such a commitment also takes creativity.

But, I ask you, who is more resourceful and creative than a woman?

I am *not* a morning person. Sorry, but 5:00 a.m. would be worthless for me! When my babies were born (two of them preemies), I could barely hold my eyes open *any* time of the day. When they grew a little older, just when things were settled and quiet, a child would cry or get upset or injured … or something! Moms with little ones have to relax when things fall apart and take what they can get. Don't lash yourself and live under a pile of guilt. Rather, enjoy the time you do have to quietly feed upon the Lord. Use a "Mother's Day Out" with no guilt, listen to a CD while your child is nursing, and by all means, make use of a small study group with friends as a means of feeding. I have done all of these things over the years. Each season of life has brought its own set of challenges and adjustments.

So find out what works for you. If a daily thing is overwhelming to you, then start with three days, or even one. Just start somewhere, and know that God is delighted in that step. Above all, use your gift of creativity. Ask God to *make* a way.

I know of one woman with five children who takes an extra thirty minutes when she goes for groceries; she literally sits in the parking lot alone in her car, reading, praying, journaling—*before* she shops (so that the ice cream doesn't melt). While she is feeding her soul, her husband, who is watching the children, thinks she is taking excessive care to thriftily shop for her family of seven! Susanna Wesley, mother of John and Charles, was known to sit in her rocker and put her apron over her head; her ten children all knew that this was her signal that it was *her* time to be left to quiet meditation and prayer, and they honored it.[17]

*But what if you are in such a dark time that you have no words to speak, no desire to even open your Bible?*

God understands what is going on in your heart better than you do. He is your Father, not your dictator. Let Him wrap His unseen arms around you and weep quietly there with you. "Draw near to God and He will draw near to you" (James 4:8). It matters not to God what state your heart is in. Just be you, and pour out your heart. The most important thing is to resist the urge to withdraw from Him, or to cease drinking the "living water" or eating the "living bread," even in the darkest hours. Especially in those hours.

God wants to be your Husband, your Sustainer, your first and greatest Hope.

When this happens, your husband will be drawn to you. There is something very appealing and inviting about a woman who is rooted and grounded.

# Chapter Fourteen

## DRAWING OUT YOUR MAN

*A plan in the heart of a man is like deep water,*
*But a man [or woman] of understanding draws it out.*
*—Proverbs 20:5*

Charles Spurgeon once observed, "I had rather put my foot upon a bridge as narrow as Hungerford, which went all the way across, then on a bridge that was as wide as the world, if it did not go all the way across the stream."

I can picture that narrow little arched bridge in the countryside of England, its ancient stones etched in moss. Nothing spectacular, perhaps, yet for centuries sturdy and sure, providing a path from one riverbank to the other.

It is ours to seek to build a Hungerford bridge.

Our men are quietly desperate for this.

Yes, they must join us of their own accord; but we can entice them—draw them in—to the close intimacy that awaits them there. The key is in becoming as skillful as any great angler in drawing out our men from their hiding places in the reef.

Consider the angler for a moment. He doesn't merely toss out a line. He studies his fish—its natural proclivities, its hideouts, its peculiarities, and its appetites. He carefully designs his rod and bait. And he works patiently, with great perseverance. Like that of a farmer, his is also a craft of faith. Spurgeon says,

It looks easy, I dare say, to be a fisherman, but you would find that it was no child's play if you were to take a real part in it. He does not sit in an armchair and catch fish. He has to go out in rough weathers. If he who regardeth the clouds will not sow, I am sure that he that regardeth the clouds will never fish.... A fisherman is a dependent person, he must look up for success every time he puts the net down ... [for] he cannot see the fish.... "Follow me and I will make you fishers of men." Keep close to Jesus, and do as Jesus did, in His spirit, and He will make you fishers of men.[1]

Salvation (of which Spurgeon speaks) can take many forms; drawing our men into the net of healthy connection is certainly one of them.

Based on all we've learned so far, how would one define healthy connection? Try this definition on for size:

*Healthy connection occurs between* **two healthy individuals** *who* **first depend on God** *as their primary rock and source of identity, and* **then reach out to their spouse** *in order to love and connect with them* **on every level— including sex.**

That is the kind of connection that doesn't happen overnight.

Healthy connection is like the creation of a masterpiece. Though the bulk of the Sistine Chapel was painted in four years (a feat of marvel in itself), it took thirty-three years to finish the project—and this from a great master. I have yet to meet a couple with a great marriage who came by it in a month or a year. As my husband often says to men, "How long have you been married? Twenty years? You're just getting started. Thirty years? Don't give up now, because your marriage is yet in its youth!"

### A Lifelong Proposition

When Steve and I first met, we talked for three weeks straight (give or take a few hours of sleep here and there). It ruined my grade-point average, but who cares about a silly number when you have just made the connection of your life?

And we've been talking ever since.

Steve will stay up all night with me if need be to work out a thorny problem, and I'm ashamed to admit that he is usually the first to acknowledge his fault in the thing. Women often tell me I am a blessed woman, and they are right.

Yet I wouldn't have you think that all has been oneness and bliss. Not only has life taken us through deserts and valleys, but we have also taken ourselves there as well. The marriage of two strong-willed, textbook first-borns is a recipe either for impasse or gut-wrenching growth. And we have had our share of both.

There was one particularly very important and difficult period in which Steve honestly didn't think he could get through to me. I was blind, and he felt so hopeless that he actually fasted and prayed. There was another very dark valley in which I felt so lonely and misunderstood by Steve that I wondered if the treasured closeness we had once shared could ever be restored again. In each case, our eyes were eventually opened and deep connection was restored. But it wasn't without a great deal of angst and prayer on the part of one—and a huge piece of humble pie on the part of the other.

Sometimes the distances were wretchedly untimely. I remember a plane flight on the way to speak together at a marriage conference in which we were completely silent. The people who heard us speak the next day had no idea that we had been up most of the night working through a stupid argument that had begun on the ride to the airport. Then there was a plane ride home after a vacation to New York City in which the two of us didn't speak a word to each other. The flight was a smooth one, but our marriage was full of in-flight turbulence. Some vacation.

Usually, however, the issue in our marriage hasn't been silence. Ours has tended to be that of *unhealthy* verbal communication. A hole in the wall of a bedroom when our kids were toddlers comes to mind. Steve put it there in the heat of a verbal fight. I'm sure it has long since been repaired, as was the anger that caused it to be put there. A plastic glass full of iced tea, tossed high into a tree outside another house when our children were older, also comes to mind. I threw it there in a moment of complete and utter frustration. I'm sure it has since been dislodged with time and the change of seasons … as was the frustration that put it there.

The last thirty-one years have seen the gradual resolving and melting away of a huge load of baggage we carried into our marriage, not the least of which was our own immaturity. "I do" has had to become "I still do" every day since the wedding.

Living with Steve has been a learning experience. A training experience. I love him more deeply today than the day I married him. And I feel more loved and valued by him. I am ever challenged each time I look into the mirror of his character. And I know where I will find him every morning—poring over Scripture and praying for me and our children. But our strong connection has been sorely tested and fraught with perils: dashed dreams, unexpected trials, prolonged illness, financial and parenting crises, to name a few.

I have found that just when you think you have arrived, life turns a new corner and there you are, learning all over again. But what richness, what treasures, what strength and surety of foot come to the one who continually crosses that bridge for the tenth and hundredth times.

How do we draw our men out from the Great Barrier Reef? We do it by …

- providing a safe place;
- listening with the "third ear";
- asking timely, important questions; and
- communicating our hearts.

With the book of Proverbs as our biblical tutor (for every passage in the following discussion will be from that book), think of this chapter as a quick crash course in the art of healthy connection.

## PROVIDE A SAFE PLACE

Men need a safe place in order to overcome their reluctance to be transparent. What makes a man feel safe?

## Verbal Encouragement

The mouth of the righteous is a fountain of life. (Prov. 10:11)

Our words set an atmosphere of either danger or safety.

Encouraging words are like a gift of flowers. They bring color, beauty, and fragrance into an otherwise drab world. They also last about as long. Men thrive on a woman's genuine words of gratitude and affirmation. But they need to hear them often. Your encouraging words are air and food and healing to your men.

Pleasant words are a honeycomb, sweet to the soul and healing to the bones. (16:24)

A man (and a boy) who lives with a verbally uplifting woman is drawn to her. And he is more readily drawn out. Our verbal encouragement is a safety net to our men. Mike Mason says it beautifully: "The tongue is a pen, which pressing deeply enough (and whether for good or for evil) will write upon the heart."[2]

This doesn't mean morphing yourself into Pollyanna. We are to be truthful, and sometimes truth hurts. But truth also needs a setting; if there is no encouragement, no spirit of understanding and appreciation, a man cannot readily hear painful truth.

Do your words create an environment of safety?

## Rejuvenation at the End of a Workday

Anxiety in a man's heart weighs it down, but a good word makes it glad. (12:25)

A man who is recharged (even just a little bit) is a man with energy to talk more deeply and connect emotionally. Think of the end of the workday as the *beginning* (or "morning") of your marital day—only both of you are exhausted. At the end of a long drive home in traffic and a God-only-knows-what kind of day, men are usually *h*ungry, *a*ngry, *l*onely, and *t*ired (counselors refer to this as HALT).

On the other hand, a woman who has been caring for children all day long is *t*ired, *a*ntsy, *l*onely, and slightly *k*ooky—which adds up to TALK. (Sorry, but it was the best I could come up with on short notice.) And women who work in a dog-eat-dog world tend to replenish through loving connection. The problem is an obvious one. What to do? The first thing to do is to acknowledge reality.

The truth is that most men (and boys) decompress at the end of the day by *not* talking or emoting. (There are those men who verbally unwind, but they like to do so freely, *without* an agenda.) In short, our men require space to switch gears from one world to another. So while you and I need to switch gears for sexual intimacy, our men need to switch gears for emotional intimacy. They need to unload, before we load them down anew. They need the good news before the bad:

Bright eyes gladden the heart; good news puts fat on the bones. (15:30)

"Don't expect us to let down in the same way you do, or to identify what we are feeling so quickly. And let us breathe a little before you ask us to go deep," say our men. It is counterproductive to dump on a man the minute he walks in the door—unless of course it's an emergency. A woman who does this regularly becomes an *extension* of her man's day rather than the person with whom he can decompress. In fact, Proverbs refers to such a woman as "vexing" (21:19) and "a constant dripping" (27:15).

However—and this is an important "however"—there should be a time in your day when serious talking *can* take place—even if it means excommunicating the children for thirty minutes (as Steve and I would often do when the kids were young). They may protest, but secretly they will love you for it. It makes them feel very secure.

But what if a man is seemingly never recharged? What if he brings his work home or is consumed by diversion? That's a different story. He has now moved from rejuvenation to avoidance—the same kind of blissful (and unhealthy) attitude my guys tend to take toward dental and doctor's appointments. If this is your situation, the time must come (*sooner* rather than later) when you do discuss important issues and communicate from your heart.

But ... the man whose wife wisely *considers his state of mind* substantially raises the chances that he will actually hear and engage her concerns.

### *Laughter and Play*

There are three things which are too wonderful for me ... [one is] the way of a man with a maid. (30:18–19)

Laughter and play are actually serious business in the art of connection.

A man needs to *enjoy* his wife. Most women have no idea how essential this is to a man's feelings of safety with her.

Think back. Did you laugh and have fun together when you were dating? These were not "trivial pursuits." Do you still laugh and enjoy each other's company?

*Rejoice* in the wife of your youth. (5:18)

The term *rejoice* in this proverb was carefully chosen. Why? Because the weight and urgency of life can rob us of these two wildly significant contributors to great connection: laughter and play.

Consider laughter. It reduces stress, lowers blood pressure, boosts the immune system, stimulates both sides of the brain (enhancing learning), and—take note—it *changes the mood*, fosters *relaxation*, and *draws us together*. "When we experience humor, we *talk more, make more eye contact* with others, *touch others*, etc."[3] What could be more conducive to connection?

Laughter brings about a certain feeling of safety and warmth. And everybody knows it's contagious.

A joyful heart makes a cheerful face. (15:13)

A home without laughter is a miserable place. How interesting that the first neuron pathways to come "online" in a newborn baby are those that enable him to smile in the first few weeks, and then laugh out loud within a few months.[4]

Babies begin their little lives laughing. But all too often they lose that natural joy on the path to growing up. By the time we become adults, its loss creates a desperate search for relief. No wonder so many adults seek out late-night TV or *Seinfeld* reruns just to meet that long-lost human need to laugh out loud. Have you ever wondered why so much adult laughter tends to revolve around sick sex jokes? My sense is that this is because sex and laughter are emotionally closely related; we have simply perverted that connection. But pure, clean laughter in a home and marriage is the greatest therapy on the planet.

I have a friend who has a gift for knowing how to make her high-strung husband laugh. And her children have caught her spirit. Recently, after an unfortunate misunderstanding with his parents, he received a bitter letter from them disinheriting him from the will. The children were present when the letter came and were as somber as he was.

After expressing her genuine sadness and compassion over the situation, she finally said, "Well, I don't know how we are going to live without that extra million dollars." (Since the inheritance was a tiny fraction of that amount, her husband was already cracking a smile.) Then her youngest child piped up and said, "I guess we'll just have to shop at Wal-Mart the rest of our lives." Everybody fell over laughing, completely diffusing the situation and putting it into perspective. Laughter has a way of putting life into perspective.

Now consider play. Play breaks down walls and causes a man to feel comfortable and safe with his wife. But not the kind of play that is all aggression and seriousness. We live in a culture that has forgotten how to really play; true play feels devoid of accomplishment, and therefore a waste in our driven generation. But nothing could be further from the truth.

Joseph Keller once said, "When I grow up, I want to be a little boy." Most men feel this way at times. True play taps into the freedom and joy of childhood. It's much like a beach: It takes you Somewhere Else—away from home, office, and routine. It diffuses stress, catches us up in the moment, refreshes and recharges us, restores optimism, stimulates creativity, and unleashes our inhibitions.

Interestingly, children who have been able to play freely (in the old-fashioned playground kind of play) have been shown to excel in first grade beyond those who haven't; and they are also less depressed. Adults who play tend to live longer and find greater happiness in marriage.[5] Why? Because *the person with whom we spend our most relaxed and enjoyable moments is the person we tend to feel closest to*. If that person is not our mate, we drift apart and are surprisingly vulnerable to involvement with someone else.[6]

Our postindustrial men *need* to play, to unwind and recreate with us. According to Dr. Willard Harley, play is a man's second-greatest need in marriage.[7] (You can guess what the first is, which we have already learned is a form of play for men.) Believe it or not, even though men enjoy being with other men (and they do need complete freedom to bond and do "men things" with other men!), recent research actually shows that most men prefer to have fun with their wives even more than with the guys. (I know. I couldn't believe that one either.)

> Most married men don't want to abandon their wife to do guy things. They want to do "guy things" with their wife. They want her to be their playmate.[8]

Harley confirms this: "Men place surpassing importance on having their wives as recreational companions."[9] This makes sense when you consider a man and woman when they are dating and in love. Dating, however, is not just for *finding* a mate; it is also for *keeping* him (or her!). Couples who continue to "date" and just flat enjoy each other's company tend to be best friends. One of the greatest disappointments to a man is to discover after marriage that his wife only did certain activities while they were dating to please him, and now that they are married, she is no longer interested.

What does your man want you to do with him? Do it. You are entering into his inner "joy" and drawing him close. And coax him to try doing things you love to do that he might not ordinarily do. Can you picture my macho Steve shopping in cute little shopping areas? He *never* did that before we were married. But he actually enjoys it now. He likes to take an afternoon of a vacation (his idea!) and saunter through quaint shops. Of course we always hit the new and old bookstores, which is like being in heaven for him.

Play need not cost money. For a man, play can involve simply going for a run (or a slow walk in the country), dancing to music in the kitchen while you do dishes, drinking a cup of hot tea and watching an old movie together, following an NFL, NBA, or NHL team together—nothing relationally intense; nothing of "great import." While women tend to think of planned affairs as romantic, these simple things often tend to be the most romantic to our guys.

Do you and your husband laugh and play together? If so, the chance of his opening up to you increases a hundredfold.

## LISTEN WITH THE "THIRD EAR"

The hearing ear and the seeing eye, the LORD has made both of them. (20:12)

Listening with the third ear is a very simple concept. It looks *beyond* and *beneath* a man's words to "hear" what lies underneath those words.

How do we listen with the third ear?

### Restrain Your Own Emotions ... Initially

When there are many words, transgression is unavoidable, but he who restrains his lips is wise. (10:19)

A good angler uses great restraint. So does a wise woman.

Anybody can get a boatload of fish by just dropping a grenade into the water. But then the fish would be decimated, and what would be the good in that?

A babbling fool will be ruined. (10:8, 10)

How easy it is for a verbal woman to become a babbling fool—to interrupt, to speak far too quickly and extensively in the midst of an argument.

Yet here is the strange phenomenon. The less emotionally we initially react in a tense situation and the more we withhold our onslaught of words, the more open our men can become with us and the better we can actually get to the heart of things. To a man, unloading emotionally feels like a loss of rational control. If he already senses that you are emotional, he will be less likely to share his emotions. (You do the same with your little children, do you not? The more emotional they become, the wise parent steps back from the emotional "meltdown" and operates out of a rational calm. Otherwise things get out of control and you have the grenade effect with your kids, right?)

By restraint I don't mean the "stuffing" of your emotions, but rather choosing how and when you will express them.

The heart of the righteous ponders how to answer. (15:28)

When your husband explodes on you, you have to make a conscious, determined effort not to take it personally. When men interact with men (and boys with boys), they rarely takes things so personally, and they wish that we wouldn't.

I know what you're thinking … easier said than done! Believe me, I fully understand what a huge challenge it can be to keep yourself from simply reacting to sharp words. Frankly, I consider this to be the second most difficult task in building the communication bridge. (We will discuss the most difficult in the next chapter.) Words violate and hurt. Anger penetrates and upsets. But those words and that anger are actually rendered powerless *when they don't produce the desired effect upon us.*

The same goes for a man who goes silent on you. Again, difficult as it may be, try not to take it too personally. We all recognize that noncommunication is degrading and intentionally dismissive. And some men can carry on this ploy for astonishing periods of time. Recognizing the ploy (feel free to calmly say that you recognize what he is doing!), refusing to let it frantically upset you, and carrying on in a state of genuine peace and joy (for until he lets you in on what is bothering him, why on earth should you be miserable too?) has a way of completely foiling such an approach.

At a certain point you might simply ask, "How long do you plan not to speak? I'd only like to know so that I can be sure to be here when you're ready to talk." They may not show it, but men respect a woman who is dispassionately unaffected by their passive-aggressive efforts to control.

We women have to work at stepping back from an emotionally charged situation. And we have to wisely refuse to be silently dismissed. It takes a certain dispassion and ability not to care *too* much (for there is such a thing as caring too much) to disarm such a tense moment.

Staying dispassionately in the moment requires enormous discipline, while acting in kind (returning insult for insult, for example) takes no discipline at all. A man respects this kind of discipline.

He who is slow to anger is better than the mighty. (16:32)

Does this mean you allow abusive language, anger, and disrespect as a matter of course in your interactions? Clearly not. That would be a disastrous, unbiblical alternative. You must insist on certain ground rules, the first being a tone of respect by *both* parties in the midst of an argument. Let your man know that this is your ground rule. It is a ground rule based upon God's commands for healthy communication ("Speak the truth in love"; "Let no unwholesome word proceed from your mouth.... Let all bitterness and wrath and anger and clamor and slander be put away from you, along with all malice. Be kind to one another," Eph. 4:15, 29, 31–32). If this is being violated, the discussion will need to end for the moment—postponed, so to speak, until respect is restored. It's okay to suspend a heated conversation—not indefinitely, but until cooler heads prevail.

> Do not associate with a man given to anger; or go with a hot-tempered man, or you will learn his ways and find a snare for yourself. (Prov. 22:24–25)

In other words, *don't let a man pull you into his emotional "soup"* and thereby find yourself drowning with him. If you get pulled in, with anger flying and verbal shots being fired from every bow, you will never be able to get to the bottom of things, much less help him to grow, or grow yourself. Take this from one who has far too quickly fallen into the soup enough times to know.

Ships, though they be great and driven by strong winds, are directed by a tiny rudder, says James. Likewise the tongue, though a small part of the body, can set a forest aflame (James 3:2–5).

Lassoing the tongue takes practice, but ... a woman's wise emotional restraint makes possible *healthy and appropriate emotional release* in her men.

### Look at the Emotion Beneath the Emotion

> The wise in heart will be called understanding. (Prov. 16:21)

In other words, don't assume that what you see on the surface is the whole story. Most often, it's not even remotely close.

Anger can be the one negative emotion that enables a man to keep a semblance of strength and control (other negative emotions carry a stigma of weakness). But anger is often a *secondary* emotion.

> Anger is almost an *automatic response to any kind of pain*.... [It is] usually the first emotion that we see. For men it's *often* the only emotion that we are aware of.... Just below the surface there are almost always other deeper emotions that need to be identified.[10]

Beneath anger can lie at least eight other "negative" emotions—fear, anxiety, stress, frustration, insecurity, shame, hurt, and grief—all of which come out in the form of anger in men. In other words, anger (whether quietly seething or foaming at the mouth) is usually *displaced* anger (or "dyslexic" anger, as one of our children used to call it), or it is *a sign of something deeper*. You can count on the fact that in most cases, your husband's excessive or unwarranted anger began somewhere earlier in the day or it has risen from a deeper issue that has nothing to do with you. (By the way, isn't this true of women as well?)

So what does this mean? It means you will have to *excavate* to find out.

Have you ever seen an archaeological dig? A wise archaeologist carefully brushes away the layers of soil and gently handles the broken bones. He doesn't blast with TNT and then go through the rubble.

How then do you excavate a man's soul?

Know well the condition of your flocks. (27:23)

"Flocks" refer to those for whom we have been given care. Our men have been given into our care, and we need to know well their condition:

- What *events* have happened in your man's day when you weren't around? Find out.
- What are the natural pitfalls of his *personality*? Is he a thinker? Sometimes a thinker thinks too much. Is he a doer? Sometimes a

doer is overdriven to succeed. Is he naturally creative and spontaneous? Then too much regimen can drive him nuts—and he'll battle even necessary structures at times. Is he organized and highly reliable? Then spontaneity and "living on faith" can create enormous anxiety. And disarray can be his undoing.

- What naturally *restores* your man? Every man restores himself differently; social interaction restores one man, while solitude restores another. Some are restored by sleep; some are restored by invigorating activity. If you are his opposite (which is often the case), then you will have to make a special effort not to judge, but rather to understand his unique path of restoration. When my husband discovered that I required sleep for restoration, he encouraged it, rather than judging it as laziness. When I learned that quiet was his greatest need, I had to work at creating that "desensitized" space for him, and teach our children to respect that as well.

- What was his *home* like? Emotions from youth remain shockingly close to the surface and intimately involved in our present-day reactions. I know of one gentle feminine soul whose husband has huge mother issues; as a result, every time she opens her mouth, he reacts as if she were his overbearing, controlling, bitter mom, though she isn't even remotely akin to his mother in her nature. (Women with father issues do the same thing with their husbands.) I know of another woman whose husband's father went bankrupt when he was growing up. She has learned to recognize his bouts of irritation as invariably a sign of deeper hidden worry over money. Childhood issues (in both husband and wife) are so closely connected to our fights and misunderstandings, it is unfortunate how we so rarely recognize it. Be wise to see this; discern when it is happening, and go to that hidden worry and angst when you see it. In due time, ask God to enable you to be a catalyst in helping your husband to recognize where that originates.

- A man's *physical health* or *stage in life* (such as the tumultuous teen years) can greatly affect his emotions. Moms can take heart in this. (In fact, anger is far better than passiveness in a teenage boy; passivity may be a sign of inward implosion or the result of self-medicating in some way.) A man who eats badly and takes ill care of his body will have a proclivity to be messed up emotionally—more depressed and negative, more readily anxious, more quickly angered.

While these don't excuse anger (or its sister reaction, silence), they surely do explain a lot.

There are obviously those times when *we* are the source of the problem. If you don't know, just ask: "Is there something I have done to upset you?" And then step back and listen with the third ear.

## DRAW HIM OUT

This is what you can do so very well. But once again, an angler's skill is needed.

### Start in the Shallow End

The heart of the wise instructs his mouth. (16:23)

In other words, start with familiar territory; start with *man-speak*.

When my youngest son was learning to swim, he had two teachers. The first teacher, Mrs. Boon, simply took him and threw him into deep water, which traumatized him. Somehow her tactics matched her name.

"Don't worry," she said, "he'll figure it out."

Well, fine. The only problem was we were paying her to do what we could have done ourselves, and this little three-year-old was waking in the middle of the night in a panic, asking, "Is today my swimming lesson?"

So we gave the boot to Mrs. Boon. The second teacher played games with him and gradually coaxed him into swimming. It was harder work to engage my son relationally, and it took a little longer, but it paid off in the end. (The problem then became persuading my son to come *out* of the water.)

Your husband can come to enjoy sharing his emotional life with you. But wisdom says not to begin with a cannonball dive into the deep end, à la Mrs. Boon. Much better to start slowly and coax him in. Otherwise he could wake up in a sweat in the middle of the night wondering if today is going to be another "emotional lesson."

H. Norman Wright recommends starting by using *less emotional language*.

> Ask a man, "What is your reaction?" rather than, "What are you feeling?" Think of communicating with a man as speaking your native language to someone from another culture. I have learned to do this with my Asian students, and they appreciate it.[11]

Jesus spoke the language of His listeners. He built a bridge to their world and spoke of what they knew. Most emotion-based words are simply out of a man's normal repertoire. Men don't normally use words like *hurt* or *wound* (unless you're talking about knife or bullet wounds). So we need to begin with their normal, more objective and action-oriented language:

- "What were you *thinking*?"
- "Did it *concern* you?"
- "What did you want to *do*?"

This is how men are used to expressing themselves in the outside world.

But you need not stay there. Gradually you can begin to put meat on his emotional bones.

- "That must have been *nerve-racking*."
- "You must have felt a little *betrayed*."
- "That had to have been *depressing*."
- "How *frustrated* you must feel."

As with the fledgling swimmer, confidence in identifying and putting words to feelings will grow. Mothers, boys learn to quickly hide emotions unless you pick up on their nonverbal language and facilitate emotional expression. There is a marked difference in boys who are blessed with such moms.

## Ask Good Questions

A wise man will hear and increase in learning. (1:5)

Wise questions are like golden keys to secret closets.

Jesus was the master of good questions. He often started discussion with a question. And He was incredibly skillful at *answering a question with a question*. Moms and wives and girlfriends, what wisdom we can gain from doing the same: "What do *you* think? How do *you* feel about this?" This gives the clear message that we are not lecturing or deciding for other people; we are encouraging their own quest for wisdom and maturity.

Jesus was also masterful at *listening*. Frequently interrupting or being overanxious to speak might work with our feminine friends, but in the male world, it's grounds for shutting down the conversation. It will make him feel frustrated or inadequate … which is no way at all to build a bridge.

Jesus' questions tended to see into the hearts of a people (their deep inner fears, desires, motives), assuring them that He understood them very well. Likewise, we need to ask questions that get to the inner core of a person. *Not all at once, but gradually over time.* The more you attempt this, the better your questions will become and the more accurate the emotional map you will have of your men.

If you are at the beginning point with an emotionally distant husband, consider this approach:

- *Pick your first moments*: a quiet meal, a weekend retreat, a time after you have had enjoyable sex, a close time that is peaceful and uninterrupted. Every couple needs time away to go deep. If life doesn't allow for it, be creative and make it happen.

- *Start with the outer concrete life,* with things that are tangible and on the surface—his career, his goals in life, his concerns, fears, disappointments. What are his dreams? Has he given up on them?
- *Move to your family and marriage.* Ask him his perspective on your children, then add your own perspective in light of his. (A woman is a man's greatest resource to knowing and understanding what makes his children tick. He will come to value this in you.) Then ask about your marriage.

"How are you feeling about our life together?" (If he is stumped, move on.)

"Do you feel respected by me?"

"Do you feel neglected at times?"

"What do you need most that I don't do for you?"

"How do you feel about our sex life?" (You *need* to ask this one.)

I have found that one of the best ways to get to the heart of the deepest inner life of my men is to *ask them how to pray for them.* It is amazing how they will tell me things I would otherwise never have been privy to. (And then I need to pray for those things and circle back around to see how they are doing. Men are heartened by knowing their women are praying for them all the time.) Prayer plays a huge role in getting to the heart of my men.

What do you do if his answers to your questions are hard to receive? *Listen to what he says and validate what he is feeling.* This is no time to be defensive. Receive it and legitimize it as real to him. The same is true with your sons. When your sons express hard things about your mothering, listen and validate; then ask them what you can do better. Our men need to be able to say these things (whether we agree or not), and we need to hear them.

Do not be wise in your own eyes. (3:7)

Listen to counsel ... that you may be wise the rest of your days. (19:20)

### Going Deeper Still

The more a man feels understood and validated, the more you can safely venture into harder, deeper places of the heart:

- What was his childhood like? What brought him happiness? What was hard for him?
- How did he feel about *himself* in those years? How did he feel about his parents' marriage? What about his relationship with his dad, his mom, his siblings?
- What experiences were most traumatic for him?
- How does this affect him in his life today, including his relationships to you and the children?

*Be prepared for an initial denial of early hurt and pain.* God will lead you as you venture into this deepest part of your husband's heart. If you hit a wall, pray about it—and don't cease praying. If it's a forty-foot-high iron fortress, you may be led to fast and pray. But hang in there. You can't rush self-revelation, but what a healing thing it is when it happens.

(Perhaps you are noticing that you are doing here what a paid counselor might do. It may be that you will unearth things at this point that could cause the two of you to consider the help of a professional counselor. But how much better for your man to see the need and *want* to pursue this.)

One last thought: Your man may tell you some disturbing things ... and you need to be very, very careful at this point if you want the pipeline to stay open. Why? Because he will immediately sense dismay and disapproval. A man needs to feel safe and understood, no matter what lies deep within. Dr. Hart says,

Men want to be open about their deep inner selves. They want to bare it all. They just don't know how to do it. So when a male finally begins to open up it must be in the context of total acceptance with no condemnation.[12]

Let me illustrate how this can work out. Recently, in one week's time, each of my three men shared some pretty raw emotional moments with me. Our exchanges were possible only because these guys have let me know them inside out, and because I was aware of particular events in their lives that week. One of them expressed that even though he appears very brave and calm, he is actually terrified a good part of his life. It was a very manly thing for him to admit, and I told him so. He needed to sense that I understood this is how most men feel a good part of their lives. He needed to know that it was okay by me, that even though he hated this fact, I wasn't freaked out by it at all. Somehow my lack of concern put him at rest and calmed his spirit.

Another one of my men teared up and said he didn't understand why at certain times he felt such a need to weep. It alarmed him. But I knew of some sad things he had been exposed to that week. And because I know him so well, I was able to verbalize that he has a tender, empathetic soul, and that because he feels these things every day of his life, it eventually builds up in him. I told him his tears were a sign that he cared deeply and passionately about the sad things of this world. And that is a very manly thing. It made all kinds of sense to him.

My third man told me he didn't understand why he had been so agitated and explosive all evening. But I knew that a good and righteous anger had been building up in him all week; it was very manly to be angered by the rampant sin and ungodliness that destroys the world around us. So because he couldn't express it anywhere else, he had gotten angry at a quarterback who couldn't seem to throw a pass to save his life. My awareness of his emotions that week helped him to understand himself that night.

## COMMUNICATE YOUR HEART

Truthful lips will be established forever. (12:19)

Connection is not a one-way street. As with a flashlight, two circuits are required: one flowing into the battery, the other flowing out to the bulb. When the circuit is complete, the light goes on and an electromagnetic field is created.

I like that image.

When we *draw out our men* and then *express our hearts to them*, the circuit is complete, the light can go on, and we are pulled together.

Our men can't read our minds—even though sometimes we think they should. Your man needs to know how you feel (the good feelings and the bad feelings), what your needs are (the ones he can meet and the ones he can't), and what makes you tick (what deflates you, encourages you, helps you, and frustrates you). He absolutely *must* hear from you.

But what does a wife do when her husband isn't listening?

And what if he truly needs to be listening?

It's a tough place to be in, but it happens in every marriage; it happens in the best of marriages, with the best of people. Like a smoldering fire, sin starts small, but if it isn't contained, it will seep under doors, ignite the curtains and furniture, and flash through your home.

Please hear this well: *Philandros* is as tough as it is tender. This chapter has been about the tender side. The last few chapters are about the tough side. *Philandros* means that you go *toward* the fire—the purifying fire of healthy confrontation.

There is no greater challenge than this: to love your husband enough to address sin wisely, immediately, and unflinchingly.

And there is nothing more healing.

*Chapter Fifteen*

# WIFE, SISTER, FRIEND (I): ENTERING THE FIRE OF TOUGH LOVE

*Courage is not the absence of fear,*
*but rather the judgment that something else is more important than fear.*
—Ambrose Redmoon

He was a young man from lowly descent, an untarnished, tender warrior destined for greatness. She was a beautiful and intelligent woman of noble class and character. They were both living in very unfortunate situations.

Though he had served brilliantly in war and in peace, he was being hunted down like a dog by a king whose sole desire was to see him dead. Her great misfortune was to have been given in marriage (no doubt at a very early age) to a wealthy sheepherder whose very name meant "fool," and those who knew him best called him the "son of Belial" (1 Sam. 25:17, 25 KJV).

That wasn't an affectionate nickname.

In the original Hebrew, *Belial* meant "death" or "perdition"; in the New Testament it was used as a reference to Satan.[1]

Such were David and Abigail of 1 Samuel 25.

They were two unlikely people who met in the most unlikely of circumstances. But theirs is a story worth telling. It jumps out of the pages of the Old Testament as one of the all-time great love stories.

The timing of our story is crucial. It was sheep-shearing time—usually a happy time that occurred after the spring grazing, when profits were distributed and several days of celebration followed.[2] Even the sheep were happy, being set free from their heavy coats of wool. But the prophet Samuel had just died, and all of Israel was in mourning. Though King Saul had repented of his death wish for David (1 Sam. 24), his word was not to be trusted— especially now that Israel's prophetic leader and David's advocate was dead. So David had fled with six hundred loyal men to the southernmost wilderness of Paran, near the camps of Nabal's shepherds.

While there, David and his men had lived honorably among them, taking nothing from the shepherds and providing a wall of protection against the ever-threatening Philistine marauders. As a result Nabal had lost none of his men or his three thousand sheep or one thousand goats, a remarkable feat in itself (1 Sam. 25:21). In those days, it was not uncommon for a farmer to hire such protectors. But David's men did so freely without remuneration.

However, feeding a small army was no small challenge, and now he and his men were running out of supplies.

So David sent an envoy of ten men to graciously request whatever food Nabal might be able to spare on their behalf. It was a little thing to ask, and any reasonable man would have given the son of Jesse a fair hearing.

But Nabal was no reasonable man. Not even close.

Nabal mocked them and called David a lowly knave, deserving of nothing from his table. In other words, Nabal returned evil for good (v. 21).

That was the spark that lit the fire in David's belly on this hot, dusty, miserable day in the wilderness. He had had it. He and four hundred of his men girded their swords to wipe out every male in Nabal's household (v. 34).

## LIFE-SAVING COMMUNICATION FROM A WISE WOMAN

When David descended the mountain that day—he was *hungry, angry, lonely,* and *tired.* (This is beginning to sound strangely familiar.)

He was *hungry* enough to eat a bear.

He was *angry* because Nabal had "spit in his face," thanklessly refusing to provide a meager gift from his overflowing celebratory coffers.

He was *lonely* not only because he had lost his mentor, Samuel, but also because he was separated from Jonathan (Saul's son and David's bosom friend who could no longer venture to meet him), he had lost his priestly friend Ahimelech, and eighty-five other priests loyal to David (all slaughtered by Saul, 1 Sam. 22), and he had lost his wife, Michal, the king's daughter (whom Saul had given away to another man, 1 Sam. 25:44).

Talk about a low point. Many of David's loneliest psalms were written during this "God-forsaken" period of his life.

Finally, he was dog-*tired*. He was sick to death of the double-tongued treachery of the king; he was at his wit's end from fleeing Saul's army; and he was bone-weary of withholding vengeance when he could have just as easily killed this crazy king and ended the whole affair.

If ever a man was "weary in well doing," David was. Now he was bent on a mission of revenge in which innocent people would be slaughtered.

To his great surprise, Abigail awaited him there at the foot of the mountain. Along with her were her servants and a pack of donkeys laden with food enough to feed an army: two hundred loaves of bread, one hundred clusters of raisins, two hundred cakes of figs, wine, grain, and sheep already prepared for his men to eat. What a very wise woman.

David came to a full stop.

He was stunned at her beauty and generosity. And he was moved by her candor and wisdom. I will summarize what she said:

"My lord, let the blame fall to me. I beg you not to pay attention to this worthless man, Nabal, for he is a fool. And I was not aware that you had sent an envoy to him. Please take these gifts for your men, and forgive me for not having dealt with them from the beginning.

"My lord, I know that you are to be king someday over an enduring house. And God has restrained you from shedding blood and avenging yourself in the most trying of circumstances. Even now you fight the battles of the Lord, and no evil has been found in you all your days. It would be a dark blot upon your good character if you were to carry through with this plan. And when you do become Israel's king, it would only bring great grief to you to have shed innocent blood without cause."

David immediately replied,

> Blessed be the LORD God of Israel who sent you this day to meet me, and blessed be your discernment, and blessed be you. (vv. 32–33)

He received her gifts, and, in accordance with God's command (Deut. 32:35), he did not take revenge upon Nabal.

Back at the ranch, Nabal feasted like a king. When Abigail returned home, he lay in a drunken stupor, totally unaware of the calamity that had just been averted. But the next morning when he was sober, Abigail told him everything. Immediately, "he became as a stone" and ten days later, "the LORD struck Nabal and he died" (1 Sam. 25:38). Some theorize that he had a stroke or a heart attack; others say he died from shock.

The Bible doesn't tell us the immediate cause of death—only the ultimate cause, which was the swift judgment of the Lord. As David put it, God had not only "kept back His servant from evil," but He had also "returned the evildoing of Nabal on his own head" (v. 39). A man who lives a lifestyle of sin eventually pays a steep price. Some die old and lonely in their big houses. Others end up in some other form of personal misfortune. Nabal's price was his life.

When David learned that Abigail was widowed, he sent for her and asked for her hand in marriage, which she gladly gave. So she became his wife. Had David remained true to her, had Abigail been his *only* queen when he ascended the throne (also commanded by God, Deut. 17:17), and had he continued to avail himself of her wise input, one can only imagine what other calamities might have been averted during his long reign as king.

## Two Kinds of Men

In this situation Abigail was dealing with two very different kinds of men. And in each case, she recognized her crucial position of influence. This we know: *Every* person falls prey to sin—even the most godly and good-hearted among us. But let's face it, there are those who are tender and teachable, and there are those who aren't.

A teachable man knows and freely admits his fallibility ("Behold, I was brought forth in iniquity, and in sin my mother conceived me," Ps. 51:5); he wants to grow and he is open to wise input. An unteachable man, on the other hand, may feel a certain sorrow over consequences, but it is not a sorrow unto repentance ("I now rejoice, *not* that you were made sorrowful, but that you were made sorrowful *to the point of repentance*," 2 Cor. 7:9). In the case of a believer, an unteachable spirit creates a condition of *willful blindness* that renders a man incapable of seeing his shortcomings and unable to gain perspective from God's emissaries of grace in his life.

David was tender and teachable at his core. Even in his hour of ugliest sin (2 Sam. 11), he responded to the tough love of the prophet Nathan and humbly received the discipline of God (2 Sam. 12). On the other hand, Nabal was, as one theologian described him, "churlish, stubborn, proud, unbending."[3] He lacked empathy and was stingy and unthankful. There was no moving such a man, for at his core, he was hardened and unteachable. David was known for his restraint and noble character in the face of great trial. Nabal was known for his lack of self-restraint and an obsessive preoccupation with his own interests and concerns.

Whether your man is teachable or unteachable, restrained or unrestrained, able to see outside of his own point of view or completely caught up in his own concerns, given to the fruits of the Spirit or given to the fruits of the flesh—there is great insight to be gained from observing Abigail's handling of these two men.

Several things are also immediately clear about Abigail. She was an honorable woman and merciful in her dealings (which is why her servants ran immediately to her when they realized the peril that awaited them). She feared the Lord and gave honor to those who feared Him (as we see in her actions toward David), but she maintained a certain respect for the human dignity of those who did not fear God (as was seen in her actions toward Nabal). She was strong and self-contained at her core, capable of acting decisively when the situation called for it and willing to take great risks when it came to protecting those under her care.

Finally, she accepted the difficulties that came her way in life and did the best she could under the circumstances. Was she superhuman? We know she wasn't. But one gets the very clear sense that she believed that God was great and righteous and good, and that He honored those who honored Him. If Nabal had not died that day, Abigail would have continued on, making the best of her life in spite of being married to a fool.

## IMPLEMENTING TOUGH LOVE

We can learn much from Abigail, for she understood the necessity of intervening when a man is caught in sin (Gal. 6:1). And she knew how to do it well. There are five things we can learn about biblical tough love from this wise woman.

### (1) Consider the well-being of your household.

Tough love matters to your children.

It was up to Abigail to stand between her foolish husband and the impending destruction of her household. Do you have children? Realize that whatever is said and done to you *is said and done to your children.* Children absorb a man's attitude and anger toward his wife just as if it had been poured out upon them. They are deeply affected by a lifestyle of sin in their father.

*But my children seem perfectly fine,* a woman may be thinking. *They are not fine.* If a man's sinful lifestyle is allowed to go unchecked, the weakest among us suffer the most. Out of instinct to survive, our children learn how to *hide the inner confusion and damage* being done to their souls. Oftentimes it does not emerge until they are in their teens or twenties, and then it is woefully late. If we don't intervene for them, who will? You must do what is necessary to protect your children now, for *they are depending on you.*

> Open your mouth for the mute, for the rights of all the unfortunate.... Defend the rights of the afflicted and needy. (Prov. 31:8–9)

If nothing else will cause you to take action, do so for the sake of the children.

## (2) Consider the well-being of the man.

David's character and honor were at stake, while Nabal's very life was at stake.

Consider what would have happened to David. He would have shed a household of innocent blood, alienated himself from God, and ruined his reputation. Things would have only gone downhill from there. Abigail understood that. What about Nabal? He faced his own gory execution because of his complete foolishness, and he would have taken an innocent household down with him.

Abigail cared enough to intervene on behalf of both men.

We've said it before, and we must say it again: *A woman cannot open the eyes of a man blinded by sin, but she can do her part. She can become a well-honed instrument in the hands of the great Eye Surgeon.*

If you love your man, you will act for *his* sake. Consider what inevitably happens to any man who falls into a lifestyle of sin and never walks out:

- God will not hear his prayers.
- His ability to lead will become effectually nil.
- His life will inevitably have a sad ending—relationally, spiritually, and in some cases, physically.

As his closest companion, you will usually be the one most cognizant of what is going on in your man's life. At those times, if you do nothing, who will? Do you love your husband enough to do the hard thing and intervene through tough love?

### (3) Be a realist.

Be discerning regarding the man with whom you are dealing.

Abigail had lived with her husband long enough to know his selfish, reckless, and harsh nature. So she didn't question for a second the report of her servants. She was able to think clearly based on what she knew of the man.

On the other hand, she also knew a great deal about David. The whole nation knew of him. His anointing by Samuel to succeed Saul as king, his skillful leadership in war, and his honorable actions in the face of unwarranted persecution had been widely reported across the land. When she learned of David's kindness to her husband's employees, it fit what she knew of him. She intuitively knew that she could appeal to his core integrity of character. "This will ... cause grief or a troubled heart to [you,] my lord [literally, 'become staggering to you'], both by having shed blood without cause and by my lord having avenged himself" (1 Sam. 25:31).

In other words, Abigail was a realist.

Is it harsh or unkind or loveless to be a realist? No. It is wise. Realism accepts the truth about the men in our lives. If we choose to think unrealistically about a man, we are doing him harm. Realism does not cling to vain dreams and wishes; it assesses the true nature of a man over time and experience. Realism is the prism through which a woman must look if she is going to live in healthy relationship with him.

If you are single, you must be a realist about the men you date. Don't overlook a sinful lifestyle just out of a desire to be married. If you do, you will be walking into a lifelong battle with that very sin. Learn from the women who are there right now; don't do that. If you are a mother, your sons need a woman who cannot be smoothed or conned. They need a realist. Don't allow those attitudes of disrespect (that inevitably occur) to persist and blossom into actions. And in a marriage, realize that although a man may possesses certain good traits while being completely blind in one area of his life, that area of blindness matters.

When a woman says, "Well, he *means* well," or excuses a man on the basis of his past, she is not being genuinely loving and merciful. David meant well, for his men were starving. Nabal may have had a tragic upbringing or been indulged as a boy. But no matter what went into the making of this man, as an adult he made his own choices and bore the consequences of them.

A generational chain of sin *can* be broken—it *must* be broken if a man is to reach maturity. But a new link can only happen through his conscious choice in adulthood to take a new path.

We do great harm when we *minimize a man's blindness* and *ignore the importance of overcoming* an unfortunate past … lest it become his undoing. A lifestyle of continual sin in one area has a rippling effect, just as "a little leaven leavens the whole lump of dough" (1 Cor. 5:6).

In the end, it is not so much a man's words as his actions that give us a realistic picture of his inner core. If a man is malleable, it will become clear. If he is hardened to wise input, that, too, will come to light. How many times did Saul weep? How many promises did he make to David?[4] But tears or promises mean nothing when a man's actions remain fundamentally unchanged.

There are men who learn from their mistakes and listen to the input of a loving woman. And those men change over a lifetime into something grand and rare. There are other men who come back to the same old sin over and over and continually hit their heads against the same impenetrable wall. Such a man needs a wife who is a realist. He desperately needs it.

Because Abigail was realistic, she could act wisely and mercifully. She could be tender and tough. Every man needs such a love.

*(4) Take ownership of your _____ percent of responsibility.*

Even if it is a miniscule .01 percent.

Even if, as in Abigail's case, it is only by accident.

Sometimes we are *greatly* at fault in a situation. That goes without saying. The question is, are we willing to look at that and admit it?

Not long ago, Steve pointed out that I had interrupted him. "I hate it when you do that!" he said in complete frustration. Why did I interrupt him? Because after living with him for thirty years, I was sure I already knew what he was going to say. But guess what? Even if I did know (which I didn't), the least I could have done was to let him finish his sentence. It's at times like these when my husband needs to hear me say, "You're right. It was rude for me to interrupt you. Will you forgive me?"

I hate admitting that I'm a jerk. So if I hate saying that I am wrong, doesn't it make sense that my husband does too? Hidden in Abigail's story is a powerful secret for engaging a man caught in sin. When a woman takes responsibility for her fault in a situation, whether it is significant or a mere .01 percent, the result is astonishing. Especially if he is a teachable man.

Consider Abigail's approach to David:

"Please forgive the transgression of your maidservant," she said to David (v. 28).

What was her transgression?

It was her simple lack of knowledge of David's appeal to Nabal. But Abigail disarmed David by her request for forgiveness for not having intervened at the moment his envoy had arrived. What a wise initial approach.

A soft approach that takes ownership where ownership is due has a way of softening the heart of the one approached. Even when a man speaks in anger, it makes a difference when we decide not to let the message bearer keep us from hearing the message. Proverbs advises that when we communicate our hearts, *it is wise to begin soft*, for "a soft tongue breaks the bone" (25:15), and "a gentle answer turns away wrath" (15:1). Is a lifestyle of angry outbursts acceptable in a man? No, it absolutely isn't. But let us not become equally harsh when we address that sin.

Abigail acted graciously in the face of David's anger. She knew that a humble approach would enable him to hear the rest of what she had to say. Does humility *always* have this effect? Not always. But if a man possesses even an ounce of teachability, it will. Softness in a woman tends to soften a man's heart. In fact, *sometimes the softest thing to do is to simply be silent.* To let a man's words just hang in the air for a moment. When your words aren't immediately filling the air, a man has a better chance of actually hearing what he just said. He is left in that moment to think about what he just said (and how he said it), instead of how he is going to rebut.

"The wise in heart will be called understanding, and sweetness of speech increases persuasiveness" (Prov. 16:21). When a woman is wise enough to stand back in a highly charged situation and let her husband know she is open to his input, the dynamics are completely changed. The *moment is diffused, the sword of defense can be sheathed, and your wrong is removed as the central focus.* Something else also happens. Your teachable tone inclines a man to be more teachable himself.

This leads me, however, to an important distinction.

There is a harmful kind of ownership that happens when a woman accepts guilt for what she has *not* done—or too quickly allows a man to wrongly make her the culprit. Oftentimes these women are by nature peacemakers who feel enormous angst over conflict. Many of them have grown up in homes where they were made to feel guilty for the dysfunction and sin of others and they have learned to become superior second-guessers. The truth is that a difficult and verbally abusive man gravitates to such a woman because she is so easily manipulated. These women aren't struggling with an inability to see shortcomings but rather an inadequate sense of healthy boundaries and self-dignity.

Hear this well: The last thing a man needs is for a woman to carry his weight of the blame.

One woman I worked with was married to a difficult man who continually degraded her and their four boys. The day came when she realized that it was not only killing her, but it was also killing her kids. She had to step into the fire of tough love for the sake of everyone. She began to calmly draw boundaries and let him know that his abusive language was unacceptable.

As you might expect, as soon as she spoke up, he would fly into a fury. He would turn up the volume and blame her (or one of the children) for *his* attitude, thinking that this would surely bring things back to "normal." Wisely (though she was often shaking on the inside) she calmly refused to accept responsibility for his attitude. So he would persist, more angrily and irrationally. He had to have control. *He simply had to be right.*

His ace in the hole was always something like, "Well, you're not perfect, you know!" or, "I'm not the only one here with issues!" to which she learned to calmly answer, "Well, you're completely right about that. I *do* have issues from my past. I *am* far from perfect." Now that is what I call taking ownership of your .01 percent. Then she would calmly and firmly return to the real problem at hand.

Gradually, it began to dawn on this hotheaded man that something had changed under his own roof. This woman was not going to be manipulated anymore. And he found himself in that strange, alien place of actually having no one else to blame but himself.

It took a considerable period of time (for he had grown accustomed to having his way) before any change was apparent. There were times when she wanted to throw in the towel. Yet all the while, she was getting better and better at engaging him and keeping the focus on the real problem at hand. She was becoming a whole and healthy woman who could stand firmly when the situation called for it. Then, amazingly and unexpectedly, there was a genuine breakthrough, a turning point at which he began to see, really see. Her willingness to own up to her own stuff, all the while staying the course without getting pulled into his soup, eventually bore fruit.

Is he always kind in his communication today? No, for old habits die hard. But he has changed; he is now able to see his own sin and own up to what he has done in a spirit of humility. That is how a new link begins to be formed. Those boys will be part of that new link, for they have received the incalculable blessing of a very courageous mother who was willing to graciously address sin and take the heat in the process.

A teachable man like David is softened by a woman who demonstrates understanding and is willing to own up to her percent of responsibility, while an unteachable man like Nabal is left with no one to blame but himself.

### (5) Be honest and forthcoming in a timely fashion.

Abigail was honest and forthcoming. And just as with my friend, it was a gutsy thing to do. In fact, in her vulnerable position, it could have cost her her life. But it was the right thing to do. She didn't walk on eggshells. Or edit the truth. She was a "straight-up woman," as my sons would say.

But we cannot miss how she wisely chose the way and the time in which the truth was to come out. In David's case, Abigail recognized his dire condition—physical and emotional. She met his immediate need for food, apologized for his ill treatment, and gave an explanation of what had happened.

Often our men don't know the full story; at the very minimum they need to hear from us what has been going on behind the scenes. David quickly realized that he was safe with her. This woman understood him. She had read him accurately, and she was on his team. Once he knew she wanted the best for him, she could speak forthrightly about the sinful path he was taking.

In Nabal's case, Abigail didn't wait for weeks and months.

She only waited until he was sober.

And she didn't soften the story or withhold any of the truth. Every man needs to know the truth very simply and honestly as it is.

I have known women to wait for years before finally addressing a sin issue openly and forthrightly—in many cases out of a terribly flawed idea of biblical submission—until something catastrophic happens. But by then, years of sinful habits have set in, and what was once very bad eyesight in a man has now become complete blindness. Would it not have been wise to have spoken the truth early on? And far more loving?

The sooner you speak up, the better. Don't let weeks and months go by. If possible don't even let a day go by (Eph. 4:26).

But if after years of passivity you are finally seeing the need to step into the fire of forthrightly addressing sin, it is not too late. It is never too late to bring truth to bear in your marriage. There are many women who, though late in the game, have seen the fruit of tough love. You may need to be in the presence of someone else (such as a counselor who gets what is going on) who can be a buffer in the situation. But truth sets people free, even in the darkest and most stubborn of places, as we will see in the next chapter.

Abigail knew that Nabal had to be sober and in his right mind to comprehend the facts. And no doubt, there were others present when she broke the news. But he needed to know the consequences of his foolishness *while the situation was still very fresh.*

Immediacy, timing, and complete honesty are all important. Ask God to give you the wisdom to implement all three. But don't hesitate for long. Even if you're still learning the art of communicating with a difficult man, *the only way to learn is by doing.* Every time you do it, you will get better at it. The war against deep-seated sin is rarely won in a single battle. And even the best generals have to learn as they go.

Here's what you need to know: A man greatly respects a woman who is honest and forthright. He may not say so at the moment, but he truly does.

## WHEN TOUGH LOVE GOES MISSING

In the end we can say that Abigail understood the crucial role of tough love.

For some of you, this chapter and the next will be the most important chapters of this book. Your home is not a place of protection and safety or healthy communication. And at this moment, you may be dying. Some of you may not even feel love for your husband anymore (for relational abuse has a way of killing love).

I have a great passion about this subject because I have seen so many lives wrecked for lack of understanding it. In the last month alone, I have talked with three of the kindest and most gracious women whose families are deeply suffering because these women did not understand their call to tough love. In each case, the woman's husband fell into a lifestyle of sin that went unchecked for years.

One man did not provide financially for his family—year after year after year. Another man was continually angry and defensive, so much so that no one dared to approach him. His wounded children lost all respect for him and could hardly wait to get away from home (and from the Christian faith he professed). The third man had chosen personal success time and again over his family, until the relationship had died and he became involved in an affair. His desire for success had been the first mistress of his life, the "other woman" who took him down.

All of these women wished that they had known years ago what they know today—that a lifestyle of unaddressed sin ends up hurting everyone, including their men. And once those years are gone, you simply can't get them back.

When tough love goes missing, it is usually because a woman has never learned the great value of biblical boundaries. In many cases, she has never seen them implemented and has very little understanding of how to integrate them into a marriage relationship.

But what a difference when she does!

# Chapter Sixteen

# WIFE, SISTER, FRIEND (II): THE CHECK AND BALANCE OF INTERACCOUNTABILITY

*[For] intimacy to develop and grow, there must be boundaries.*
—Drs. Henry Cloud and John Townsend

*How beautiful is your love, my sister, my bride!*
—Song of Solomon 4:10

I will never forget a conversation over lunch with two women who were going through a seminary class with me several years ago. As we ate, we talked openly and deeply about our lives. We discovered we had much in common: We were all about the same age, married to men in ministry, and very involved in ministry to women. One of them led the women's ministry in a well-known church in the area. The other worked on her church staff as a counselor to women. Knowing of my husband's work with men, they began pumping me with all kinds of questions on what is happening among men today.

Then out of the blue, one of them said, "Mary, this is probably going to sound strange, but can I ask you a personal question?"

"Sure," I said.

"I just wondered … what does it feel like to be loved?"

I was a little stunned. "What do you mean?"

"Well, it's hard to find someone to tell your problems to when you and your husband are in leadership. You know how that is."

I did know and I was listening.

"Well, I can just tell by the way you speak of your marriage that Steve really loves you. I can tell that you guys have a genuine partnership." Hesitating, she went on. "I have never had that. I have never felt loved by my husband."

You could have knocked me over with a leaf.

"What does he do to make you feel so unloved?" I asked.

The words began tumbling out. "He won't let me get close to him, and he never says anything that would make me feel loved. I honestly don't think he knows how to love. Our entire marriage he has talked down to me with such disrespect that I haven't known what to do with it. Every problem ends up being my fault, and I can never seem to please him. I feel like he is angry at me half the time, and the rest of the time he is somewhere else. Our marriage has always been all about him—making his life happen, meeting his needs, ensuring his success."

She paused as the tears started to flow. Then gathering herself, she continued on: "The worst moment was recently when he actually threw me against the wall. It was horrible. Now that our two boys are growing into their teens, I see them becoming just like him, treating me just like he has done all these years. It terrifies me. I don't know where to turn."

I felt sick. And angry.

I had been sitting beside this woman for three months with no inkling of the pain in her life. Not only was she paralyzed in personally dealing with his abuse, but he had clearly not been called into account by others in the body of Christ. I knew what Steve would have done had this happened to any woman he knew. "Did the church not know of this?" I asked.

"I've tried to talk to different leaders who are close to us, but they've never seen this side of him. I honestly don't think they grasp the problem ... or even believe me. No one wants to ruffle feathers or upset the status quo. No one has encouraged me or helped me. And he refuses to go to counseling."

Well, that happens often enough. A man living one way publicly and another way privately. A church that is passive when it comes to addressing sin and reluctant to take a wife seriously when the outer shell of a man is so very smooth.

Sure, it may not be all that unusual. *But it is completely inexcusable.*

Then the second woman spoke up. "This is probably going to surprise you both, but I'd also like to hear what it is like to be loved, Mary. I haven't felt free to speak to anyone else about this. But I haven't felt loved by my husband for years. When I've tried to express this to him, he just doesn't get it. It's as if we live on two separate planets. The love between us has died."

I just sat there. These weren't the kind of women who would walk around making a man's life miserable. They were not only attractive, but if anything, they were *too* sweet-natured and kind. They just wanted to love and be loved. Did they have their problems that contributed to the situation? That goes without saying; there are no perfect wives. But too many wives tolerate distance and abuse out of the woefully misconstrued idea that this is their role in love. God's love, however, *addresses* sin and refuses to let it gain a foothold.

I attempted to answer their genuine question first.

How do you describe what it is like to be loved? To trust a man utterly and completely when he walks out the door because you know his heart belongs to you? To have him share his soul with you, even at his lowest times? To know that he values you and believes in you and desires for you to express your gifts? How do you explain what it is like to be married to a man who takes care of you when you're sick, holds you in his arms when you're depressed, and daily encourages and prays for you? Is it possible to recount the blessing of not being immediately questioned or blamed when something has gone wrong? Or the relief of knowing that conflict between you will be resolved, come hell or high water?

Unless you have lived with that kind of love day in and day out, you simply cannot fathom the incomprehensible gift of it. Being loved and cherished by the man you married is the greatest blessing a woman could possibly have.

I don't usually get emotional, but we all had wet eyes.

"Do you know what's really sad?" one of the women said. "I counsel women every day, and the most common problem that comes through my door is a woman who doesn't feel loved by her husband. But what is she to do? She can't *ask* him to love her."

When an unloving man says irritably, "What do you *want* from me?" your only answer can be that you want to be loved *without asking*. You want to be understood, respected, valued, loved. But these must come voluntarily from a man's heart or they are meaningless. (By the way, if your man asks you that question, you must express it in just that way.)

At this point, I found myself thinking, *What on earth is going on? These two women are married to Christian leaders and teachers. Their churches are widely known. They believe in the same Bible. Where have we gone wrong?*

But I already knew at least part of the answer.

## GOD'S CHECK AND BALANCE: *INTER*ACCOUNTABILITY

In conservative Christian circles where biblical headship is embraced and taught, we have tended to neglect something essential to a healthy marriage.

We have done a superb job of teaching our women to honor their men; but we have done a lousy job of teaching them what to do when their husbands are entrapped in sin. We have welcomed the idea of godly biblical leadership, but we have shied away from the tough side of biblical love that stimulates a man toward that godly leadership.

Let me be very clear. The Bible teaches male leadership in the church and home expressly and unequivocally. *But as certainly as it teaches male leadership, it also teaches **interaccountability** in marriage and in the church.* In fact, God designed male leadership to guard over the church body (rather than to take advantage of it, see 1 Peter 5:1–3) and to *prevent* abuse and *protect* women and children. Christian leadership has never been about power or titled positions. It has always been about *character* and *responsibility*.

Our Reformation leaders of the sixteenth and seventeenth centuries decried its abandonment by the church in their day, when leadership abuse had become rampant and out of control. So it always is when we depart from the biblical teaching of character, responsibility, and accountability among leaders. How revealing of God's nature is the New Testament's teaching that a leader's *primary role* is that of sacrificial responsibility, and his *primary qualification* is that of character. This idea is so countercultural and revolutionary that we find no other system or religion in the world that comes anywhere close. God's plan has always been countercultural, has it not?

Can sinful men ever use a position of leadership as license for abuse? They can and they have. But such abuse of leadership is anathema to God. *God hates abuse; it is a mockery to His very name.* That is why God has built a check-and-balance system of interaccountability into our relationships for the express purpose of countering such abuse. He has given a clear pathway for discipline, and He has commanded that it be implemented swiftly and completely.

Should we throw out male leadership because of the potential for its abuse? God forbid! We should not throw it out any more than we should throw out its requirement of selflessness—just because someone might take advantage of that. No, both are essential. I am as passionate about male leadership as I am about its abuse. The health of our homes and churches depends on a man taking seriously his role of leadership. When male leadership is abandoned, another kind of abuse takes place—the emasculation of men and the breakdown of protection, provision, and godly oversight. Women were never intended to be the primary protectors, providers, and overseers. Your children need to see their dad step into his manly role. They need to know you are 100 percent behind his doing that.

*But they also need for him to do it well.* A woman must understand that she is *a key player in making that possible.* He cannot do it without her tender *and* tough love.

This means that not only is the church to teach male headship (as it is found in passages like Ephesians 5, Colossians 3, 1 Peter 3, 1 Timothy 2, and Titus 2), but we are also to put that teaching in the entire *context* of those books—a context that *teaches biblical tough love and interaccountability* in marriage as well as the church. Indeed, that teaching is at times so strong that it stuns the sensibilities of postmodern, politically correct "niceness." But the Bible is crystal clear. Sin is serious, and we must treat it with seriousness. There can be no toleration for a lifestyle of sin, especially among those who are leaders and teachers (James 3:1).

Here is what we are saying.

Context is everything! When we pull ideas out of context, we lose the full teaching of God, and abuses of every form rush in to set up shop. *Male leadership is always taught in a context of interaccountability.* And without that context, we go seriously awry.

### The Context of Interaccountability

For the sake of example, let us consider just three of those contexts.

In the first epistle to Timothy, where men are given the role of authoritative teaching in the church body (2:12), we read the command to treat "older women as mothers, and the younger women as sisters" (5:2). We also read that leaders are to be men of integrity and characterized by a spirit of sacrificial service (3:1–15). When a leader falls into a lifestyle of sin, he is to be held accountable, as an example to the church ("so that the rest also will be fearful of sinning," 5:19–20). This is strong stuff.

When we read in Ephesians 5 that men are to lead in the home (v. 22), we discover in the preceding chapter that *every* member in the body is to speak the truth to one another in love (Eph. 4:15, 25). This applies to a wife with her husband. And in the verses that follow 5:22, we learn that husbands are to love their wives as they *love their own bodies*, for "he who loves his own wife loves himself; for no one ever hated his own flesh, but *nourishes* and *cherishes* it, just as Christ also does the church" (5:28–29). This is an earthshaking perspective of God's call upon our men.

The corresponding passage in Colossians 3 on male leadership (3:18) is also preceded by the command to all brothers and sisters in Christ to put on a heart of compassion, kindness, humility, and gentleness (v. 12). And it is followed by the command to husbands to love their wives and not to be embittered against them (v. 19), and to fathers not to exasperate their children, lest they lose heart (v. 21). The very last verse of this chapter is particularly gripping. It contains a most sobering warning that "he who does wrong will receive the consequences of the wrong which he has done, and that without partiality" (3:25).

### Interaccountability in the Church

One of those consequences is the discipline of the church.

Paul instructs Titus to "reject a factious man after a first and second warning, knowing that such a man is perverted and is sinning" (Titus 3:10–11). Wow. Jesus also gave clear guidelines for addressing sin among brethren in Matthew 18:15–20. And 1 Timothy 5:20 is a mirroring passage regarding accountability for sin when it comes to a church leader. These are only a few of the many passages in the Bible that are surprisingly strong when it comes to rooting out sin. When sin is addressed, God's holy name is exonerated. When it is not, we become just like the world—only worse. For we defame His name.

Tragically, we rarely see this implemented today. Far too often the church waits until a man has "hung" himself by becoming publicly exposed to the world at large. How much better to address a lifestyle of sin when it first rears its ugly head and before it gets completely out of control! Early and certain intervention is God's call to the church.

Didn't the weak and immature church of Corinth do just that? There was a young man among them who was having sex with his father's wife (a fact well known to its leaders, 1 Cor. 5). Paul was sickened by the willingness of the church to look the other way. So he wrote a letter to be read publicly in their midst. He wrote it in tears over the man's condition and with an eye toward his restoration. But he didn't mince words. That tough-love approach resulted in this man's discipline by the Corinthians, which in turn led to his repentance and restoration (2 Cor. 2:1–11). If that weak little church of Corinth can implement such discipline, why can't we?

*Interaccountability in Marriage*

But interaccountability is also meant to be part of a healthy marriage. God intended that a husband and wife treat each other with the tough and tender love of a brother and sister, and the concern of a true friend.

Here's the kernel of what we have been saying.

*If your husband is an unbeliever, you are his friend.*

*If your husband is a believer, then you are his sister in Christ.*

Cain said to God, "Am I my brother's keeper?" Yes, he was. And so are you. What does a sister in Christ do? Every passage addressed to members of the body of Christ applies to you as your husband's sister in the Lord. Let me give you only a taste. You are to …

- speak the truth in love (Eph. 4:14–16, 25);
- address your brother's sin gently with an eye to restoration (Gal. 6:1);
- rescue him from sin, lest he perish (James 5:19–20);
- stimulate him to good works (Heb. 10:24);
- admonish the unruly, encourage the fainthearted, help the weak, be patient with all men (1 Thess. 5:14);
- be bold as a lion (Prov. 28:1), yet humble in spirit (Phil. 2:3).

Please hear me on this: *You simply cannot be a true friend and sister to your husband without lovingly addressing sin.* In fact, if you don't, you are contributing to the problem. You are enabling it to go on.

How does a woman build interaccountability into her marriage? She does it best by implementing *boundaries*.

## THE BLESSING OF BOUNDARIES

Boundaries are biblical.

They are also the hallmark of great marriages.

What is a boundary? It is a fence that promotes healthy individuality and safety. Without them, civilization cannot exist. We have boundaries in every part of life—on our highways, at work, even in the boxing ring.

God is the Author of boundaries. The Ten Commandments are boundaries.

(Our forefathers saw those boundaries as so foundational that they had them etched on the walls of our Supreme Court.) Boundaries like "love your neighbor as yourself" (Lev. 19:18) and "preserve justice and do righteousness" (Isa. 56:1) are found throughout the pages of Scripture. Open the Bible to any page, and you will inevitably find a boundary. They are there to protect us and to set us free!

In every marriage there *must* be healthy boundaries—physically, relationally, spiritually, and sexually. Otherwise we become "like a city that is broken into and without walls" (Prov. 25:28), and things get dysfunctional very fast. Human dignity and individuality are violated, and healthy communication dies. When healthy boundaries are present, individuality is preserved, and love and communication flourish.

Boundaries establish *inter*dependence and *inter*accountability, so that the "two" can then become "one." As Drs. Henry Cloud and John Townsend wisely say, *it is impossible to have a healthy "one" without first having a healthy "two."*[1]

Think about Siamese twins—cojoined together, sharing vital organs and life-sustaining systems, tragically unable to grow to full health and vitality. In a marriage without boundaries, two people can become emotional/relational Siamese twins. They are so intertwined that individuality is swallowed up, a sick sort of *co*dependence replaces *inter*dependence, and one person tends to dominate—controlling, engulfing, literally draining the life out of the other. Yes, they are united, but it is a debilitating union. Neither partner is able to mature into the person God uniquely created them to be.

The only way to break such a deadly tie is to step back lovingly and establish life-giving boundaries. You cannot wait for your partner to do this. You are responsible before God for *your* life and decisions. It is up to *you* to perform emotional surgery and draw lines of safety. Can you change your partner? No, but you can become healthy yourself. And you can teach him what *your* boundaries are.

A woman who does this actually changes the entire dynamics of a relationship; and that can go a long way toward setting the stage for her man to become healthy.

### *Three Fundamental Boundaries*

Every marriage needs at least three boundaries: the boundary of *commitment*, the boundary of *protection,* and the boundary of *respect*. When these boundaries are present, there is safety and trust, there is space for disagreement and discussion, and communication thrives.

I realize I am introducing a subject here that cannot be handled fully in a few brief pages. But let's at least put it on the table and begin the discussion.

Look at the boundary of *commitment*. It says, "I am committed to you for better or for worse, for richer or poorer, in sickness and in health, till death do us part." In other words, no matter how hard things get—he's not going anywhere, and neither is she. What blessing to the man or woman who experiences this kind of commitment day in and day out! What freedom, what trust, what possibility for growth and healing. And how tragic when this boundary is thrown to the wind, as it is in our day. Civilization cannot survive its loss.

What about the boundary of *protection?* It says, "I will come between you and anything that threatens to harm you. I will take care of you." The man who honors this boundary provides for the needs of his family and stands between them and the onslaught of the outside world. The woman who honors this boundary makes her home an environment of nurture and care. There are some men who have gone their entire lives and never understood how their lack of provision is a repudiation of the very faith they espouse (1 Tim. 5:8). And similarly, there are women who have just as seriously neglected the care of their homes and the nurture of their families. Such a breakdown puts an almost unbearable strain on a marriage, and makes "orphans" of children who depend upon both.

Finally, consider the boundary of *respect*. It says, "I will treat you with dignity—physically, relationally, spiritually, and sexually." In other words, a man will never hit a woman or abuse her physically. Nor will he descend to degrading, abusive language or condescending attitudes. (Nor will his wife do so with him.) Let us stop to say imperatively that *physical abuse of any kind can never be allowed—ever.* When it happens, immediate and severe consequences must be put into effect. And let us also say that *verbal abuse is completely unacceptable.* Never underestimate the profound damage of verbal abuse.

The boundary of respect is life-giving on every front. It extends to a person's spiritual journey (where the expression of questions and struggles are encouraged and a person's pathway to faith is honored). And as we have said before, it certainly extends to the sexual relationship, where each partner is unselfishly approached and treated with honor.

Doesn't this sound wonderful? It *is* wonderful. Marriages with boundaries are a beacon of hope to the rest of the world. A woman can express her heart freely because her husband values her input and empathizes with her feelings. And he feels safe with her. He knows that she is on his team and that she believes in him. When she questions him, he knows that it is because she cares deeply about him and that she wishes the best for him.

Expressions like "I want to understand what you are really feeling," "I see what you mean," and "I'm so sorry, will you forgive me?" are *commonplace, daily expressions* by both partners in a marriage where boundaries prevail. What a breath of fresh air in a selfish, dysfunctional world!

But what happens when boundaries are continually violated?

What is a woman to do when a man breaks down those fences and ignores her honest communication?

Then consequences must be put into place.

Boundaries without consequences are mush. We know this as parents and as citizens. It is just the same in the marriage relationship.

### The Good Work of Consequences

There are two great challenges in the good work of consequences. The first is in knowing which consequences are appropriate. And the second is in enacting them with an equal amount of firmness *and* graciousness. In other words, the skill is in learning *what* to do and *how* to do it. We have to combine wise consequences with an attitude of unflinching firmness and grace.

The basic rule of thumb is this: Consequences must seek to meet the level of violation, and if there is no response on the part of the violator, they must increase in severity. This is how we implement consequences in a civilized society. But more important, this is how our Lord commanded that we approach sinfulness in relationships with friends and fellow believers (Matt. 18).

Jesus taught that when the first step is not effective (a one-on-one communication and implementing of consequences between you and your spouse), you must move to the next, more significant step (involving other people with discernment and strength of character in addressing the sin and establishing accountability). A step-by-step approach allows a person to stop and reconsider and take a new course of action. The further along you go, the more public becomes the matter and the more severe become the consequences.

For example, I was once on a long overseas trip in which the guide (a Christian leader) denigrated his wife in front of the entire group on a regular basis. It was embarrassing to her and utterly discomforting to the entire group. It was clear he had become so comfortable in this role that he didn't even see what he was doing. (This is common with a man who is allowed to speak disrespectfully at home.)

At that moment, what could she have done? She could have stayed at the hotel the next day after it happened—just stepped out of the trip for a day, letting her husband clearly know why. If that didn't change things, she could have altered her flight plans (no matter what the expense!) and gone home. It would have been a compelling consequence for that man and a relief to the rest of the group as well to see a woman take a gracious but very firm step to address such sinful humiliation.

Don't let these kinds of things just go on and on. It hurts you, it hurts your man, it hurts everyone around you, and it hurts the name of Christ.

If you are married to a difficult man for whom very tough consequences must be brought to bear, let me encourage you to get some help. Perhaps the most practical biblical book on the subject I have come across to date is the classic work *Boundaries in Marriage* by Drs. Henry Cloud and John Townsend. I encourage you to get it and consume its pages.

The bottom line is this: The single goal in implementing consequences is *restoration.* James put it this way:

> My brethren, if any among you strays from the truth and one turns him back, let him know that he who turns a sinner from the error of his way will save his soul from death and will cover a multitude of sins. (James 5:19–20)

Such a life-changing path of restoration isn't easy, but what rewards to those who choose it!

God does the unexpected, the unthinkable, the remarkable when we walk *toward* that purifying fire. Our men are stimulated to growth and change, and in the process, so are we!

There is one last very important word of advice to the woman who chooses this life-saving path.

*Never go it alone.*

The support of others in the foxhole may be the single most important factor in your life.

## The Power of the "Two or Three"

God never intended for a woman to live out this kind of purifying love in a place of isolation. An isolated woman is a vulnerable woman. We are nurturers by nature, sensitive to a man's anger, wired to complement and seek oneness, and physically more vulnerable. It takes a lot for a feminine woman to love with a tough love—even if she possesses a strong personality. All of us need the encouragement and wise counsel of others.

Just as Moses needed the additional strength of Aaron and Hur when his arms grew weary (Ex. 17:11–12), and as Paul needed Epaphrus and Luke and

Mark (Philem. 1:23–24), we need the encouragement of one or two friends who will pray with us and encourage us in the heat of life's fire.

It's no accident that at the conclusion of our Lord's instructions on tough love, He said, "Where two or three have gathered together in My name, I am there in their midst" (Matt. 18:20). Prayer among close friends is the great secret weapon in the battle "against the rulers, against the powers, against the world forces of this darkness" (Eph. 6:12). Where "two or three" are gathered, we are not only counseled and emboldened, but we are also bonded together in beseeching the mighty help of God.

There is something *very* powerful in that.

I have been praying with a dear friend on a weekly basis for the last eight years. We have filled journal upon journal of God's answers to our prayers. Many times in seemingly impossible situations, we have been like the persistent widow of Luke 18 who refused to give up in her requests of an uncaring, unrighteous judge—until finally he relented (vv. 1–5). So we, too, have persisted, knowing that God—unlike that cold judge—is a caring and righteous judge.

And what prayers He has answered for our husbands and children! It has become quite the thing now for our children to call with requests for our prayertime together, or for our husbands to give us specific things to pray about. They have come to see the power of the "two or three," and they love it that we are bonding together in prayer.

So uplifting is this time to us personally, if we miss for a week or two, we feel it. There is something about being able to let down your hair and come before the throne with a very good friend. It sets your boat aright and puts fresh wind in your sagging sails. That kind of "two or three" is a treasure worth finding.

By the way, when we pray, we do so as if everything depended upon it.

Because in the end—it truly does.

In the purifying fire, *only God can do the shaping and welding.*

## THE BLACKSMITH'S SHOP

*"Under a spreading chestnut tree the village smithy stands."*

So wrote Henry Wadsworth Longfellow. Until the last century there was a blacksmith in every town. His skill was indispensable to life, and his hammer and anvil were as essential to civilization as water and food. He made every tool needed for farming, cooking, building, traveling, hunting, even fighting wars.

But the blacksmith was also an artist who used welding, riveting, chasing, and punching to build the most delicate and intricate pieces of work. If you visit the twelfth- and thirteenth-century churches of Europe, you cannot help but be struck by the exquisitely wrought ironwork: elaborate gates and fences, door hinges, knockers, window grilles—all skillfully crafted in the smithy's shop.

Whether crafting horseshoes or elaborate ironwork, the blacksmith's work was hard and laborious. He had to be a man of strength and durability. Upon entering his shop, your senses were assaulted with the mixed odors of burning metal and fire, and the ear-splitting clangs of his huge hammer pounding upon the anvil. And the heat! It was stifling. Temperatures were so hot that the smithy dared not build a second floor to his shop, lest it burn down.

But heat was the smithy's best friend.

It was the heat that caused the iron to become malleable for shaping and welding. Every day he would arise and build his fires—stoking them to temperatures of 1,500–2,000 degrees or even more, till a brilliant yellow-white hot center was formed. But the blacksmith always guarded against too much heat, for if the metal got too hot and sizzled with flying sparks, it would be burned and rendered useless. And no blacksmith relished tossing away good metal.

When the fire was right, the smithy took his tongs and placed the unformed iron in the fire's center till it was turned to a brilliant red. At the right moment he quickly pulled it out and laid it on the anvil, pounding and hammering it into the shape he desired. "Strike while the iron is hot" was his byword.

But even then, his work wasn't finished.

Back into the fire it would go, this time on the cooler outer edge of the fire to be heated just enough for the dents and sharp corners to be smoothed out. When the shaping was completed, his finished piece was placed into the water to "quench" and set it.

Welding was the greater skill, however. It was the welding of *two* pieces of iron together that produced the works of greatest beauty. The heat (though only around 400 degrees) needed to be perfect for the bond of iron on iron to occur. Such a skill took years to perfect if a man wished to produce a true masterpiece.

In the forge of marriage our great Blacksmith also toils. And it is a great transforming kind of work that He is about. Heat is inevitable, for we are all born to adversity. But when the Blacksmith takes us in His hands, He is purposeful and skillful. He knows exactly how to shape us as individuals and then to weld us together—iron upon iron.

As He works, He takes great joy in our shaping, and He guards our hearts in the heat. If we allow Him to do His good work, we are shaped, not ruined in the fire. Even in moments of the most intense heat, our wise smithy sees us through, shaping and reshaping—until He has made of us a thing of beauty.

The marriage of two individuals who have each been softened and shaped and then welded together skillfully in His hands is a marriage that becomes a masterpiece to behold.

And the world will look on and say, "Who did this work? We wish to know Him!"

# *Addendum*

# TRICKS PORNOGRAPHERS PLAY

## *(1) Porn-napping*

When a Web site owner forgets to renew a current domain name (as often occurs), pornographers quickly *purchase the expired name* and set up shop. The unwitting visitor, expecting the oft-used legitimate site, suddenly finds himself on a porn site. (For example, the accounting firm Ernst and Young let a registration lapse on "moneypolis.org," a children's money-management site. Visitors suddenly found themselves at "euroteensluts.com.")

## *(2) Cybersquatting*

"Cybersquatting" is when pornographers purchase *domains named for legitimate topics*, only the site is explicit pornography. Words often used in homework research or popular children's toys and character names are often used in this scam. (For example, civilwarbattles.com, tourdefrance.com, or whitehouse.com were at one time porn sites. The official site for finding info on the president is whitehouse.*gov*.) Once discovered, these sites disappear, only to reappear elsewhere. A 2006 study by the Justice Department found that nine out of ten school-age children were exposed to pornography most often while doing their homework online. At least twenty-six different children's character names (like Pokémon and Action Man) have been linked to thousands of porn sites.[1]

## *(3) Misspelling*

Easily *misspelled words* are also commonly used as porn sites. For example, not long ago if someone accidentally typed an extra "l" in "Google," he ended up at an Asian porn site. Pornographers like to work off trendy, high-traffic sites with hard-to-spell names (such as abercrombieandfitch.com). One wrong letter can land the surfer at a porn site.

### (4) Doorway Scams

A "doorway scam" is when a pornographer carefully constructs a Web site around *nonpornographic themes*, then gets these sites *placed high on search-engine lists*. Once the unsuspecting surfer clicks onto what appears to be a legitimate site, he finds himself on a porn site. Another doorway scam is to *create a pornographic Web page around an innocent search* (such as "livestock," with the unsuspecting user opening up a page depicting bestiality).

### (5) Entrapment

*Once a person has actually entered a porn site*—even if it was unintentional—a new bag of tricks is employed. For example, there are *"cookies," "start-up file alterations," "Trojan horses"* (placed into your hard drive when downloading from another site; it can occur while a person is downloading something as simple as a pretty calendar, screensaver, or children's puzzle), and a program called *"spyware"* (enabling a porn site to monitor keystrokes, scan files, snoop applications, collect e-mail addresses, and gather all kinds of personal information).[2]

The most vicious form of entrapment is called *"mousetrapping."* We discussed this in chapter 7. But for those who have not read that chapter, mousetrapping is when a site alters the "back" or "close" button, preventing a person from exiting the pornographic Web site. This is called mousetrapping because it renders the mouse useless.

Many children have found themselves mousetrapped: 26 percent of those who were inadvertently exposed to pornography while surfing the Net reported they were *brought to another sex site when they tried to exit* the site they were in. A 2001 survey revealed that two-thirds of porn sites *did not indicate the adult nature of that site* up front, and most disturbingly, 25 percent of those sites *hindered the user from leaving*.[3]

# NOTES

## Chapter 2

1. All information taken from three Web sites: (1) *The Great Flu Pandemic of 1918*, vol. 6, no. 2, fall 2004, University of Michigan Medical School, www.medicineatmichigan. org/magazine; (2) Roland Anderson, *Bald Mountain Childhood*, http://home.swipnet.se/ roland/flu.html; (3) "Could SARS and the 1918 Influenza Pandemic Be Caused by the Same Virus?" by James A. Marusek, May 11, 2003, http://personal.galaxyinternet.net/ tunga/SARS.htm.

## Chapter 3

1. Hara Estroff Marano, "The New Sex Scorecard," *Psychology Today*, July/Aug. 2003, http:// psychologytoday.com/articles/pto-2832.html.
2. Ibid., 1.
3. Ibid., 2.
4. Ibid., 2–3.
5. Jessica D. Gatewood, et. al., *The Journal of Neuroscience*, Feb. 22, 2006, www.jneurosci. org.
6. Marano, "Sex Scorecard," 2–3.
7. Peg Tyre, "The Trouble with Boys," *Newsweek*, Jan. 30, 2006, 44–52.
8. *Reformation Study Bible* (Lake Mary, FL: Ligonier Ministries, 2005), notation.
9. Daniel Akin, *God on Sex* (Nashville: Broadman & Holman, 2003), 183.
10. Roy Edgar Appleman, *Abraham Lincoln: From His Own Words and Contemporary Accounts* (Washington, D.C.: U.S. Government Printing Office, 1961), 3, www.questia. com/PM.qst?a=o&d=30393218.
11. Sheri and Bob Stritof, "Issues and Problems in Mary and Abraham Lincoln's Marriage," About.com, http://marriage.about.com/od/presidentialmarriages/a/abelincoln_2.htm.
12. *New York Times Service* article written at time of Churchill's death, www.winstonchurchill.org/i4a/pages/index.cfm?pageid=768.
13. "Lady Randolph Churchill," http://en.wikipedia.org/wiki/Jennie_Jerome#Marriage_ and_adultery.
14. Mary Soames, *Clementine Churchill: The Biography of a Marriage* (New York: Houghton Mifflin, 2003), 201.
15. Ibid., from various passages throughout the book.

## Chapter 4

1. H. Norman Wright, *What Men Want* (Ventura, CA: Regal, 1996), 93.
2. Wendy Shalit, *Girls Gone Mild* (New York: Random, 2007), 4.
3. Michele Weiner-Davis, *The Sex-Starved Marriage* (New York: Simon and Schuster, 2003), 23.
4. *Annie Hall*, Directed by Woody Allen, Rollins-Joffe Productions, 1977. (Wanderlust Alvy admits that love and relationships are something we require, despite their often painful and complex nature.)

5. Harry W. Schaumburg, *False Intimacy* (Colorado Springs: NavPress, 1997), 68.

6. Theresa L. Crenshaw, *The Alchemy of Love and Lust* (New York: Pocket, 1996), 125.

7. For an in-depth explanation of the male-female sexual physiology, see Douglas E. Rosenau, *A Celebration of Sex* (Nashville: Thomas Nelson, 2002).

8. Feldhahn, *For Men Only*, 130. (Eight out of ten women wish their sex drive was as great as their husbands', and among happily married women, that desire is almost 100 percent.)

9. Akin, *God on Sex*, 55.

10. C. F. Keil and F. Delitzsch, *Eerdmans Commentary on the Old Testament, Volume I, The Pentateuch* (Grand Rapids, MI: Eerdmans, 1980), 90–91.

11. H. C. Leupold, *Exposition of Genesis, Volume I* (Grand Rapids, MI: Baker, 1942), 137.

12. Wright, *What Men Want*, 99.

13. Archibald D. Hart, *The Sexual Man* (Dallas: Word, 1994), 76–77.

14. Mike Mason, *The Mystery of Marriage* (Portland, OR: Multnomah, 1985), 72.

15. Ibid., 46–47.

16. Schaumburg, *False Intimacy*, 30.

17. Mason, *Mystery of Marriage*, 53–54.

18. Thomas V. Morris, *Making Sense of It All* (Grand Rapids, MI: Eerdmans, 1992), 134.

19. J. I. Packer, *Knowing God* (Downer's Grove, IL: InterVarsity, 1973), 29.

### Chapter 5

1. The Associated Press, "Female British spy's exploits during World War II are revealed," *International Herald Tribune*, Apr. 1, 2008, www.iht.com/articles/ap/2008/04/01/news/Britain-World-War-II-Spy.php.

2. Regis Nicoll, "Men in the Muddle," *BreakPoint Worldview Magazine*, July 20, 2007, www.breakpoint.org/listingarticle.asp?ID=6776.

3. Stephen B. Clark, *Man and Woman in Christ* (Ann Arbor, MI: Servant, 1980), 635.

4. Harvey C. Mansfield, *Manliness* (New Haven, CT: Yale University, 2006), 18.

5. Clark, *Man and Woman in Christ*, 635.

6. Ibid., 635–36.

7. Ibid., 636.

8. Ibid.

9. Ibid., 637.

10. Ibid.

11. Ibid., 636–37.

12. Ibid., 636.

### Chapter 6

1. Giorgio Vasari, *Lives of the Artists* (Oxford, England: Oxford University, 1998), 415–16.

2. See www.michelangelo.com/buon/bio-index2.html.

3. Shaunti Feldhahn, *For Women Only* (Sisters, OR: Multnomah, 2004), 68.

4. Mansfield, *Manliness*, 14.

### Chapter 7

1. Rocky McElveen, *Wild Men, Wild Alaska* (Nashville: Nelson, 2006), 149–64.

2. Eric Griffin-Shelley, "The Internet and Sexuality: A Literature Review—1983–2000,"

vol. 18, no. 3, Aug. 2003, Sexual and Relationship Therapy series, www.drgriffin-shelley. com/articles/articles/netsex.html.

3. Ibid.

4. Ibid.

5. David Hiltbrand, "On Line—Out of Control," *Philadelphia Inquirer*, Nov. 2, 2003, www.pornnomore.com/OnLineoutofControl.htm, 1.

6. Ibid.

7. Ibid.

8. Daniel L. Weiss, "Children and Pornography," Apr. 3, 2007, www.family.org/socialissues/ A000001155.cfm, 1.

9. Jerry Ropelato Research Company, "Internet Pornography Statistics," TopTenReviews. com, http://internet-filter-review.toptenreviews.com/internet-pornography-statistics. html.

10. Weiss, "Children and Pornography," 1.

11. Mark Penn, *Microtrends* (New York: Hachette, 2007), 276.

12. Jerry Ropelato Research Company, "P2P Networking: Kids Know! Do Mom and Dad?" TopTenReviews.com, www.internet-filter-review.toptenreviews.com/peer-to-peer-file-sharing.html. Also, Daniel Sieberg, "Study: Children Bombarded with Online Porn," CBS News AP, Feb. 5, 2007, www.cbsnews.com/stories/2007/02/05/tech/printable2431433. shtml, 1.

13. R. Albert Mohler Jr., "Custom Pornography for a Consumerist Age," quoting *USA Today*, May 14, 2006, www.AlbertMohler.com/blog_read.php?id=650.

14. Holman W. Jenkins, "Pornography, Main Street to Wall Street," *Hoover Institution Policy Review*, Feb.–Mar. 2001, http://hoover.org/publications/policyreview/3479067.html, 4.

15. Ibid., 4–5.

16. Mohler, "Custom Pornography."

17. James Sunday, "iPods & Porn," Family Research Council, July 1, 2006, www.frc.org/get. cfm?i=CU05K17.

18. Tony Perkins, "Pornographic Cell Phones," Family Research Council, May 2, 2006, www.frc.org/get.cfm?i=CM06E02.

19. Penn, *Microtrends*, 276.

20. Dirk Smillie, "Dangerous Curves," *Forbes Magazine*, Apr. 7, 2007, 56–59.

21. Penn, *Microtrends*, 277.

22. *The Village Pub* 2, 2005, http://thevillagechurch.net, 1.

23. Pam Mellskog, "XXX: Bringing sexual addiction out of the shadows," *The Longmont Times-Call*, Feb. 23, 2006, www.longmontfyi.com/health-story.asp?ID=6360.

24. Jerry Ropelato Research Company, "Internet Pornography."

25. Ibid.

## Chapter 8

1. Mary Farrar, "1949," Feb. 2008.

2. Hiltbrand, "On Line," 3.

3. Ibid.

4. Three recent books reporting these disturbing patterns among young women (from adolescent girls through college/postcollege single women) are *Girls Gone Mild* by Wendy Shalit; *Unhooked* by Laura Sessions Stepp; and *Prude* by Carol Platt Liebau.

5. Mellskog, "XXX," 2.
6. Ibid., 3. Also, Jenkins, "Pornography," 3.
7. Hiltbrand, "On Line," 3.
8. Ibid.
9. Steve Watters, "The XXX Files," *New Man Magazine*, June 2000, 32–33.
10. Jenkins, "Pornography," 3.
11. Mark Laaser, *Faithful and True* (Grand Rapids, MI: Zondervan, 1992), 22.
12. "How Common Is Pastoral Indiscretion?" *Leadership Magazine*, vol. 9, no. 1 (winter 1988): 12–13.
13. Such studies were reported by H. Norman Wright (*What Men Want*), Dr. Archibald D. Hart and his landmark study of men and sex in the 1990s (*The Sexual Man*), and Dr. Harry Schaumburg (*False Intimacy*).
14. Donna Rice Hughes, "Archive of Statistics on Internet Dangers," Protect Kids.com, 2000, www.protectkids.com/dangers/statsarchive.htm.
15. Ibid.
16. Penn, *Microtrends*, 276.
17. Ibid.
18. *AFA Journal*, "Research Shows Early Porn Exposure Has Lasting Effects," AFA Online, Apr. 21, 2006, http://headlines.agapepress.org/archive/4/afa/212006g.asp.
19. Jerry Ropelato Research Company, "Internet Pornography."
20. *AFA Journal*, "Early Porn Exposure."
21. Frank York and Jan LaRue, *Protecting Your Child in an X-Rated World* (Wheaton, IL: Tyndale, 2002), 12–13.
22. Jerry Ropelato Research Company, "Internet Pornography."
23. Weiss, "Children and Pornography," 2.
24. Ibid.

*Chapter 9*
1. Ken Druck and James C. Simmons, *The Secrets Men Keep* (New York: Doubleday, 1985), 1.
2. Tyre, "Trouble with Boys," 44–52.
3. Joseph LeDoux, *The Emotional Brain* (New York: Simon and Schuster, 1996), 99.
4. Marano, "Sex Scorecard," 2.
5. Simon Baron-Cohen, *The Essential Difference* (Jackson, TN: Cohen Perseus, Basic, 2003), 29–30, 61.
6. Feldhahn, *For Women Only*, 77.
7. Ibid., 84.
8. Ibid., 83.
9. Ibid., 56.
10. Hart, *Sexual Man,* 24.
11. Feldhahn, *For Women Only*, 92–94.
12. Wright, *What Men Want*, 94–95.
13. Max Lucado, *No Wonder They Call Him the Savior* (Sisters, OR: Multnomah, 1986), 106.
14. Dorothy C. Finkelhor, *How to Make Your Emotions Work for You* (New York: Berkley Medallion, 1973), 23–24.
15. Gary J. Oliver, *Real Men Have Feelings Too* (Chicago: Moody, 1993), 64.

16. Druck, *Secrets*, 15.
17. Ibid., 27.
18. Oliver, *Real Men*, 71.
19. Ruthy Levy Guyer, "Emotions and Disease," National Institutes of Health Office of Science Education, http://science-education.nih.gov.
20. "Frontiers of the Mind," National Library of Medicine, www.nlm.gov/hmd/emotions/frontiers.html, 1–6.
21. B. B. Warfield, *The Person and Work of Christ* (Philadelphia: Presbyterian and Reformed, 1950), 141–42.

## Chapter 10
1. Hart, *Sexual Man,* 37–38.
2. Shalit, *Girls Gone Mild,* 107.
3. Ibid., 94.
4. Laura Sessions Stepp, *Unhooked* (New York: Penguin, 2007), 28.
5. Ibid., 8.
6. Shalit, *Girls Gone Mild*, 95.
7. Weiner-Davis, *Sex-Starved Marriage*, 23.
8. University of California, San Diego School of Medicine, "Men's Health News," June 2007, www.newmedical.net/print_article.asp?id=26094.
9. Hien T. Nghiem and Pauline Anderson, "Low Testosterone Linked to Higher Risk for Depression," *Archives of Psychiatry*, Mar. 2008, www.medscape.com/viewarticle/571198.
10. University of California's San Diego School of Medicine, "Men's Health News."
11. "Low Testosterone in Men Doubles Their Risk of Bone Fracture," Garvan Institute of Medical Research, Jan. 2008, www.garvan.org.au/news-events/news/low-testosterone-in-men-doubles-the-risk-of-bone-fracture.html.
12. "Low Testosterone Levels in Men May Mask Presence of Prostate Cancer," *Journal of the American Medical Association*, Dec. 18, 1996, www.pslgroup.com/dg/ed8a.htm.
13. Feldhahn, *For Men Only*, 128.
14. Ibid., 132.
15. Ibid., 129.
16. Feldhahn, *For Women Only*, 44.
17. Mason, *Mystery of Marriage*, 127.
18. Wright, *What Men Want*, 93.
19. Ann F. Caron, *Strong Mothers, Strong Sons* (New York: Harper Perennial, 1994), 29.
20. William J. Petersen, *25 Surprising Marriages* (Grand Rapids, MI: Baker, 1997), 15–21.
21. Ibid., 34.
22. "St. Augustine of Hippo," *New Advent Catholic Encyclopedia*, www.newadvent.org/cathen/02084a.htm.
23. "Augustine of Hippo," Wikipedia, http://en.wikipedia.org/wiki/Augustine_of_Hippo.
24. Albert C. Outler, trans., *St. Augustine Confessions—Book Ten,* www.sullivan-county.com/id3/confessions/augcon10.htm#chap30, 17.

## Chapter 11
1. Stephen Arterburn, et. al., *Every Heart Restored* (Colorado Springs: WaterBrook, 2004), 49–50.

2. Iris Krasnow, *Washington Post*, Sept. 11, 2000, quoted in Akin, *God on Sex*, 39–40.

3. Wright, *What Men Want*, 103–4.

4. Feldhahn, *For Women Only*, 111–22.

5. Ibid., 13.

6. Wendy Jaffe, *The Divorce Lawyers' Guide to Staying Married* (Los Angeles: Volt, 2006).

7. Willard F. Harley Jr., *His Needs, Her Needs* (Old Tappen, NJ: Fleming H. Revell, 1986), 100–13.

8. *In Touch Magazine*, Feb. 18, 2008, 68.

9. Ashley Pearson, "Hollywood's Dirty Diet Secrets," *New York Daily News*, Mar. 24, 2008, www.nydailynews.com/lifestyle/2008/3/24/2008-03-24_hollywoods_dirty_diet.

10. Ibid.

### Chapter 12

1. Marvin Olasky, "Washington's War," *World*, Feb. 23/Mar. 1, 2008, 61.

2. Ibid.

3. Ibid.

4. Hart, *Sexual Man*, 39.

5. Akin, *God on Sex*, 15.

6. John Piper, *Future Grace* (Sisters, OR: Multnomah, 1995), 332.

7. Jonathan Aitken, *John Newton: From Disgrace to Amazing Grace* (Wheaton, IL: Crossway, 2007), 111.

8. John Piper, "Sexual Relations in Marriage," message series on marriage, Feb. 15, 1981, www.desiringGod.org.

9. "Martha Dandridge Custis Washington," www.whitehouse.gov/history/firstladies/mw1.html; also, http://clinton4.nara.gov/WH/glimpse/firstladies/html/mw1.html; also, www.firstladies.org/biographies/firstladies.aspx?biography=1.

### Chapter 13

1. Petersen, *25 Surprising Marriages*, 193.

2. Ibid., 198.

3. Ibid., 200.

4. Ibid.

5. Poem by Galeain ip Altiem MacDunelmor.

6. C. H. Spurgeon, *The Treasury of David,* vol. I (Byron Center, MI: Associated Publishers and Authors, 1970), 1.

7. Ibid., 1, 4.

8. J. J. Stewart Perowne, *The Book of Psalms* (Grand Rapids, MI: Zondervan, 1980), 107.

9. *Reformation Study Bible*, 739.

10. Craig C. Broyles, *New International Biblical Commentary on Psalms* (Peabody, MA: Hendrickson, 1999), 43.

11. Ray C. Stedman, *Folk Psalms of Faith* (Glendale, CA: Regal, 1977), 7.

12. Donald M. Williams, *The Communicator's Commentary: Psalms 1—72* (Waco, TX: Word, 1986), 25.

13. Spurgeon, *Treasury of David*, 2.

14. Susan Olasky, "An Old Deception," *World,* June 28–July 5, 2008, 60.

15. Cheryl and Jeff Scruggs, *I Do Again* (Colorado Springs: WaterBrook, 2008).

16. Available at www.songofsolomon.com.

17. Gary L. Thomas, *Sacred Pathways* (Grand Rapids, MI: Zondervan, 2002), 100.

### Chapter 14

1. C. H. Spurgeon, *The Soul Winner* (Grand Rapids, MI: Eerdmans, 1963), 292–93.

2. Mason, *Mystery of Marriage*, 67.

3. Leslie Lindeman, Gina Kemp, and Jeanne Segal, "Humor, Laughter and Health," HelpGuide.org, Sept. 2007, www.helpguide.org/life/humor_laughter_health.htm, 1–2.

4. Ibid., 3.

5. Ibid.

6. Harley Jr., *His Needs, Her Needs*, 78.

7. Ibid., 74.

8. Feldhahn, *For Women Only*, 147.

9. Harley Jr., *His Needs, Her Needs*, 74.

10. Oliver, *Real Men*, 99–100.

11. Wright, *What Men Want*, 87.

12. Hart, *Sexual Man*, 78.

### Chapter 15

1. J. D. Douglas, F. F. Bruce, and J. I. Packer, eds., *The New Bible Dictionary* (Grand Rapids, MI: Eerdmans, 1970), 138.

2. Ralph Gower, *The New Manners and Customs of Bible Times* (Chicago: Moody, 1987), 143.

3. A. W. Pink, *The Life of David* (Grand Rapids, MI: Baker, 1998), 147.

4. See references in 1 Samuel 13:10–14; 15:13–31; 18:9–13; 18:22; and 19:1; 19:6, 11; 24:16–22; 26:17–25.

### Chapter 16

1. Henry Cloud and John Townsend, *Boundaries in Marriage* (Grand Rapids, MI: Zondervan, 1999), 86–87.

### Addendum

1. Jerry Ropelato Research Company, "Tricks Pornographers Play," TopTenReviews.com, www.internet-filter-review.toptenreviews.com/tricks-pornographers-play.html.

2. Ibid. (This Web site is an excellent resource for learning about these and other updated tactics used on the Web.)

3. Weiss, "Children and Pornography," 1–2.

BOLD MEN OF GOD ARENT BORN, THEY'RE BUILT

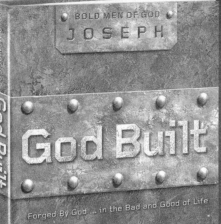

Explore the defining spiritual process that makes men "men of God" through the story of Joseph who overcame tremendous odds to become an influential leader.

**ISBN: 978-1-4347-6850-6**

David C Cook

800.323.7543 • DavidCCook.com